PrimaFacie 1987

An Anthology Of New American Plays

Previous Editions:

PrimaFacie 1985

Ringers
Frank X. Hogan
The Immigrant
Mark Harelik
The Female Entertainer
Elizabeth Levin
A Woman Without A Name
Romulus Linney
When The Sun Slides
Stephen Davis Parks
Christmas Miracles
Laird Williamson and
Dennis Powers

PrimaFacie 1986

Pleasuring Ground
Frank X. Hogan
Hope Of The Future
Shannon Keith Kelley
Circe & Bravo
Donald Freed
Goodnight, Texas
Terry Dodd
The World Of Mirth
Murphy Guyer

PrimaFacie 1987

An Anthology Of New American Plays

Max and Maxie
James McLure

Rachel's Fate
Larry Ketron

Shooting Stars
Molly Newman

Koozy's Piece
Frank X. Hogan

Veterans Day
Donald Freed

With a Foreword by Romulus Linney

The Denver Center Theatre Company

Sponsored by **US WEST**

PUBLISHED BY THE DENVER CENTER THEATRE COMPANY
Copyright 1987© The Denver Center Theatre Company

ISBN: 0-936947-52-7

First printing December 1987

Editors: Coleen Hubbard, Peter Hackett
Editorial Assistant: Larry Bograd

Cover design by David Sevick
Printed and bound by Johnson Publishing Company, Boulder, Colorado

U S West sponsors the PrimaFacie program because we believe that American Corporations have a responsibility to further the arts in this country for the benefit and joy of all.

PrimaFacie provides an avenue for innovation and a forum for new playwrights in the American theatre.

U S West is proud that a national resource for the performing arts is located in our territory, and we are pleased to support it.

CONTENTS

Foreword   vii
Romulus Linney

Max and Maxie   1
James McLure

Rachel's Fate   69
Larry Ketron

Shooting Stars   115
Molly Newman

Koozy's Piece   165
Frank X. Hogan

Veterans Day   227
Donald Freed

Afterword   269
New Play Development at the
Denver Center Theatre Company

FOREWORD

When the American Theatre began its transformation after World War II, the first consideration was physical space. It was discovered, at the Alley in Houston, the Arena in Washington, and by the work of Glen Hughes on the West Coast, among others, that almost any play could be perfectly well produced for small audiences in the round. This meant that an American theatre did not have to be either an enormous 19th century proscenium house in a big city or a dreary high school stage at one end of an auditorium. The resident theatre movement in the United States began.

In the slow fifties these theatres struggled with their useful but very modest spaces, and many other problems. It was difficult to attract actors eager to succeed in the New York theatre, and almost impossible to dent the national consciousness. The existence of their schedules was confined to small notices in the one existing theatre magazine, *Theatre Arts,* now defunct. The difference between a resident and an amateur theatre was by many in the theatre considered a very small one. But the work continued, each new theatre gaining experience with the classics and experimenting with modern work. Most important of all, a style of performing began to emerge: less dazzling and pyrotechnically overwhelming than the best productions in New York and on tour; it was also more human, closer both physically and emotionally to the growing number of people who came to love living theatre.

In the sixties, with the realization that a nation's identity is nowhere written larger than in its art, the United States began to fund these theatres. They were able for the first time to develop their staff, attract by more stable employment, very gifted actors, and build, finally, their castles—the dramatically imposing state-of-the-art theatres that now serve American cities across the country.

In the seventies, again stimulated by funding sources, theatres began to encourage, ask for and even subsidize playwrights. The result was not only plays going on to win Pulitzer Prizes, but the creation of a large number of gifted and dedicated dramatic authors who for the first time could feel it very likely, if they ever managed to write a decent play, that it would be produced. A whole subculture of workshops, dramaturgs and literary managers now testify to the vitality of the search for new plays, as do the schedules of the theatres, which abound with premieres.

The point of this mini-history is "what now?" What is the next step, from our present castles producing new plays along with the old and doing it very well? What's next?

I suggest that while the castles are wonderful, they flourish in a theatrical civilization a bit medieval. They are isolated. When one does a superb production of an old play, the others most often do not hear about it, and if they do, they have their own work to think about. Only when a new play is a sensational success does anyone pay it national attention, or is it likely to move on to New York or to other theatres. World class productions end their runs with little notice. Few theatres exchange productions.

But rescues are afoot. Theatre Communications Group's *American Theatre* magazine does its best to cover the enormous span of America's theatrical life, with increasing effectiveness. Theatres like the Milwaukee Repertory concern themselves with theatre abroad. And the Denver Center Theatre Company's program takes all this one step further.

Now in its fourth year, the DCTC's PrimaFacie program stages readings of up to ten new plays every year. The theatre then produces three or four of them in the following season, and publishes the premieres in this Anthology of New American Plays, which you hold in your hand.

Here you may read the work itself: a harrowing military psychodrama by Donald Freed; a delicious female basketball comedy by Molly Newman; a bittersweet theatrical love story by James McLure; a fierce struggle between Denver generations by Frank Hogan; a shocking explosion of erotic guilt by Larry Ketron.

The Denver Center Theatre, under the artistic direction of Donovan Marley, is with this third edition of its PrimaFacie Anthology helping to move our national theatre toward a wider knowledge of itself, as well as toward a richer and deeper future.

—Romulus Linney

Romulus Linney is a playwright, novelist, and teacher, living in New York City. His plays have been produced on Broadway, Off-Broadway, and in regional theatres across the country. His play, *A Woman Without A Name*, was developed in *PrimaFacie I*, produced during the Denver Center Theatre Company's 1985 season and subsequently published in *PrimaFacie 1985*.

Max and Maxie
James McLure

The Denver Center Theatre Company, Donovan Marley, Artistic Director, presented the world premiere of *Max and Maxie* in December, 1984 in the Source Theatre, as part of the DCTC's 1984-85 season, with the following artists:

MAX AND MAXIE
by James McLure

Directed by Peter Hackett
Sets, Costumes, and Lights designed by Pavel M. Dobrusky
Stage Manager, Lyle Raper

THE CAST

Max .... Bill Buell
Maxie .... Penelope Miller
The Boy .... Ken Sonkin

TIME AND PLACE
A rehearsal hall in Miami in 1956

Max and Maxie

ACT ONE

SCENE ONE

(Blackness)

A VOICE: Five minutes, Mr. Love.

(Strains of "I Can't Give You Anything but Love." They fade. The sound of tapping.)

VOICE: Five minutes, Mr. Love.

(Lights up suddenly. A bare rehearsal room. A hat rack, a prop bed, a dressing screen, chairs. MAX, an old man, stands smoking. He coughs. Throws smoke away. Stamps it out. Lights another one. Paces. Stops. Upstage a BOY enters. He's somberly dressed. He stands very still. MAX senses his presence. Turns)

3

BOY: Good morning. How are you, Mr. Love?

MAX: Talented. Who are you?

BOY: Am I on time?

MAX: On time for what?

BOY: We haven't met.

MAX: Obviously, or otherwise I'd know you.

BOY: Didn't they tell you I was coming?

MAX: I'm an old man. They don't tell me anything. Who are you?

BOY: I'm sorry I'm late.

MAX: You're late?

BOY: Yes, sir.

MAX: Don't be late again.

BOY: No, sir.

MAX: Ever!

BOY: No, sir.

MAX: What're you late for?

BOY: For you. I've come for you.

MAX: For me? You've come for me? Where are you taking me?

BOY: Nowhere, sir.

MAX: Then what are you here for?

BOY: To cue you on your lines.

MAX: You're not taking me anywhere? You're sure?

BOY: No, sir. I don't know, sir.

MAX: You're here to cue me on my lines.

BOY: Yes, sir.

MAX: You're not a chauffeur?

BOY: No, sir.

MAX: You're just here to cue me on my lines.

BOY: Yes, sir.

MAX: Why didn't you *say* so? Why didn't you *say* so?

BOY: I'm sorry, sir. My name's Tommy.

MAX: My name's—oh, you know my name.

BOY: Oh, yes, sir! I've read everything about you. Absolutely everything! Everything!

MAX: Everything?

BOY: I'll bet I know things about you that even you don't know.

MAX: Well, keep it to yourself! I don't ask you about your personal
life. You probably don't even have a personal life. Look at you,
you're just a kid. How'd you get this job?

BOY: My cousin's the producer.

MAX: Jesus.

BOY: Actually, second cousin.

MAX: Second cousin. Not even a first cousin.

BOY: Sorry I'm late. I was walking to the theatre, it was such a
beautiful day. You know, sir.

MAX: Don't call me sir. No one ever called me sir in my life.
BOY: No, sir.
MAX: Of course you *could* start a precedence.
BOY: Yes, sir.
MAX: Show a little respect.
BOY: Yes, sir. Uhhh . . .

(MAX *unpacks his bag, bending over the chair. The* BOY *approaches* MAX. *Startles him*)

MAX: What?—
BOY: Nothing, sir, it's just that.
MAX: What? What? Spit it out! Spit it out!
BOY: It's just that my grandfather was a friend of yours.
MAX: All my friends are dead.
BOY: He knew you in vaudeville when you did a doubles act called
        Max and Maxie.
MAX: What's his name
BOY: *(Proudly)* Dimitri Kravovitz. *(Pause)* Dimitri
        Kravovitz?
MAX: I don't know a Dimitri Kravovitz.
BOY: He said he knew you in New York as boys. In vaudeville.
MAX: Never knew a Dimitri Kravovitz. Never. Never.
BOY: His stage name was Tommy Lark.
MAX: . . . Tommy Lark? Tommy Lark was Dimitri Kravovitz.
BOY: Yes.
MAX: Tommy Lark. I never knew that! We used to swim off the
        pier in the East River together.
BOY: I know that, sir.
MAX: Tommy Lark! So where is ol' Tommy now.
BOY: He died of cancer. Last year in St. Petersburg.
MAX: Where's my thermometer? Where's my thermometer?
BOY: Are you feeling bad, Mr. Love? Are you not feeling good?
MAX: At my age feeling bad *is* feeling good! At least you're feeling.
        Let's just do the lines—okay?
BOY: Yes, sir.
MAX: And don't call me sir . . . Call me . . . Mr. Love.
BOY: Yes, Mr. Love.
MAX: We'll start with the part where the two bums discuss death.
BOY: *(Turns to the table)* Ready?
MAX: Yes.
BOY: "This place . . ."
MAX: No . . . wait . . . *(He sets down the script.)* Okay. Go.
BOY: "This place has not . . ."
MAX: Wait—

(Pause. HE *tries to group his memory.)*

BOY: Are you ready?

MAX: Of course, I'm ready! I'm always ready! I was born ready! Go.

BOY: "This place has not changed since yesterday."
       (Pause. MAX *blinks.)*

MAX: I wasn't ready. Do it again.

BOY: "This place has not changed since yesterday."
       (Pause)

MAX: Don't tell me. Don't tell me.
       (Pause)
  Okay. Tell me.

BOY: "This place never changes."
       (Pause)

MAX: Then what?

BOY: Then I say: "Some places never change."
       (Pause)

MAX: Then what do I say?

BOY: Then you say: "This one in particular." Then I say: "We've been here before." Then you say: "We have?" Then I say: "Certainly." And then you say: "What did we do?" And I say: "What we always do." And you say—

MAX: Young man.

BOY: Sir?

MAX: Are you trying to turn this into a singles act?

BOY: Why . . . no, sir.

MAX: Then just give me a general idea where we're headed . . . got it?

BOY: Yes, sir.

MAX: I'm in this play too, y'know.

BOY: Yes, sir. You're coming to the part about the dust and the bones.

MAX: Let's not get personal, son. Let's just say the character's coming to the part about the dust and the bones . . . the dust and the bones . . .

BOY: Yes, sir.

MAX: The dust and bones?

BOY: Yes, sir.

MAX: *(Suddenly brightening)* I know the dust and bones! Why didn't you say so? Why didn't you say so? Take it from the top.

BOY: "This place has not changed since yesterday."

MAX: "This place never changes."

BOY: "Some places never change."

MAX: "This one in particular."

BOY: "We've been here before."

MAX: "We have?"

BOY: "Certainly."

MAX: "What did we do?"

BOY: "What we always do."

MAX: "We do the act?"

BOY: "We do the act."

MAX: "As usual."

BOY: "As always."

MAX: "Do we kill 'em?"

BOY: "We knock 'em dead."

MAX: "We slay 'em in the aisles!"

BOY: "We murder 'em!"

MAX: "As dead as a doornail, as dead as a mackeral." *(HE counts out the pause for the* BOY.*)*   Pause. Two. Three. Go.

BOY: "We always do the act."

MAX: "It's so we'll feel safe."

BOY: "It's so we won't feel."

MAX: "It's our only safe ground."

BOY: "When we're alone."

MAX: "We don't know who we are."

BOY: "We don't know what to say."

MAX: "We say nothing."

BOY: "Our silences are dreadful."

MAX: "They sound like dust."

BOY: "Like bones."

MAX: "Like dust." *(HE counts out the pause.)* Pause. Go.

BOY: "The dead keep talking."

MAX: "They wander."

BOY: "They cannot keep still."

MAX: "They cannot rest."

BOY: "They wander."

MAX: "Their voices are like silences."

BOY: "Like cries."

MAX: "Like dust."

BOY: "Like bones."

MAX: "Like dust." Where the hell is everybody?

BOY: Who, Mr. Love?

MAX: They should be here by now!

BOY: *(Cautiously)* Mr. Love—

MAX: Don't interrupt me. The director, the other actors, if you could call 'em that. Where are they? Who are they to keep me waiting? Don't they know who I am? Don't they know? I have half a mind to walk out on this show. Then where will they be? Hah! Then they'll see. Where will they be then? Who will they get? Who? Tell me who? Who's as good as me?

BOY: Milton Berle.

MAX: What? They want Berle?

BOY: Sir?

MAX: What do you know that you're not telling me?

BOY: Nothing.

MAX: Who else?

BOY: Jackie Gleason?

MAX: What Gleason? First Berle, now Gleason. I was probably third on their list.

BOY: Mr. Love.

MAX: I feel sick. Where's my thermometer?

BOY: No, you asked me who's as good as you—I just said Mr. Berle and Mr. Gleason.

MAX: C'mon! Tell me! Have they been having conferences?

BOY: I don't know—

MAX: You know, but you're not saying!

BOY: No, sir.

MAX: Aw, yeah, you do! Talk! It's my memory, isn't it? They say I can't handle the lines. Isn't that right!

BOY: No, sir. I don't know, sir.

MAX: *(Shouting)*   Are you afraid of me?

BOY: Yes, sir.

MAX: *(Shouting)*   Why?

BOY: I don't know, sir.

MAX: Yes, you do! Why are you afraid?

BOY: *(Shouting)*   You're shouting.

MAX: *(Shouting)*   Okay! Let's not shout! We'll be calm! We'll be civilized! We don't have to shout! Who needs the aggravation?!   *(Finally in a normal voice)*   Okay. We're not shouting.

BOY: No, sir.

MAX: Are we happy?

BOY: Yes, sir.

MAX: Y'know something, son, if I may make a personal observation?

BOY: Yes, sir?

MAX: You're too sensitive for show business. Take up another occupation. May I suggest aluminum siding.

BOY: Why aluminum siding?

MAX: Why not? It's terrific stuff. Lasts forever. You don't have to paint it.

BOY: I really don't think so—

MAX: Do you have a house?

BOY: No, sir.

MAX: Then how would you know?

BOY: Do you have a house?

MAX: What a question! What a question! Do I have a house!

BOY: Do you?

MAX: No, I live in Manhattan. I have a building.

BOY: I thought so.

MAX: You thought what?

BOY: That you lived where you live.

MAX: We all live where we live.

BOY: It's just that I read all about you. I mean, I looked you up
  when I heard we were going to be working together.

MAX: You're cueing me on my lines. That's not the same thing as
  working together. Even my fellow actors and I aren't working together.

BOY: They're wonderful, though.

MAX: They don't understand.

BOY: What?

MAX: Comedy.

BOY: Isn't comedy either funny or it isn't?

MAX: As I told somebody once a long, long time ago. "A laugh is
  the hardest thing to give birth to and the easiest thing to kill." I
  mean, I'm a funny man. Look.
      (HE *makes a series of funny faces and moves.*)
  Okay. I know you didn't laugh. Because it's not in the right sequence.
  They were just poses, masks. If they'd been connected to the right
  material, they'd have been funny. They'd have been funny.
      (*Pause*)
  Where the hell are they?

BOY: Who?

MAX: Them. The others.

BOY: Mr. Love—

MAX: They think I ain't got it. But they're wrong! I still got it.
  Whatever it is I had—I still got it. Hell, I've forgotten more than
  they'll ever know. Memory? I still got my memory—I'm sharp as a
  tack. Memory like a steel trap. I don't forget. I don't forget. Where
  are they?

BOY: They're not coming. This is the day off.

MAX: Oh, right. I forgot . . . you threw me off. All this talk. Where
  were we?

BOY: The part where they commit suicide.

MAX: First bones and dust, now suicide. And my agent told me this
  was a comedy. What does he know? My agent. He once got me a
  gig on the Andrea Doria.

BOY: The Andrea Doria. What's that?

MAX: Aw, grow up, wouldja?

      (MAX *sits, lights another cigarette, pours himself coffee from
  a thermos.*)

Where are my pills? I've lost my pills.

BOY: Mr. Love, as long as we're on a break . . .

Max: This is not a break. And I have not stopped. This is merely a pause.

BOY: I just wanted to ask you something.

MAX: Well, don't! I'm looking for my pills. I'm having a heart attack here without my pills. You're asking me questions. Andrea Doria. Okay, okay. What is it?

BOY: How do you get started in show business?

MAX: Start.

BOY: But how? Movies and television are so hard to break into. I mean, it was easier for you. You had vaudeville.

MAX: Young man, there are two hardest things in the world to do. One is breaking into vaudeville. The other is breaking into vaudeville.

BOY: But today, there is no vaudeville.

MAX: See, they've made it even harder.

BOY: But how did you get into it?

MAX: I had an act.

BOY: An act?

MAX: Yeah.

BOY: With a partner.

MAX: Yeah.

BOY: I mean, I know you had an act with Maxie L'Amour.

MAX: *(Startled)*   How did you know that?

BOY: I told you, I read all about you, especially in *Vaudeville's Favorite Faces*. But it didn't tell how Max and Maxie started . . . or what happened to her

MAX: We just started. One thing led to another . . . I'd been travelling the country for years. They did things different then.

SCENE TWO

(There is the sound of tapping in the distance. Then the sound of applause. MAXIE enters, dancing. As she comes into place the sound of the tapping and applause fades. The BOY clears the stage of rehearsal props used in the present rehearsal scene, then crosses to the theatre seats. During MAXIE'S entrance MAX has gotten his hat and rolled up his pants legs.)

MAX: Hiya. My name's Max. I seen ya dancin' over there.

MAXIE: I wasn't dancin' over there. I was dancin' over here.

MAX: But I was over there. I caught you right out of the side of my eye.

MAXIE: Well, at least your eyesight's okay.

MAX: Yeah, well I—hey, what's that supposed to mean?

MAXIE: You got a funny face, mistah.

MAX: Thank you.

MAXIE: That wasn't a compliment.

MAX: Oh, yes it was.

MAXIE: It was?

MAX: Sure. You bet.

MAXIE: Huh?

MAX: Do you see my nose?

MAXIE: Are you kiddin'? I could see that nose if I was in Hoboken.

MAX: Hey! We're in Cleveland.

MAXIE: Exactly.

MAX: Well, that's my point. I gotta funny nose. I got funny eyes. I got a funny mouth. I got funny hands. Funny feet.

MAXIE: You must have a swell time laughin' at yourself.

MAX: Yeah, well I . . . hey! You got some mouth on ya for a lousy hoofer.

MAXIE: (SHE *continues tapping.*)   Comic, huh?

MAX: That's right. Comic.

    (SHE *keeps tapping.* He *regards her dancing feet.*)

Hey, don't those tootsies ever stop? You look like somebody put a nickel in ya.

    (SHE *ignores him.*)

You know, I'm a funny fella.

MAXIE: So I hear.

MAX: (*Delighted*)   Oh, yeah? Word's already gotten around, huh? Who ya hear that from?

MAXIE: You.

MAX: Oh. (*Pause*)   Well, I am. I'm the best. I'm the funniest. I'm the funniest there ever was. And even if there's somebody funnier, I'm still the best.

MAXIE: Look at ya. You're just a kid.

MAX: It doesn't matter. I make 'em laugh. I make 'em all laugh. I can make you laugh.

    (SHE *keeps tapping.*)

I said I can make you laugh.

MAXIE: Okay, make me laugh.

MAX: Okay, stop with the tapping.

MAXIE: Look, mistah, I'm working here. I don't know about you.

MAX: How can I make you laugh if you're doin' the feet?

MAXIE: You say you make a livin' with your face.

MAX: Yeah.

MAXIE: I make a livin' with my feet.

MAX: How can I make you laugh if you're doin' the clickety-clickety-clickety?

MAXIE: That's your problem.
   (Clickety-clickety-clickety)
MAX: She's doing the clickety-clickety-clickety and it's driving me
   nuts. Can't you do nothin' but clickety-clickety-clickety?
MAXIE: Oh, I can do a few things.

   *(SHE stops tapping and begins dancing around the room—
   graceful Ginger Rogers swoops and movements.)*

MAX: Hey, for a hoofer, you ain't bad.
MAXIE: *(SHE'S heard this a zillion times.)*   But I'm no comic, huh?
MAX: Nope.
MAXIE: And being a comic's tougher than being a hoofer?
MAX: Yep.
MAXIE: Do you work this hard?
MAX: I work harder.
MAXIE: Comic, huh?
MAX: Yeah. Comic.
   (SHE dances by him again.)
MAXIE: Yeah, well, I ain't laughin'.
MAX: That's 'cause I ain't makin' you laugh.
MAXIE: Nobody can make people laugh.
MAX: I can.
MAXIE: I still ain't laughin'.
   (HE stops her.)
MAX: You will.

   *(HE pulls her to him. THEY begin to tango together. HE does
   an eccentric dance with MAXIE with several clownish movements
   of his own.)*

MAXIE: Hey!! Heeeyyyy—you can dance.
MAX: A little.
   (Pause)
MAXIE: You're pretty good.
MAX: Wrong. I'm not good. I'm great. I'm the best.
MAXIE: How can you be the best—the best comics on this circuit
   are Frank Fay and Benny Fields.
MAX: Used to be. In six months, it's me.
MAXIE: Don't think much of yourself, do you?
MAX: I think a lotta myself. Why not? Nobody takes care of nobody
   in this world. Who's lookin' out for you, but you? I'm gonna be
   somebody in this business.
MAXIE: *(Fascinated)*   I've never known anyone who really thought
   they were the best—really the best.

MAX: So? Do you like me?

MAXIE: I don't know you.

MAX: Ya don't have to know a person to like a person. I know I like you.

MAXIE: How come?

MAX: Saw ya dancin' over here. I knew. I just knew I like ya. You got some good moves.

MAXIE: You don't know anything about me.

MAX: All I need to know. I seen your act every night for a week! That act you do with the swish dancer.

MAXIE: Yeah, I seen you out there.

MAX: Liked me, huh?

MAXIE: I thought you were some kind of nut.

MAX: I am nuts. Nuts about your dancing. How about your act with that guy.

MAXIE: What about it?

MAX: Quit it.

MAXIE: Why should I?

MAX: A comic, a girl dancer. What could beat it? You could make more money with me. You like money, Lady?

MAXIE: I never met anybody yet that didn't.

MAX: Bet on me, Lady. I'm going all the way.
     (Pause)

MAXIE: Okay.

MAX: Okay, what?

MAXIE: Ya got yourself a partner.
     (HE goes into a routine. Shy, goofy fella. Making funny faces)

MAX: Oh golly—she said yes! *(Goofy laugh)*   She said she'd do it. She said she would! *(Goofy laugh)*   You all heard her! I can't *believe* it! I can't believe it.

     (MAXIE laughs. MAX suddenly drops the goofus act, does a few suave dance steps. MAX takes out a small leather bag from around his neck.)

MAXIE: What's that?

MAX: It's my boodle bag. It's where we'll keep our money.
     (HE extracts a penny.)
  Here. Kiss it.

MAXIE: What for?

MAX: Ya kiss a penny for good luck. A penny for your thoughts.

MAXIE: Why don't we kiss a quarter?

MAX: I ain't got a quarter.

MAXIE: *(Laughs)* Okay.
     (SHE kisses it. HE does too.)

MAX: Shake. See, I do this cop act—
MAXIE: *(Laughing)* I can't believe you talked me into this—
MAX: Not only that. I made you laugh.

*(The BOY comes in dressed as the stage manager gesticulating—
they're late; it's time to go.)*

BOY: Come on. They're waiting. You're on.

SCENE THREE

*(MAX and MAXIE coming offstage. Applause. We see shadows
projected against the wall of backstage representing the succeeding
act. The BOY is standing here, smoking a cigar—the Stage Manager.)*

MAX: You were off in the dancing and you threw me off. I didn't
get my laugh.
MAXIE: God, I'm hot.
MAX: It's when you did the turn.
        (HE illustrates.)
You put a little tick in there. Where'd that tick come from?
MAXIE: What tick? Jesus, I'm hot.
MAX: What tick? That tick I saw! And don't tell me there wasn't a
tick in there 'cause I know a tick when I see a tick.
MAXIE: A tick? You mean a take.
MAX: I don't mean a take. Don't you think I know the difference in
a tick and a take? We're talking tick. Here is a tick.

*(HE demonstrates a lascivious dance turn and as he does so,
he does a little tick with his eyes and his hips.)*

That was a tick. That's what you did.
MAXIE: Jesus, it's hot.
MAX: Are you watching here?
MAXIE: I'm watching. I'm watching. It's just that I'm about to die.
MAX: How come?
MAXIE: Because I'm so goddamn hot!
MAX: Okay. Now that was a tick. This is a take.

*(HE does the step again; this time does a more elaborate eye
roll and hip movement.)*

Now that's a take.

MAXIE: I didn't do a take.
MAX: I'm not accusing you of a take. I'm accusing you of a tick.
MAXIE: Tick! Take! What's the difference.
MAX: Difference! Difference! I'll tell you the difference. Everything affects the act. Everything. Learn something.
MAXIE: It's too hot to learn something.
MAX: I'll tell ya another difference in the tick and the take.
MAXIE: What's that?
MAX: For a tick ya get bawled out. For a take I break your neck.
MAXIE: Oh yeah? What if I ad-lib a line.

(HE *gasps, clutches his chest in true horror.* SHE *exits.* HE *runs after her.*)

MAX: Ad-lib! Ad-lib! So help me God, Maxie, if you ever ad-lib a line I won't be responsible for my actions!

(*Blackout*)

SCENE FOUR

(*The* BOY *sets up the dressing table as the diner.* HE *is dressed as a short order cook. Toothpick dangling from his mouth.* HE *sets down cups of coffee for* MAX *and* MAXIE. THEY *are about to take a sip, get half-way.*)

BOY: That's a nickle a cup.

(THEY *look at each other.* MAX *pulls out the boodle bag, extracts the money, miserably.*)

MAX: Where's the crackers?
BOY: What crackers?
MAX: The crackers with my coffee.
BOY: You get crackers with our soup. You don't get crackers with our coffee.
MAX: What do I get with your coffee?
BOY: Heartburn.
(*The* BOY *crosses to theatre seats.*)
MAXIE: My feet are killing me.
MAX: You and your feet.
MAXIE: Where are we?
MAX: Davenport.
MAXIE: I thought we were goin' to Davenport.
MAX: Chicago. (*Pause*)   They didn't laugh enough.
MAXIE: They never laugh enough.

MAX: You ever played Rochester?

MAXIE: Yeah. You ever play Kansas City?

MAX: Murder. People don't laugh in Kansas. State law.

MAXIE: You ever play the Aching Heart circuit?

MAX: That's nothin'. You ever play the Death Trail circuit?

BOTH: Right.

    (Pause)

MAX: How much money we got?

MAXIE: $4.35.

MAX: Gee. That's better than we cleared last week.

MAXIE: Yeah, a coupla more weeks like this and we can retire in the lap of luxury. Easy street. Us and the Rockefellers.

MAX: Yeah, I wonder what the Rockefellers are eating tonight.

MAXIE: Well, it wasn't a 15-cent lamb chop.

MAX: 15 cents. That's outrageous.

MAXIE: Say, do you recognize this place?

MAX: This restaurant?

MAXIE: The restaurant, the boarding house, the trains, the girls: they are all the same. What's today, Friday?

MAX: Right. Then it's the Orpheum, Cleveland, 16th through the 22nd; then Keith's, Toledo, 23rd through 29th; Temple, Detroit, 30th through the 5th; then Keith's, Indianapolis; Keith's, Cincinnati; Keith's Dayton; Keith's, Louisville, Keith's, Columbus; Keith's, Canton; then the Palace—

MAXIE: The Palace?

MAX: That's right. The Palace—in Akron, Ohio.

MAXIE: There oughta be a law.

MAX: What?

MAXIE: Against calling something the Palace in Akron, Ohio.

MAX: We'll make it to the Palace.

MAXIE: Not tonight, we won't. I'm going to sleep. Wake me up in time for the train.

    (SHE props herself on her elbows. Almost immediately begins to snooze)

MAX: *(To himself)*   Great, who'm I supposed to talk to? The salt shaker? How can she fall asleep that quick?

BOY: *(From the seats)*   Pssst. Why doncha wake her up.

MAX: I can't.

BOY: I thought you wanted to talk to her.

MAX: I do.

BOY: But why?

MAX: Because.

BOY: 'Cause why?

MAX: I'm lonely.

(SHE *shifts to one elbow—her head resting on the palm nearest* MAX. HE *moves closer to her.* SHE *takes her head off her palm and leans into his shoulder.* SHE *rests her head there.* HE *doesn't know what to do.* HE *seems ill at ease. Finally,* HE *wakes her up by tapping her gently on the shoulder.)*

MAXIE: What's the big idea? I just got to sleep.
MAX: I know, but . . . uh . . .
MAXIE: But what?
MAX: I wanted to talk about the act.
MAXIE: The act.
MAX: Yeah.
MAXIE: We just did the act.
MAX: I thought we'd go over it.
   (The BOY *crosses to the table and removes cups.)*
MAXIE: *(Sarcastically)*   Maybe you'd like to do a little of it.
MAX: *(On his feet)*   Okay!
BOY: Yeah. You better work on the act. I caught it yesterday night.
MAX: *(Brightening)*   Oh, ya caught it, huh?
BOY: Yeah, I'd been better off catchin' a cold. The girl was okay. You stank.
MAXIE: Oh, Jesus.
MAX: *(With dignity)*   For you and your kinds I have but one word. Pphhhht!!   *(To* MAXIE*)*   Now then, you know when I do the hat bit?
MAXIE: *(Acting dumb)*   The hat bit? The hat bit? What's the hat bit?
MAX: What's the hat bit? Jesus! You forgot the hat bit?
MAXIE: You jerk. We been doing this act for six months. Don't you think I know what the hat bit is? Jesus!
MAX: It's just that you scare me when you do that! Just don't do that! Don't do that.
MAXIE: You know, you don't trust anybody, do you?
MAX: No. Not with the act.
MAXIE: The act. The act. Boy, one track with you.
MAX: That's right. I don't trust anybody. I know where I been and I ain't going back there.
MAXIE: And you think *I* am?
MAX: Look, nobody trusts anybody in this world. Everybody's got to go their own way. You got yours, I got mine. Right now we're headin' down the same road together.
MAXIE: So what happens when you wanna ditch me?

MAX: That's not gonna happen—we're partners. Look, I know comedy.

MAXIE: How? How do you know? You're broke. You're nothin'. I got a bigger name than you—have you ever been a headliner?

MAX: Well . . .

MAXIE: No. I have. So how do I know? You say you know comedy? How do I know?

MAX: Trust me.

MAXIE: You said not to trust anybody.

MAX: With the act. You can trust me, okay?

MAXIE: Okay.

   (THEY shake.)

MAX: So, okay! The hat bit. When I do the hat bit, hold for a titch longer. I know I can get another laugh there. Just a titch.

MAXIE: Just a titch.

MAX: Just a titch.

MAXIE: *(Kidding)*   Not a take.

MAX: Christ, no! Not a take! That'd ruin it entirely! Christ! Look!

   (HE demonstrates. SHE watches, loving him for his pursuit of excellence.)

Hold, two, three, then say your line.

MAXIE: That's a titch?

MAX: Yeah that's a titch.

MAXIE: Looked like a tick to me.

MAX: Oh my God no. No relation. Different animal entirely. As a matter of fact, I'm beginning to get a little worried about your titches.

MAXIE: My titches are terrific.

MAX: Oh, yeah? Lemme show you the difference.

   (HE is about to demonstrate. The sound of the train whistle)

MAXIE: Saved by the B&O Railroad!

   (THEY run to meet their train.)

SCENE FIVE

   (The BOY dressed as a bellhop showing MAX and MAXIE into the room)

BOY: Nice clean bed.

   (BOY tests bed. Rubs fingers indicating soiled linen.)
Got a night light.

   (The light flickers. BOY taps bulb. It comes back on. HE goes to window.)

Nice view.
(A cat screeches from the fire escape.)
C'mon! Beat it, will ya! Gotta bathroom right outside the door, folks.

(Sounds of toilet flushing. Loud. BOY crosses to door. Stamps on roach)

Well. Nighty-night.

(Waits for a tip. MAX does a "wait-a-minute" take and extracts something from his pocket. HE shakes hands with the bellhop, discreetly exchanging the bill in his hand with the BOY.)

MAX: Here. Have a bill.
BOY: This ain't money. It's a laundry bill!
MAX: It's a bill, ain't it?
BOY: What about a tip?
MAX: If I had money for a tip I'd have money for the laundry. Get outta here.
MAXIE: I've seen worse rooms, but not for people.
MAX: I'm sorry, kid. It's the best I could do. I mean, I know you're used to your own room or bunkin' up with one of the other girls, but this is only for one night.
MAXIE: Hey, look. Who's complainin'? I'm a pro. Ain't I a pro? I carry my own bags, don't I?
MAX: You sure do. That's one thing I like about you. You carry your own bags. You're a real pro.
MAXIE: Some of the other girls, they get guys to carry their bags for 'em. All that gallantry stuff. That ain't bein' a pro.

(THEY set their bags down. There is one chair. One window. One double bed. A flashing light goes on and off, on and off, etc.)

Well, okay, we got one chair. One bed.
MAX: Well, I'll take the chair.
MAXIE: Like hell ya will.
MAX: Huh?
MAXIE: None of that gallantry stuff. I'm a pro. We'll flip for it.
That's awfully sportin' of ya. We'll flip a quarter.
(MAX digs deep for a quarter.)
I coulda sworn I hadda quarter.
MAXIE: Well, what ya got? We can flip anything.
(HE pulls out an empty pocket.)
MAX: Can ya flip a pocket?
(MAXIE pulls out a quarter.)

MAXIE: Here. Call it in the air.
  (SHE *flips it.*)
MAX: Heads.
  (SHE *catches it. Looks at it.*)
MAXIE: You get the bed.
MAX: Oh, boy!
MAXIE: My own lousy quarter.
  (SHE *holds out the quarter. Speaks to it.*)
  Traitor!

  (*Meanwhile,* MAX *begins to make up the bed—fluffing pillows,
  etc. Suddenly,* HE *gets guilty.*)

MAX: Hey, look. I was only kiddin'. You take the bed.
MAXIE: Forget it! You won the toss fair and square.
MAX: Yeah?
MAXIE: Yeah.
MAX: Oh, boy! A bed! Brother, am I sleepy!
MAXIE: Yeah? Well, don't tell sister about it.

  (SHE *goes behind the screen to undress.* MAX *begins undressing
  also.*)

MAX: You were good tonight.
MAXIE: Thanks.
MAX: Not *great*, but good. If you'd only think about what you're
  doing more. Remember basically our bread and butter is laughs. We
  gotta get the laughs.
  (SHE *sticks out her head.* HE *covers himself with his overcoat.*)
MAXIE: I'm a dancer, okay? Not a comic, okay?
MAX: That's okay. I'm good enough for both of us.
MAXIE: Thanks awfully.
  (SHE *goes back in.*)
MAX: It's always the laughs. You gotta make 'em laugh. Otherwise
  you get a dog and juggle something.
MAXIE: I'm a dancer! I dance.
MAX: That's right! So dance. But don't dance on a laugh. No move-
  ment. Stillness. Still like a grave. You can't even breathe. Never
  breathe on a laugh, not even an eyebrow moves. Remember, a laugh
  is the hardest thing to give birth to and the easiest thing to kill.

  (MAX, *by this time, is in underwear and shirt.* MAXIE *emerges
  from the bathroom.* SHE *wears a long, thin nightgown. The light
  behind her silhouettes her form through the nightgown. It is nearly
  transparent.*)

A laugh is the most beautiful thing in the world.
>   *(HE turns. HE sees her for the first time—sexually.)*
Uh . . . yeah, well, it's one of the most beautiful.
>   *(SHE goes to the chair.)*
MAXIE: Lemme have a pillow for the chair.
MAX: Pillow? Oh, yeah sure!
>   *(HE brings a pillow and the blanket off the bed.)*
Here we go.
MAXIE: Thanks.
>   *(HE regards the blinking light.)*
MAX: Are you gonna be able to sleep okay?
MAXIE: Yeah, sure.
MAX: Here, lemme fix it.

>   *(HE covers himself with the sheet and goes to fix the window-shade.)*

G'night.
MAXIE: G'night.

>   *(HE turns to go, the shade pops up again.)*

MAX: Active little thing, ain't it?

>   *(HE gets up, uncovered and fixes it. Turns to go—before it can pop up again, he turns and growls, the shade stays put.)*

Well . . . g'night.
MAXIE: G'night.
>   *(HE walks halfway across the room. Turns)*
MAX: I didn't know you slept in one of those.
MAXIE: One of which?
MAX: Those.
MAXIE: Nightgowns.
MAX: Yeah.
MAXIE: Well, I didn't know you slept in striped underwear.
MAX: Well, you know . . . anything for a laugh.
MAXIE: They look kinda cute.
MAX: Oh, yeah?
MAXIE: Yeah.
MAX: Well . . . g'night.
MAXIE: G'night.

>   *(HE goes back to bed. SHE goes to the chair. THEY both try to get comfortable.)*

MAX: Tough gettin' to sleep.
MAXIE: You said it. *(Pause)*   Are you gonna turn out the light
or what?
MAX: Oh, yeah.

> *(HE does so. Darkness. Suddenly her window shade rolls up.
> We have the light going on and off. Note:* THE BOY *is operating
> the window shade.)*

MAXIE: You want me to fix it?
MAX: It ain't botherin' me.
MAXIE: Good, 'cause I'm too tired.
MAX: You work hard. You're a pro. No wonder you're tired.
MAXIE: That's the nicest thing you've ever said to me.
MAX: Well, kid, you can take it.
MAXIE: . . . I wonder if I can take it sometimes.
> *(MAX sits up in bed. Turns on light)*
MAX: Are you kiddin' me? We're going all the way! All the way!
MAXIE: All the way.
MAX: We're gonna make it, you and I, 'cause we're both just alike.
We're not gonna let anything get in the way of the act. I mean, a
lot of people, they mess things up. They get their professional and
the personal all mixed up.
MAXIE: Like with romance.
MAX: Yeah! But that's the good thing about us.
MAXIE: What?
MAX: We're too professional to let that happen.   *(Pause)*   Aren't
we?
MAXIE: Sure we are.
> *(HE turns light off. Pause)*
MAX: You asleep yet?
MAXIE: No.
MAX: You know, Maxie . . . something hit me the other day. We
do another year of the act, then we hit New York.
MAXIE: New York. Wouldn't that be swell. Not being on the road.
No more flea bag hotels. No more trains to catch . . . New York.
MAX: Yeah, New York. See the old neighborhood. See all the guys.
I wonder what Tommy Lark's up to these days. Wouldn't it knock
him for a loop to see me—a headliner. To be able to walk down the
street and have people recognize me. Have people I don't even know
say—"Hi ya, Max"—"Loved the show, Max"—"Can I have your
autograph, Mr. Love?" To be somebody in New York—Now wouldn't
that be swell? How's your chair?
MAXIE: It's okay.
> *(HE turns on the light.)*

MAX: 'Cause y'know you're half of this act. If I lose you, I'm sunk.

MAXIE: Yeah . . . so?

MAX: Well, I was thinking half of the act is entitled to half of the bed. You got two shows tomorrow. You should take care of yourself! Get a good night's sleep! Like in a bed!
      (Pause)

MAXIE: You want me to sleep with you? Over there? Thanks but no thanks. What do you think, I was born yesterday? Probably be trying to sell me the Brooklyn Bridge next. I won't sleep over there . . I won't . . . I won't unless . . .

MAX: Unless what?

MAXIE: Unless there was something between us.

(SHE *looks at the suitcase.* HE *gets the idea and drags the suitcase up on the bed.)*

Oh . . . well . . . in that case.

(SHE *goes to the bed, gets in, with the suitcase between them. The sexual tension between them is incredible.)*

MAX: This way we can both get a good night's sleep. What could be more sensible?

MAXIE: You're right. It's sensible.

MAX: Well . . . g'night.

MAXIE: G'night.
      (HE turns out light.)
      You forgot something.
      (HE turns light on.)

MAX: What?

MAXIE: *(Professionally)* You forgot to kiss me goodnight.

MAX: Oh . . . g'night.
      (HE kisses her quickly, turns out light. SHE turns it back on.)
      This is all still professional, right?

MAXIE: Right.

MAX: It's just I don't want to do anything to hurt the act. *(Pause)* This isn't gonna hurt the act, is it?

MAXIE: This is gonna help the act.

MAX: Y'know, I know I should want to do this but . . .

MAXIE: But what?

MAX: I'm a little nervous.

MAXIE: Sure you're nervous. You're finally doing something where you don't want to get a laugh.
      (Pause)
      Turn out the light, Max.

(HE *turns out the light. Blackout. In the dark, the sound of the suitcase being knocked off the bed.)*

SCENE SIX

BOY: *(As* HE *turns on the light)* Max and Maxie—five minutes.

(THEY *get up and go behind the screen to get dressed. The* BOY *returns to the seats.)*

MAXIE: Max . . . am I good?

MAX: God, I hate matinees. Three shows a day and they make us do matinees.

MAXIE: Max . . . am I good?

MAX: Mmmmm?

MAXIE: Am I good?

MAX: Babe, you're a heckuva dancer.

MAXIE: Thank you, Max. I come from a long line of dancers, you know.

MAX: No, I didn't know that.

MAXIE: Oh, yes. My mother was a dancer. She lived in Spain. She danced for the King of Spain as a matter of fact.

MAX: That's good, babe.

MAXIE: It was great. My mother danced in the gardens of the King of Spain. Where the swans played in the orchestra and the musicians sailed their violins across the royal pond. It was a private performance. No one was there. They were alone, as alone as you and I.

MAX: That's great, babe.

MAXIE: *(Laughing)* Isn't it funny. You call me "babe" and everyone else calls me "mom."

MAX: Yeah, babe.

MAXIE: Max. . . I need to know. . . Was I good for you last night?

MAX: You were terrific the other night! You were great the other night! Don't change anything! You fed me brilliantly!

BOY: Is that the way it happened?

MAX: Yes, that's the way it happened.

MAXIE: Max . . . I need to know . . . Am I good?

MAX: You were wonderful. You were marvelous! Babe. I love you.
    (Slight pause)

BOY: Is that the way it happened?

MAX: Yes, that's the way it happened.

MAXIE: Max . . . I need to know . . . Am I good.

MAX: You were okay. Not good. Okay. Okay? Take your timing off me.

(Slight pause)

BOY: Is that the way it happened?

MAX: *(Feebly)*   No, that's not the way it happened.

MAXIE: Max . . . I need to know . . . Am I good?

MAX: No . . . your timing was off . . . you're just a lousy . . .

BOY: Don't you remember. How long we've been together? Don't you remember?

MAX: . . . It was a long time ago. I don't remember.

(The BOY *begins to clap.* MAX *and* MAXIE *go and get into the bed.)*

SCENE SEVEN

(A hotel room. Night. Darkness. Suddenly, a bedside light goes on. MAX *and* MAXIE *in bed.* MAX *gets out of bed, excitedly runs to bureau to get his pencil and script.)*

MAX: Babe! Babe! Quick, wake up, babe!

MAXIE: What! What is it? What is it? Is the hotel on fire? Fire!! Fire!! We're on fire!!

(SHE jumps out of bed.)

MAX: No, we're not. No, we're not.

(SHE sees the script.)

MAXIE: What's that?

MAX: It's the script. I just had a great idea for the act. Come on, babe, get up.

MAXIE: Now? Get up now?

MAX: Babe, when you hear this idea, you're gonna be glad I woke you up.

MAXIE: Wanna bet?

MAX: C'mon, babe
   (SHE sits up.)
   Atta girl.

MAXIE: Where do we start?

MAX: Start where the cop says "It was July. It was July. I was patrolling my vegetable."

MAXIE: "Vegetable?"

MAX: "I mean, patrolling my beat . . ."   *(Pause)*

MAXIE: What're you doing?

MAX: Holding for my laugh.

MAXIE: What laugh?

MAX: The laugh I'm going to get when you say, "vegetable" and I
say, "patrolling my beat." *(Pause)* Beet. As in beet. The vegetable.

MAXIE: You think you're going to get a laugh on "patrolling my
beat?"

MAX: I will if you say "vegetable" right.

MAXIE: Oh, brother.

MAX: " . . . When I heard a woman scream. I rushed upstairs.
When I reached the second floor, the yelling was louder; when I
reached the third floor, the yelling was still louder. Then I stopped . . ."

(HE *points to the line he wrote for* MAXIE *to speak.)*

MAXIE: "To get your gun?"

MAX: "No, I was in the wrong building. Gnong, gnong, gnong! So I
rushed down again, up the right building, came face to face with a
man holding a gun! He was going to shoot his wife. I said, 'Stop.'
He turned around, looked at me, and laughed. Oh, what a dirty
laugh! Then he started toward me with fire in his eyes. Nearer and
nearer he came with fire in his eyes. Four feet. Three feet. Two
feet. One foot. Laughter in his face, the gun in his hand . . . fire in
his eyes."

(HE *points to the line.)*

MAXIE: "What did you do?"

MAX: "I sang (HE *sings:)* 'When Irish Eyes are Smiling . . .'"

MAXIE: "What did he do?"

MAX: "He shot himself." *(Pause)* Well, is it funny?

MAXIE: Not in the middle of the night.

MAX: Look, I gotta know you like it. I gotta know it's funny. I can't
sell you and the audience at the same time.

MAXIE: Here we go, it's always me. Whatever's wrong with the
act, it's always me. You're the funnyman. If it's so funny, you tell
me. Whatever you say, Max.

MAX: But you like it?

MAXIE: Sure.

MAX: You sure?

MAXIE: Sure I'm sure. Let's go to bed.

(THEY *begin to get in bed.)*

MAX: I think it's funny.

MAXIE: I do too, let's go to bed.

MAX: It just needs a little work.

MAXIE: Sure it does.

MAX: It's a new bit.

MAXIE: We'll have to work on it. *(Turns light out)* G'night.

MAX: Maybe patrolling my broccoli.

MAXIE: G'night.

(The train whistles. MAX crosses and puts on his overcoat and hat, gets the umbrella. MAXIE puts on her dress and hat, picks up her suitcase and runs to catch the train which has left.)

BOY: All aboard . . . train for Minneapolis, Vancouver, Winnepeg and all igloos in between . . . all aboard!!!

SCENE EIGHT

(A railway station. Night. Rain. MAXIE alone, sitting. The BOY comes in dressed as an impoverished newspaper boy. MAXIE comes in. The BOY comes up to MAX. Offers him the headline.)

BOY: "Death in Europe," read all about it.
MAX: Beat it, will ya.
   (The BOY exits.)
MAXIE: You're back.
MAX: We missed the train.
MAXIE: You're here to tell me that. We saw it pull outta the station.
MAX: Okay. Okay.
MAXIE: I know a train when I see a train.
MAX: Okay. Okay.
MAXIE: When's the next train to Winnepeg?
MAX: Three hours. There's a milk run.
   (HE sits.)
God, my arm.
MAXIE: Your arm? What about my feet?
MAX: I do falls on this arm three shows a day.
MAXIE: What d'ya think I'm doin', sittin' in an easy chair?
MAX: Three shows a day.
   (Pause)
MAXIE: I thought maybe you'd skipped.
MAX: When?
MAXIE: When you left.
MAX: You knew I'd come back.
MAXIE: Why? Sometimes guys skip.
MAX: Hey, we got the act.
MAXIE: Yeah, but you had the look in your eye.
MAX: What look?
MAXIE: The look when people skip.
BOY: Extra, extra, read all about it! Love thinking of leaving partner! Ditching her in parts unknown!
MAX: Getta outta here, willya? *(Pause. To MAXIE)* Are you wet?

MAXIE: Am I wet?
MAX: Good.
MAXIE: . . . What?
MAX: Nothing.
MAXIE: C'mon.
MAX: I just didn't wanna be the only one who was wet, that's all.
MAXIE: So if you're wet, you want the whole world to be wet. That's some attitude.
> (HE *shrugs.* SHE *takes out a sandwich, unwraps it.)*
MAX: What're you gonna do with that?
MAXIE: What'd ya think?
MAX: I thought you didn't have any left.
MAXIE: Why?
MAX: 'Cause I don't have any left.
MAXIE: You ate yours.
MAX: I was hungry.

> (SHE *begins to take a bite, can see he wants it.* SHE *offers him a bite.)*

Thanks.

> (HE *savors his bite.* THEY *chew in silence. Finally,* HE *pulls out a bit of chocolate.)*

MAXIE: What's that?
MAX: Dessert.
> (HE *breaks off a bit for each of them.* THEY *eat.)*
Gotta new one. A guy runs into a guy, he says, "Hey, how's tricks," says "Didn't you know?" Says, "Know what?" Says, "Got married." Says, "Married?" Says, "Yeah, honeymooned in Maine." Says . . .
MAXIE: "What'd you do, Bangor?"
> (*Silence. The rain)*
MAX: You knew the joke.
MAXIE: I'd heard it, yeah.
MAX: You could've told me.
MAXIE: I would've if I'd known what you were going to say.
MAX: I'm your partner. You're supposed to know what I'm going to say before I say it.
MAXIE: Believe me, it's getting to that point.
MAX: Are you complaining?
MAXIE: I'm a pro. I don't complain.
> (*Silence. The rain)*
We're broke. I'm wet and I'm hungry.
MAX: Things could be worse.

MAXIE: How?

MAX: Hey, look, at least we're still in show biz.

MAXIE: Winnepeg.

MAX: What?

MAXIE: What's in Winnepeg?

MAX: Work is in Winnepeg.
    (Pause)

MAXIE: I thought a guy was going to attack me.

MAX: Who?

MAXIE: While you were gone.

MAX: Who?

MAXIE: A guy.

MAX: Which guy.

MAXIE: He called me names.

MAX: Nobody calls you names! He does it again you just let me
    know! I'll be on him like a shot. I'll be all over him! Like white on
    bread! How big was he?

MAXIE: He was big, Max.

MAX: Ah, he was probably drunk. Out of his head. Pay no attention.

MAXIE: See, you can't protect me.

MAX: Am I supposed to protect you?

MAXIE: We're partners.

MAX: I know.

MAXIE: We have the act.

MAX: *(Weakly)* He was drunk. He was out of his head.

MAXIE: *We're* out of our heads.

MAX: Why?

MAXIE: We're waiting in the rain for a train to Winnepeg.
    (Silence. The rain. SHE *laughs.)*

MAX: What's so funny?

MAXIE: My mother thinks I'm in a convent.

MAX: Really? Why?

MAXIE: I write her telling her I'm in a convent.

MAX: Oh.

MAXIE: She wouldn't like the idea my being in show business.

MAX: Oh.

MAXIE: My mother's old world Catholic.

MAX: She wouldn't like the idea of my being Jewish, huh?

MAXIE: My mother's old world Catholic.
    (The BOY *comes in with newspapers shouting headlines.)*

BOY: Extra, extra! Read all about it—Old world Catholics hate Jews.
    Marriage doomed from beginning. Love skips out before it's too late.

MAX: C'mon! Beat it, will ya?
    (The BOY *exits.)*
    Babe?

MAXIE: Yeah?
MAX: Are you happy with me?
       (SHE *laughs. Silence. The rain*)
  You've given up a lot for me.
MAXIE: We thought it would work out.
MAX: So, you think we oughta split up?
MAXIE: Maybe do a singles act.
MAX: . . . okay.
MAXIE: . . . okay.
MAX: Shake.
       (THEY *shake.*)
  Here.

       (HE *takes out the boodle. Divides the money.* HE *gives her her
       share.* SHE *holds up a penny.*)

MAXIE: A penny for your thoughts.
       (HE *shrugs, hopelessly.*)
  No hard feelings?
MAX: No hard feelings.
MAXIE: What'll you do?
MAX: I dunno. Go to Winnepeg.
       (*Pause.* SHE *picks up her bags.*)
MAXIE: Well, so long.
MAX: You going?
MAXIE: Yeah.
MAX: What about that guy. The one that bothered you.
MAXIE: He's still as big as he ever was, Max. He's bigger than both
  of us.
       (*Pause*)
  Well, buena suerte. Good luck.
MAX: Good luck. You deserve it.
MAXIE: You too.
MAX: You're a good dancer.
MAXIE: You're a funny fella.
       (SHE *turns and begins to walk away.*)
BOY: Extra! Extra! Read all about it! Love deserts comedy partner,
  ends possibility of great career. Loves her so much he can't see
  straight.
MAX: Maxie! Wait!
MAXIE: (*Turning*) What?
MAX: You can't leave!
MAXIE: Why not!
MAX: Because I . . . because I . . .
MAXIE: Yeah?

MAX: You can't walk out on the act.

MAXIE: The act.

MAX: Stick with me, babe. One more month. Please. Please. Look, you got talent. I got talent. We got the act. I just got it in my head that we can make it.

(HE *kneels.*)

I swear by the moon and all the stars that this dream of mine will come true.

MAXIE: Oh. For a second, I thought you were proposing.

MAX: Why would I do that?

MAXIE: *(Sitting on bags)* Winnepeg.

(MAXIE *goes behind the screen to change into costume.* MAX *exits to get the life jacket and change.*)

SCENE NINE

(Lake Lackawanna, 1922)

(MAX *and* MAXIE *outside the cabin. A beautiful day. The lake just beyond them, the clouds moving slowly across the horizon.* MAX *is blowing up a life jacket.* THEY'RE *both in swimsuits.* HE *wears a straw hat.)*

MAXIE: Max?

MAX: Yeah, babe.

MAXIE: Where do clouds come from?

MAX: I dunno, babe.

(Pause)

MAXIE: Where do they go when they're gone?

MAX: I dunno.

(Pause)

MAXIE: Where do they go when there's no place else to go?

MAX: They go hang out over China. How the hell do I know where clouds go? It's one of them things.

MAXIE: You know, I never thought we'd make it up here to the lake.

MAX: Why not?

MAXIE: Things looked so bleak right before Winnepeg. We didn't have any bookings.

MAX: But, babe, I said we'd get here.

MAXIE: I just never knew.

MAX: Don't ya like it up here?

MAXIE: I love it up here. All these trees.

MAX: Yeah, it's like a tree factory.

(Pause)

MAXIE: You don't miss it?

MAX: Miss what?

MAXIE: The business.

MAX: *(HE misses it.)* This life-jacket's givin' me the business.
(Pause) I think I'm gettin' a heart attack. I'm too young to die of
a heart attack.

MAXIE: C'mon over here.

(HE goes over to her, lies in her lap.)

Ya happy?

MAX: I'm exhausted.

MAXIE: But are ya happy?

MAX: Yeah, sure, babe.

MAXIE: I never feel like you're happy.

MAX: Of course, I am. I got my work. I got my girl. It's all terrific.
(Pause) How much longer we got here?

MAXIE: One week. *(Pause)* We got a lot of friends up here. We
have bar-be-ques. We got the sunsets on the lakes. It's all great
here. Isn't it all great here?

MAX: Yeah.

MAXIE: Did ya ever get to spend much time in nature as a kid?

MAX: Nature? Nature was the East River.

MAXIE: Was it nice?

MAX: *(HE slaps a mosquito.)* We lived near the 90th Street pier.
They used to deliver ice there from ferryboats that came from As-
toria. On Sundays over in Queens, there'd be these dollar beer parties
in the summer. My old man was an upholsterer. I can remember all
the presents I had in my childhood. A bag of candy, a five dollar
sailor-suit, and a trip with my father to the Yiddish theatre. My
mother did sewing. I had a dog named Fanny. One Christmas, I put
up my stocking and next day there was nothing in it. My mother
took in sewing and that was my childhood. *(Pause)* Oh yeah. And
I swam off the pilings in the East River with my best friend, Tommy
Lark. C'mon, let's do this boat thing.

MAXIE: What boat thing?

MAX: It's the thing we talked about. Y'know, safety on the lake.
We could drown ourselves if we put our minds to it.

*(HE leads her over to the boat. SHE stops and picks up the
picnic basket.)*

What's with the picnic basket?

MAXIE: We'll have a basket. I want this to be realistic.

MAX: Realistic! She wants it realistic! Now, we're gonna do this with the boat onshore.
    (MAX hands her the parasol from the bed.)
  Okay. This is a paddle drill.
MAXIE: Paddle? I thought we had a motor.
MAX: We do. But sometimes motors go out.
MAXIE: You're tellin' me. What about last night?
MAX: Look, don't gimme a hard time 'bout last night.
MAXIE: That's fair. You didn't give me a hard time.
MAX: Look, I'm not used to all this relaxation. The crickets last night were murder. I couldn't sleep a wink.
MAXIE: That's not all ya couldn't do.
MAX: Pipe down! Pipe down! Okay? This is a paddle. Ya got that much?
MAXIE: It's a strain, but I'll manage somehow.
MAX: Okay. You get one. I get one.
MAXIE: We both gonna do the rowin'?
MAX: You're a professional, ain't ya?
MAXIE: Yeah, but not on a lake.
MAX: This is only in case of dire emergency. Okay. You get in this end. I get in this end.
MAXIE: You come from the East Side, how come you know so much about boats?
MAX: My folks came across the Atlantic in one. It's in the blood. Okay. So you go back there.

    (MAXIE goes to middle of boat. Picks up paddle. MAX turns, leans over to get a life preserver.)

  Don't forget your life jacket.
MAXIE: My what?

    (MAXIE turns with paddle and inadvertently smacks MAX on the behind—MAX loses his balance.)

MAX: Aahh!
MAXIE: Aahh!
    (HE falls, tipping boat over. THEY both fall out on the ground.)
MAX: What's the matter with you? Don't ya know you're not supposed to stand up in a boat? Who do you think you are? George Washington?
MAXIE: I was findin' my paddle!
MAX: C'mon! C'mon, get in your life jacket.

    (THEY both take out the life preservers. THEY get in the boat, MAX in the front, MAXIE in the back.)

Wait a minute. Something's wrong.
MAXIE: What is it now, Captain Courageous?
MAX: I should be in the back.
MAXIE: Why?
MAX: 'Cause I'm stronger, I can steer. C'mon, let's change.
     (MAXIE starts to get out of the boat.)
Hey, I know you're Catholic, but you can't walk on water.

(THEY stand and begin to swap places. THEY meet in the middle. It's very cramped. It's awkward because THEY both have paddles and the picnic basket is right under their feet. But, naturally, THEY don't think of stepping out of the boat and walking around each other.)

Excuse me.
MAXIE: Excuse me.
MAX: Little cramped, isn't it?
MAXIE: Don't step on the picnic basket.
MAX: Shall we dance?
MAXIE: Here, hold my paddle and I can just scoot by.
MAX: *(Taking her paddle)*   Hold your paddle. What do I look like, a door man?

(SHE begins to try to move around MAX and the paddles. MAX, however, keeps wriggling the paddles into different permutations. SHE can't easily scoot by. Makes an effort to climb over him.)

MAXIE: Just hold still.
MAX: What're you doing?

(SHE accidently pushes his hat down over his eyes. MAX panics. SHE climbs up on his shoulders.)

Hey! Hey!
MAXIE: Aaaahh!

(The boat wobbles. THEY topple onto the grass. THEY disentangle themselves, stare at each other.)

What do you call this boat?
MAX: The Lusitania.

(THEY get back into the boat, MAX silently placing MAXIE in the front. HE goes to the rear.)

Okay. Ya ready?

MAXIE: Aye, aye, cap'n.

MAX: Stroke! Stroke! No! No! No! You gotta stroke on the other side.

> *(SHE switches to opposite side.)*

Okay. We do it again.

> *(HE watches over his shouder this time.)*

Stroke! Stroke! . . . No! No! No! You gotta stroke when I stroke.

MAXIE: I'm strokin', I'm strokin' already!

MAX: But your strokes gotta be in time with my stokes. Otherwise we go like this.

> *(HE makes a zig-zag movement with his hands.)*

. . . and we never get where we're going! Okay, let's do it again and see if you can do it right. Do it in time, this time.

> *(THEY get set again.)*

Okay. Stroke! Stroke! No! No! No! Keep in time! Keep in time!

MAXIE: How can I keep in time when you're back there and I'm up here?

MAX: You're a dancer, ain't ya?

MAXIE: Yeah, but I ain't got eyes in the back of my head.

MAX: You ain't got eyes in the front of your head!

MAXIE: You're a fine one to be talkin' about eyes. You're so cross-eyed I bet you see everything in double. I bet you *think* everything in double.

MAX: That's not true. That's not true.

MAXIE: There, ya just did it!

MAX: Hey! Look can't you just steal a look like this?

> *(MAX demonstrates. HE paddles, then quickly jerks his head around to check the imaginary paddler several times, in rapid movements of paddle and head. The annoying thing is HE does it so well.)*

Okay?

MAXIE: Okay!

> *(THEY try it again.)*

MAX: Stroke! Stroke! Stroke! Stroke! Stroke! Stroke! Stroke!

> *(As HE yells out strokes, SHE paddles furiously, jerking her head around. SHE'S hopelessly out of rhythm. Suddenly stops with her head in a funny position)*

MAXIE: Stop! Stop! Stop already!

MAX: What's the matter? You were just getting the hang of it.

> *(SHE stands, turns, goes to the middle of the boat, her head in an odd position.)*

MAXIE: C'mere.

> (MAX *comes to her in the middle of the boat, the picnic basket in between them.*)

Notice anything?
MAX: Yeah, your head's on crooked.
MAXIE: Right. A pain in the ass gave me a crick in the neck.
> (SHE *straightens the crick in her neck with her hands.*)
Don't go away.

> (SHE *bends over, takes a selzer bottle out of the picnic basket, stands and squirts him in the face.*)

MAXIE (Penelope Miller) sprays MAX (Bill Buell) with a seltzer bottle.

MAX: Mutiny! Mutiny!
MAXIE: Yeah, and you're going to get more mutiny if ya keep yelling at me.
MAX: Look, Maxie. You're thinkin' of this all wrong.
MAXIE: Oh yeah?
MAX: Yeah. See this paddling is like. . . like. . . like a marriage!
MAXIE: A marriage?

MAX: Yeah. See your paddlin' has to complement paddlin'. Otherwise, we do this . . .

(HE *does the zig-zag motion with his hands.* SHE *imitates the
zig-zag.)*

That's it, and we never get to where we're going.
MAXIE: If we do it together . . .
MAX: Then . . .

(He *makes a straight hand gesture.* SHE *imitates it.* THEY
get back into position.)

MAXIE: It's like marriage, huh?
MAX: Just like marriage. Okay. One, two, three. Stroke! Stroke!
Stroke! Stroke! Stroke!

(THEY *are in perfect unison. Long, slow strokes)*

That's it. You got it! We're together. Smooth sailin' all the way.

(THEY *paddle in silence. From time to time, exchange warm
glances)*

Take a break, kid. Ya done good.
(SHE *reclines in the boat.* SHE *opens the parasol.)*
MAXIE: Where ya takin' me, Max?
MAX: I'm takin' ya any place you want to go.
MAXIE: Any place in the world?
MAX: You bet.
MAXIE: Then take me . . . take me . . . take me to where the
clouds go! Take me to China.
MAX: China, comin' up! First floor, Kansas City, Wichita Falls,
novelties, Nevada and women's lingerie.
MAXIE: All ashore that's going ashore. Are we to China yet?
MAX: Nah, not yet. We just made it to . . . Honolulu!
MAXIE: Did you say Honolulu?
MAX: I certainly did.

(THEY *both reach down into the boat and bring out ukelelies.*
THEY *stand up and begin to sing.)*

BOTH: "Honolulu Baby
   Where'd you get those eyes
   And your dark complexion
   That I idolize?

Honolulu Baby
Where'd you get those eyes
And your dark complexion
That I idolize."

    (SHE begins the third verse. HE stops and looks at her.)
MAXIE: "Honolulu Baby
Where'd you get that style
And those ruby red lips
With that sunny smile."

C'mon! Sing! Don't stop singing!

"Honolulu Baby
Where'd you get those eyes."

C'mon, Max, sing! I'm having fun!

"Honolulu Baby
Where'd you get those eyes . . ."

    (HE stops her.)
MAX: Marry me, Maxie.
MAXIE: What?
MAX: Marry me.

    (Pause)

MAXIE: Oh, Max. You've been out in the sun too long.
MAX: I mean it.
MAXIE: I mean it too, Max. I was raised a nice Catholic girl. When
it comes to marriage, you don't mess around with a nice Catholic girl.
MAX: Honest, Maxie. I'm crazy about you. I want to marry you.
MAXIE: All right, then, marry me right here.
MAX: Huh?
MAXIE: Marry me, Max. Right here in front of God.
MAX: But, it ain't legal.
MAXIE: Sure it is. Captains on boats marry people. Well, this is a
boat.
MAX: I still don't think it's legal.
MAXIE: We'll get legal later. Just take off your hat and marry me,
Max.
    (HE takes off his hat.)
MAX: Well. Ahem. "We are gathered here today to join this man
and woman together in marriage. And they'll love each other and
be good to each other for as long as they're married. By that I mean
till they die. I'll work hard"—I mean, "he'll work hard to take care of
her in sickness and in health because he loves her and he'll do all he

can to make their act the best in vaudeville. So without further
ado—Do you Irving Laskowitz . . ."
MAXIE: Irving?
MAX: Yeah. "Do you, Irving Laskowitz, take this woman . . ."
MAXIE: Maxine De La Fuente.
MAX: De La Fuente? Not Maxie L'Amour?
MAXIE: L'Amour is a stage name. De La Fuente.
MAX: "So do the both of you take each other as man and wife, no
matter what the breaks, in sickness and in health till one of both of
you dies?" I do.
MAXIE: . . . I do.
MAX: You do?
MAXIE: I do, Max.
MAX: "Well then—for better or worse, I now pronounce you man
and wife." *(Pause)* Whew! Well, we done it.
MAXIE: You may kiss the bride.
      (THEY *kiss tenderly.)*
And now we'll be happy.
MAX: Yeah, sure.
MAXIE: And you'll love me.
MAX: Yeah, of course.
MAXIE: Nothing bad is going to happen to us. Right?
MAX: What can happen to us?
MAXIE: Nothing. Nothing bad happens to people in love. My mother
said so.

      (SHE *laughs suddenly. Loud hollow laughter. Chilling
laughter)*

MAX: What is it?
MAXIE: *(Suddenly silent)*   Look. A cloud.
      (SHE *points.* THEY *freeze.)*

      (MUSIC: *"I Can't Give You Anything But Love")*

      (The BOY *comes up from the seats with a rope and noose.* HE
puts the noose over her neck.)

BOY: Shall we make her dance? Oh, my, how she used to dance.
Dance. Dog. This will be fun. Dance.

      (HE *shakes the rope.* SHE *taps out upstage. The* BOY *follows
her upstage. The rope is dragged off.* MAX *joins the* BOY *upstage.)*

SCENE TEN

(The Rehearsal Hall)

*(*MAX *and the* BOY *going over the scene.* MAX *suddenly turning towards the* BOY*.)*

MAX: "You there! You there!"
BOY: "Who me, sir?"
MAX: "Come over here!"
BOY: "What, sir?"
MAX: "Come over here! Come over here!"

(The BOY *reluctantly comes over.* MAX *grabs him violently, shakes him.)*

"Where are the others?"
BOY: "What others?"
MAX: "All the others."
BOY: "There are no others!"
MAX: "Liar! Liar!"
BOY: "There's only me."
MAX: "Yesterday there were millions."
BOY: "There's only me."
MAX: "Where are they? They couldn't have slaughtered them all! Where would they have hidden the corpses?"
BOY: "The diggers are devoted."
    (Pause)
MAX: "Yesterday there were others?"
BOY: "Yes, sir."
MAX: "And today there are none?"
BOY: "No, sir."
MAX: "We are all that are left?"
BOY: "Yes, sir."

*(*MAX *clasps the* BOY *to his breast. Looks about in anguish. The* BOY *pushes him off.)*

"You stink!"
MAX: "Of garlic?"
BOY: "Of mortality."
MAX: "Doesn't everybody? *(Pause)* You met no one on the road?"
BOY: "No, sir."
MAX: "Someone was with me. I don't remember who. Someone was with me. I don't remember where."

BOY: "When was this?"
MAX: "Ages ago . . . yesterday."
BOY: "And you don't remember?"
MAX: *(Angrily)* "I'm not a scholar of ancient history" . . . How
the hell should I know?
      (Pause)
BOY: That's not in the script.
MAX: What?
BOY: That line—"How the hell should I know."
MAX: *(Desperate)* Just go on. Just . . . go on. We've got to get to
the end . . . finish.

      *(Pause. HE gets back into character. The BOY turns as if to
      leave.)*

"You there, boy! Where are you going?"
BOY: "Home."
MAX: *(Imploringly)* "Home?"
BOY: "Yes, sir."
MAX: "How do you get there?"
      (Silence)
"Do you know me, boy?"
BOY: "No, sir."
MAX: "You've never seen me?"
BOY: "No, sir."
MAX: "I am your father." *(Pause)* "It doesn't matter. It's getting
dark. We'd best seek shelter. We can't stay out here on the road."
BOY: "Why not?"
MAX: "Fool! They'll beat us."
BOY: "Why?"
MAX: "Because we're human."

      *(MAXIE appears upstage. MAX takes the BOY by the shoulder.
      THEY begin to move away. MAX turns and looks.)*

"And yet, I know someone was with me. Someone I've lost. I don't
remember who. Someone was with me. I don't remember where."
BOY: "But yesterday."
MAX: "Yes, perhaps it was yesterday."
BOY: "Did you love them?"
MAX: "It was such a long time ago."
BOY: "How long?"
MAX: "Years ago . . . yesterday . . . come fool. Come."
      (THEY start to take a step, stop.)

      (Blackout)

END OF ACT ONE

ACT TWO

SCENE ONE

(The Rehearsal hall. The BOY *and* MAX. THEY *are in the same position as at the end of Act I.)*

MAX: "Let's go."
BOY: "We can't."
MAX: "Why not?"
BOY: "We're waiting."
MAX: "For who?"
BOY: "For him."
MAX: "For who?"
BOY: "You know."
       (Pause. MAX *tries to remember his lines and can't.)*
MAX: What? What'd you say?
BOY: Nothing, sir.
MAX: Yes you did! Yes you did!
BOY: No, I . . .
MAX: Don't interrupt me! Don't contradict me! Don't leave me!
BOY: "The dead have many faces."
MAX: "The dead have many faces."
BOY: "They will not let us sleep."
       (MAX resumes the gesture. It's no good. HE *can't remember.)*
MAX: Uh, let's take a break. I'm a little . . .
BOY: Tired?
MAX: I am not tired. I'm hungry.
BOY: Yes.
MAX: And you don't need to finish my thought for me.
BOY: No, sir.

(Pause. THEY *sit down on the two chairs.* THEY *each begin unwrapping their lunch sandwiches in silence.)*

   You're doing much better on your lines.
MAX: I'm doing lousy on my lines. That's why we're taking a break.
       (Pause)
BOY: Do you mind if I say something?
MAX: . . . What?
BOY: I just think you're an inspiration. I mean, here you are on your day off, coming in to work on your lines.
MAX: I'm just doing my job. I'm paid to be the best.

BOY: *(Enthusiastically)* Well, that's what you are in my book. You're the best. You're the best I've ever worked with.

MAX: . . . Who have you worked with?

BOY: I've done two years at the Cleveland Playhouse . . . I guess that doesn't mean much to you . . .

MAX: No.

BOY: This is my first job since coming to New York. I mean, I got it in New York. Of course, I don't always want to stage manage . . . do you know what I plan on doing?

MAX: *(Uninterested)* Okay. What?

BOY: I want to be an actor.

MAX: Oh yeah? Who's your favorite actor?

BOY: Marlon Brando.

MAX: Unnhhmmmm.

BOY: I like him because he's so subtle . . . Oh! But I've learned a lot from you, too, Mr. Love.

MAX: Never! Never copy me! *(Irritably)* You can't copy from someone like me. I'm an original. You can learn from excellence. You can study from someone who's excellent. But never try to copy an original. What works for me won't work for you. It took me a long time to figure that out.

BOY: You mean you tried to copy someone else's style?

MAX: No. But I tried to make someone else copy *my* style.

BOY: Who was that? You mean Maxie?

MAX: *(Coldly)* It's none of your goddamn business!

    (Silence. MAX sees that HE has hurt the BOY'S feelings.)

    Hey look, kid . . . you want some of my sandwich?

BOY: No thanks.

MAX: C'mon. It's a good sandwich . . . my wife made it . . . what's the matter? You got something against my wife's cooking?

BOY: No, sir.

MAX: That's because you never had my wife's cooking. Here, take it.

    (HE gives the BOY his sandwich. MAX immediately regrets doing so. The BOY takes a big, healthy bite.)

    What's the matter? Don't they feed you at home?

BOY: I'm sorry, Mr. Love. I can't eat your sandwich.

MAX: Oh, yeah? You were giving me a good impression of it.

BOY: Here, you take it.

MAX: You're right, I need my strength. I may have a temperature.

BOY: You think you're coming down with something?

MAX: I'm *always* coming down with something! I'll probably die of something one of these days.

(MAX opens a thermos of hot soup. Pours himself some. Blows on it. Elaborate preparations for the first sip. Sips. Spits it out spraying the BOY in the face. Simply:)

Not enough salt.

(The BOY wipes. MAX adds more salt. A lot of salt. Way too much salt. The BOY does a "take" to the audience. We know what's coming. MAX sips. Sprays. The BOY sits there. MAX closes thermos. The BOY smiles, face dripping.)

BOY: Lemme guess . . . too much salt.
MAX: Way too much. I have to be very careful with salt. High blood pressure, y'know. I mean, let's face it.
    (The BOY wipes his face.)
BOY: Yes, well, I definitely faced it.
MAX: Oh, yeah? You too? Gee, you're too young for high blood pressure. You oughta take it easy.
BOY: Look Mr. Love, I'm sorry if I got too personal a moment ago. I mean, bringing up your partner and all.
MAX: Ah, forget it, kid. It's okay. Forget it. Sometimes people do insensitive things and they don't even know it. It's just something that happened a long time ago. Her and me. I'm not good at talkin' about things like that . . . And it's this crazy play!
    (HE picks up speech.)
I mean, I know it's supposed to be tragic, but I think there's a lotta gags in here. I mean, what the hell does it all mean?
BOY: *(Blurting)* I think it means—
MAX: Yesssss?
BOY: *(Catching himself)* No, I, uh—
MAX: No—I—um—what—second cousin?
BOY: It's just that—
MAX: It's just that what?
BOY: I shouldn't tell you about the play, Mr. Love.
MAX: Why not? Is it a crime that I should know something about this play? You know something about this play—what is it?
BOY: Well, as long as you asked, the theory that I'm about to espouse is the exegisis of the notion that the play matriculates on various levels of reality, surreality, consciousness, unconsciousness, a sort of post-Joycean stripped to the bare bones theatrical kind of stark, stark, starkness. That includes the manifold aspects of theatrical devices, totalling, to the breathing mosaic of the spontaneous and the cerebral, culminating in the author's serio-comic, Gaelic Gaullic, post-impressionistic, pseudo-expatriotic, Viconian, Proustian vision of the time remembered, impotent vision of human fallibilities, co-joined, coupled, linked and juxtaposed with an ear and eye for the

sorrow and the pity of the manifest . . . manifestation of the human
spirit, in spite of pain, in spite of confusion, in spite of reality and
illusion, the life of the mind, the life of the body, the brain—Groin
Matrix, that since the Greeks, since the Romans, for that matter
has polarized, split, divided the consciousness of the leading thinkers
of our time. Leading thinkers that in spite of, in regards of, think
they know something, but in point of fact do—KNOW NOTHING—
but continue to pontificate, illustrate, elucidate—as if they knew,
knew, something—to continue, to return, to reiterate—

MAX: Hey, kid.

BOY: Yes.

MAX: You say you've been to college.

BOY: Yes.

MAX: It figures. I didn't understand a word you said.

BOY: Let me be more concise—

MAX: No. Don't be concise. Just make it short. What's this play
about?

BOY: It's about two hours long.

MAX: Yes.

BOY: That's a joke.

MAX: You don't tell the jokes. I tell the jokes. Got it?

BOY: Got it.

MAX: What's the play about?

BOY: Life.

MAX: I see.

BOY: Death.

MAX: That covers a lotta territory.

BOY: Yes. It's about everything and nothing.

MAX: You sound like the director.

BOY: *(Brightening)* Oh really?!

MAX: That's not a compliment.

BOY: Oh.

MAX: I gotta trust somebody—there's gotta be somebody on this
thing I can trust.

BOY: You can trust me.

MAX: Yes. But I can't understand you.

BOY: I mean the style of the play is very stichomythic.

MAX: See, I can't understand you.

BOY: It's a term. It means two actors speaking in alternate lines.

MAX: When?

BOY: Anytime.

MAX: Anytime?

BOY: Yes.

MAX: Alternate lines.

BOY: Yes.

MAX: Like right now?

BOY: Yes.

MAX: I don't understand.

BOY: It's a dialogue, an altercation, especially a dispute.

MAX: That's bullshit.

BOY: That's it.

MAX: No, it isn't.

BOY: Yes, it is!

MAX: I don't know what you're saying.

BOY: You've got it.

MAX: What am I doing?

BOY: Stichomythia.

MAX: I can't even say it and I'm doin' it! Do you think what I'm doin' is okay?

BOY: No, sir.

MAX: Where's my pills? Where's my thermometer. Go away! Go away!

BOY: No. I think you're brilliant.

MAX: Mmmmmm.

BOY: I think you have an instinctive knowledge of the text.

MAX: Yeah, but I don't know what it means.

BOY: The play is about two people trying to get along.

MAX: Yeah! Yeah! Two bums. I mean they shouldn't be together. They're lousy partners. But they pass the time.

BOY: Yes! They tell stories!

MAX: They tell jokes!

BOY: They do bits.

MAX: They do takes.

BOY: They do gags.

MAX: Now I understand! No—I don't understand.

BOY: It's about two people trying to make it down the same road even when it's hopeless.

MAX: How do you know so much?

BOY: I read all about the play in the library.

MAX: In the library?

BOY: Yeah, you're in the library too.

MAX: They have my name inna library?

BOY: What's so strange about that? You're famous.

MAX: You never think of living long enough to get your name in a library. I gotta tell my son I'm inna library. He'll getta laugh out of that. Very bright kid, my son. I called him once. I had a bet with a guy about who wrote the Canterbury Tales. My kid knew it was Chaucer right off. Didn't even have to look it up.

BOY: *(Laughing)* Oh, that's funny.

MAX: What is?

BOY: That's a joke, isn't it? I mean everybody knows it was Chaucer.
MAX: I didn't.
BOY: Oh.
MAX: Now, that *is* funny. 65 years old and never read Chaucer.
BOY: Well, no . . .
MAX: Is it good?
BOY: Yeah, it's, uh, not bad.
MAX: Funny language though, ain't it?
BOY: Well, Old English.
MAX: I'm having enough trouble with new English.
BOY: *(Begins to laugh. Suddenly stops)*   Excuse me, that *was* a
    joke, right?
MAX: He doesn't even get my jokes. Goddamnit, of course, it was
    a joke!
BOY: Sorry. Sorry.
MAX: What're you here for, to make me look bad?
BOY: No, sir.
MAX: To undermine my confidence?
BOY: No, sir.
MAX: I'm the comic in this thing.
BOY: Yes, sir.
MAX: Yeah. You went to college?
BOY: Uh, yes, sir.
MAX: Well, that doesn't mean you know funny.
BOY: No, sir.
MAX: I know funny.
BOY: Yes, sir.
MAX: You think you know funny?
BOY: Well, I have a sense of humor.
MAX: My dog has a sense of humor but he doesn't know funny. Who's
    your favorite comic?
BOY: Lenny Bruce.
        (MAX makes a gesture to God.)
MAX: Do you mind if we don't talk for a while?
        (Pause. MAX smokes. Coughs.)
BOY: Are you all right?
MAX: Somebody put fresh air in my cigarettes.
        (The BOY laughs.)
BOY: That reminds me of the W.C. Fields line where a new person
    on the set went out to replace Fields' thermos of grapefruit juice
    and when Fields tasted it he spit it out and said, "Who put grapefruit
    juice in my grapefruit juice?"
        (The BOY laughs. Stops. MAX expressionless)
    There was no vodka in the grapefruit juice. Get it?
MAX: I get it. Bill was good. 'Course he couldn't do what I do.

(Pauses. Smokes)
Two drunks are on a railroad track. Crawling . . . Two drunks . . .
crawling . . . one says . . . sure are a lotta stairs . . . the other
says . . . the other says . . . it's not the stairs I mind. It's the low
bannisters . . . Get it? Low bannisters . . . they're crawling.

BOY: *(Forces laughter)* Oh yes! I get it. Very funny.

MAX: Don't gimme a mercy laugh! Nothing worse than a mercy
laugh. Either it's funny or it isn't.

BOY: I was laughing at the joke, Mr. Love.

MAX: I thought you were giving me a break.

BOY: No, sir.

MAX: Let's just do the lines.

BOY: From where?

MAX: From where we stopped.

BOY: "Look at him."

MAX: "He's awful"

BOY: "He's panting."

MAX: "He's dribbling."

BOY: "He's suffering."

MAX: "Of course he's suffering. He's human, isn't he?"

BOY: "It's not certain."

MAX: "No, nothing is certain."

BOY: "But he's in pain."

MAX: "Why should he be spared? Let 'em all suffer."

BOY: "That was pleasant."

          (MAXIE enters. Slight pause)

   "It's good to be back here."

MAX: "I've never seen this place before in my life."

BOY: "But you've been here in this country. Don't you remember?"

MAX: "What country is this?"

BOY: "A country called the past."

*(The BOY sets up the make-up area with MAXIE. Then HE
goes to the seats.)*

SCENE TWO

(Lights up)

*(MAXIE at the dressing table, staring at herself in the mirror.
SHE strokes her cheeks, slowly with great deliberation, fascina-
tion.)*

(The BOY enters.)

BOY: Love and L'Amour: Five minutes.

MAX: Okay.

BOY: Say, you seen the Great Marcellus?

MAX: The Great Marcellus with the trained seal act?

BOY: No, all the other Great Marcelluses runnin' around here.

MAX: No, I haven't seen him, why?

BOY: 'Cause the Great Marcellus' trained seal just took a shit in the hall. Seal shit. I'm dealing with seal shit!

    (HE exits. MAX sits next to MAXIE.)

MAX: What did you do all day?

MAXIE: Nothing.

MAX: Nothing? You should've done something, babe, gotten out. Gorgeous day outside.

MAXIE: It's not a gorgeous day. It's an ordinary day.

MAX: Hey, what're you talking about? It's a beautiful day. Sun's shining, people out walking.

MAXIE: People are doing the same thing they always do.

    (HE sits with her. Begins putting on his make-up)

MAX: What do you mean?

MAXIE: Oh, you know. People. Things.

MAX: Like what?

MAXIE: Eating.

MAX: Well, of course, they were eating. Do you have any cream?

    (SHE hands him the cream. HE begins to apply the cream.)

MAXIE: Do you think they're happy?

MAX: Who?

MAXIE: All the others.

MAX: Sure. They're like us.

MAXIE: No.

MAX: How we doing on time?

MAXIE: We've got all the time in the world.

    (THEY make-up in silence.)

MAX: I think the leg bit works, don't you?

MAXIE: I guess.

MAX: What d'you mean, you guess? It's a great gag. It's a great idea.

MAXIE: It's your idea.

MAX: I know.

MAXIE: They're all your ideas.

MAX: I know. I'm the comic. You're the dancer. What have you done with the eye pencil?

MAXIE: I haven't *done* anything with it, it's right there.

MAX: Oh.

MAXIE: On top of everything else, are you going blind?

MAX: On top of everything else. What does that mean?

    (Pause)

MAXIE: Their faces are never right.

MAX: Whose?

MAXIE: Them. All those others.

MAX: What're you talking about?

MAXIE: The ones out front. They just stare at you.

MAX: They paid their money.

MAXIE: That doesn't mean they should stare.

MAX: They're not staring. They're laughing.

MAXIE: They didn't laugh in Kansas City.

MAX: They never laugh in Kansas City. State Law.

    (Pause)

MAXIE: They're more than rude. They're not human.

MAX: Who are?

MAXIE: They just stare at you with faces like pie pans. They're just blank. They don't have features. They're like the people in the park.

MAX: What people in the park?

MAXIE: Today, when I went to the park and there were some very unpleasant people in the park. They stared at me. They made fun of me. They laughed at my dress. So I took it off and showed them I didn't care.

MAX: You what!!? Oh, jeez. Come on, that's not funny, babe.

MAXIE: Well, I'm not a comedian, am I? I'm just the dancer. Isn't that what you always say?

    (MAX checks watch.)

MAX: My God, do you know what time it is?

MAXIE: We've got all the time in the world.

    (The BOY enters.)

BOY: Max and Maxie: you're on.

    (HE exits.)

(The lights darken. Side lights go up. THEY go upstage and step beyond the performance curtain. THEIR shadows are cast on the curtain. Footlights go up. THEY begin to do the "cop act" in silence. Every gesture by MAX is greeted with enormous laughter. After only a few moments of this, THEY bow to tremendous response. THEY return to the dressing room.)

MAX: They loved me.

MAXIE: They loved *us*.

MAX: Right. But it was *my* stuff that really killed 'em. We're almost there, babe. We're almost there.

MAXIE: Where is "there"?

MAX: There is where we want to be. There is furs and minks and diamond stick pins and decent rooms, a place to stay out of the rain, Packards and swank hotels away from the East River and box seats

at the Polo Grounds, and Saks Fifth Avenue and more and more
and more. It's our time, babe, and we're gonna get it. It's Gershwin
and Garbo and great, great things, babe.

MAXIE: What're you talking about?

MAX: It's everything we've always worked for, babe. Remember
the night in the rain waiting for the train to Winnepeg?

MAXIE: Ya lost me.

MAX: And we made a promise to the stars and our talent and how
we'd never desert the dream?

MAXIE: I remember . . .

MAX: Well, this is it. I felt it tonight. I've got it. Well, we almost
got it. I could feel it in the audience. I could feel it, babe, like you
could feel flesh. I suddenly *knew*, that we can do it all. That audience
was *with* us. They weren't just laughing. They were crying too.
They were remembering their mothers. Their childhood. I don't
know, it was everything at once and it was all so wonderful. It was
like God had put a big light bulb on the Empire State and gone—
Happy New Year! Click! Everything was bright and burning.

MAXIE: I love you, Max.

MAX: *(Perfunctorily)* Yeah . . . I'm crazy about you too.

MAXIE: Not many people get to feel about something the way you do.

MAX: Huh?

MAXIE: You feel, you're an artist. You know what it is. I know *you*
don't know. But it's there in you. And I'll understand if you ever
have to leave me behind. But I want . . .

MAX: Leave? Are you thinking of leaving? We got the act.

MAXIE: Yeah, we got the act.

> *(Pause. We hear laughter.)*

MAX: C'mon, we gotta go.

MAXIE: Why?

MAX: Them.

MAXIE: Who?

MAX: The act. We gotta go.

MAXIE: Oh.

> *(HE drags her, slowly, slowly to the stage. The footlights go on.
> THEY again perform the act in silence to enormous response.
> THEY take their bow, return to their dressing rooms.)*

MAX: It's getting better. Better. The act, I mean. Did you read
those reviews we got last week? Watch your timing though on the
police station line. You came in a little too soon. When you move
your head, even that much, it steals focus and kills the laugh. Keep
your arm still until I do the take, and don't grin until I do the eye bit.

MAXIE: Anything else?

MAX: What's the matter?

MAXIE: I'm not a machine, y'know.

MAX: I know.

MAXIE: I used to be a dancer.

MAX: There you go! Flyin' off the handle.

MAXIE: What do you care? I do the act, don't I?

MAX: Yeah.

MAXIE: Then shut up. You got nothing to criticize . . . I do the act.
   (The BOY *comes in.)*

BOY: Max and Maxie—you're on. Say, anybody seen the Flying
   Dellasandros?

MAX: Maybe they flew the coop.

BOY: Very funny. You're on.

MAX: C'mon. We've got to go.

MAXIE: Do you think I should cut my hair?

MAX: Sure. Good idea. Get it bobbed. It'll be good for the act.

MAXIE: I think I will cut my hair.
   (SHE gets scissors. Cuts a piece of her hair. HE stops.)

MAX: What're you, crazy . . .

MAXIE: I thought it would be good for the act.
   (Fanfare. The BOY *comes in.)*

BOY: Max and Maxie, you're on.

MAXIE: Where we going?

MAX: We've got to go. They're waiting.

MAXIE: Who?

MAX: Them.

MAXIE: Who are they?

MAX: Come on.

MAXIE: Why?

MAX: They're expecting us.

MAXIE: Who?

MAX: The audience.

   (MAX and MAXIE *move upstage.* MAX *holds the curtain.* SHE
   goes out onstage. HE *is about to go when the* BOY *stops him.)*

BOY: Telegram, Mr. Love.
   (MAX reads it. The BOY *looks over his shoulder.)*
   Hmm. Nice offer. Are ya gonna take it?

MAX: I can't. It'd mean breaking up the act.

BOY: Think about it.

MAX: My career.

BOY: What about her?

MAX: You're right. I can't leave her alone!
   (MAX about to enter stage. The BOY *stops him.)*

BOY: You can't keep doing the act.
MAX: Yeah. I can't keep doin' the act.
BOY: You gotta do what you gotta do.
MAX: Yeah.
BOY: To be a star.
MAX: Yeah! No! I can't leave her alone.
BOY: She'll be all right.
MAX: No. She's alone.
BOY: You have to be tough to be a star! To make sacrifices! You gotta do what you gotta do!
MAX: But she's alone! Babe!

(MAX rushes onstage. Applause. Shadows. THEY return. THEY wear huge dark, somber clown costumes with red noses. The costumes dwarf them.)

I just learned.
MAXIE: What?
MAX: Harry Delmar wants me for the Follies.
MAXIE: Harry Delmar! When do we leave?
MAX: After Boston.
MAXIE: Finally, New York.
MAX: He wants me, babe.
MAXIE: What do you mean?
MAX: He wants me, babe.
MAXIE: . . . Okay.
MAX: I love you.
MAXIE: Okay.

(Blackout)

SCENE THREE

(Late night)

(MAX and MAXIE onstage, after a performance. One work-light)

MAX: Well . . . last show for awhile.
MAXIE: Yeah.
    (Pause)
MAX: Don't have another gig till Buffalo, then Rochester, then Boston.
MAXIE: Yeah. *(Pause)* Then you do the Follies.

Photo Credit: Nicholas De Sciose

MAX (Bill Buell) and MAXIE (Penelope Miller) leave the theatre after a performance.

MAX: Yeah, we'll have lots of money.

MAXIE: Yeah.

MAX: You won't have to work.

MAXIE: Yeah.

MAX: Easy street . . . worries are over . . . what's the worst that can happen to us now . . .

MAXIE: I could get pregnant.

      (THEY both laugh. Stop)

MAX: Are you pregnant?

MAXIE: No!

      (THEY laugh.)

I was making a joke.

      (THEY laugh.)

Yeah. I'm pregnant.

      (Silence)

I know I'll have to leave the act. You'll have to hire someone to complete the tour. Someone with quality, not someone that's cheap. Whoever takes my place can't be cheap. Will you marry me, Max?

MAX: Yes.

MAXIE: Good. Good. That's good. Now I'll dance for you.

MAX: You don't have to, kid.

MAXIE: No, this will be a good dance. It will be a wedding dance. I used to be a wonderful dancer, Max.

MAX: You are a dancer, babe.

MAXIE: No, not now.

(SHE *begins to tap.* HE *watches.*)

SCENE FOUR

(*Bedroom.* MAXIE *practicing her tapping. As she hears* MAX *coming in she sits on the bed.*)

MAX: Hey, babe, I'm home. Honey, our ship has finally come in! Look at this.
   (HE *takes out the boodle bag and empties it on the bed.*)
I got a raise in salary! $2,500 dollars a week! It's more than we used to make in six months on the road!

MAXIE: Oh, Max, that's wonderful!

MAX: Not only that, but I'm getting to be quite a celebrity!

MAXIE: (*Coyly*)   My husband? A celebrity?

MAX: That's right! There's a men's store on Broadway. Times Square no less. They gotta picture of me in the window, with a beautiful babe and me in this great gray suit! And the caption says, "Max Love—Broadway's Best-Dressed Comedy Star says—'I demand only the best, in my wine, in my women, in my tailored suits by Howards.'" It's real classy.
   (*Slight pause*)

MAXIE: (*Smiling*)   There's a woman in the picture?

MAX: Yeah, just a model.

MAXIE: Is she pretty?

MAX: Well, you know, a model.

MAXIE: . . . So, how's "Harry White's Revels of 1927" doing?

MAX: "Harry White's Revels of 1927—Starring Max Love," are doing very well, thank you.

MAXIE: How's Dorrine?

MAX: Dorrine? She's fine.
   (HE *embraces her.*)
Did'ja have a good day, babe?

MAXIE: A good day? What's that?

MAX: Gimma a hug!

MAXIE: I don't feel like it.

MAX: What's the matter?

MAXIE: I don't feel like being hugged.

MAX (Bill Buell) teases MAXIE (Penelope Miller) in their New York apartment.

MAX: Why not?

MAXIE: I'm not attractive. I'm pregnant. I'll never be attractive again.

MAX: Of course you're attractive. It's just a thing. Because you're pregnant. But it'll pass.

MAXIE: You like to be by yourself.

MAX: When?

MAXIE: You leave me alone.

MAX: I never leave you alone.

MAXIE: You leave me alone all the time.

MAX: When?

MAXIE: All the time.

MAX: Just to go to the theatre.

MAXIE: You want to be by yourself. *(Pause)* You're happier without me.

MAX: No, I'm not.

MAXIE: The act goes better without me.

MAX: No, it doesn't.

MAXIE: Something's happening.

MAX: It's just the baby.

MAXIE: It's not the baby. It's me. You're never going to let me
back in the act.

MAX: After the baby.

MAXIE: No! That's just an excuse! We built the act together, but
now you're taking it away from me! You're going to let them have me.

MAX: Who?

MAXIE: Them.

MAX: Them who?

MAXIE: Them that wants you to be like the others. It's easy for you.

MAX: It's not easy for me! I'm scared, too! Scared all the time.

MAXIE: It's easier for you. You make people laugh.

     (Pause)

Do I make you happy, Max?

MAX: Yes.

MAXIE: Say "I do," even if I don't.

MAX: Babe, don't you remember the lake?

MAXIE: When?

MAX: At the lake.

MAXIE: The lake?

MAX: You can't have forgotten the lake.

     (Pause)

The theatre! You were happy in the theatre. It'll all be that way
again. I promise.

     (Silence)

MAXIE: What shall we talk about now? I know, let's talk like the
others.

MAX: The others?

MAXIE: The normal people. The people outside of show business.
The ones on the other side of the lights. How do *they* talk?

MAX: I wouldn't know.

MAXIE: They sound so confident.

MAX: They sound secure.

MAXIE: Like they know who they are.

MAX: Like they know what they're doing.

MAXIE: Like they know their dreams.

MAX: Like they don't sweat.

MAXIE: What do they talk about?

MAX: The others?

MAXIE: The normal people.

MAX: Who knows?

MAXIE: They talk about things.

MAX: They talk about selling.

MAXIE: About buying.

MAX: About selling.

MAXIE: Profits and losses.

MAX: Gains and rewards.
MAXIE: Cars.
MAX: Credit.
MAXIE: Kids.
MAX: Bank accounts.
MAXIE: Homes.
MAX: Mortgages.
MAXIE: Clothes.
MAX: Money.
MAXIE: The rent.
MAX: Money.
MAXIE: Furniture.
MAX: Money.
MAXIE: Everything.
MAX: Money . . . what the hell do you want to be like the others for?
MAXIE: Yeah? What the hell do I want to be like the others for?
   (Pause)
MAX: I'm going to go shave. I have a show.

   (HE *exits to bathroom.* MAXIE *goes to the side table.* SHE *takes out a box of matches.* SHE *returns to the bed.)*

(Off)   You'll see, honey, it'll be different from now on. From now on, we won't have any more problems. From now on, we'll have all the money we need.
   (MAXIE *lights the match.)*
You'll see, honey. Things'll be so different after the baby. We'll be rolling in the dough. You'll have the baby and come back to the act, and everything will be like it used to be.
MAXIE: Who'll take care of the kid?
MAX: We'll hire someone.
MAXIE: How will we afford it?

   (SHE *extracts several bills from the wad and lights them.)*
MAX: *(Off)*   I keep telling you. Our money worries are over.
MAXIE: No, they're not, Max.
MAX: *(Off)*   Oh, yes they are!
MAXIE: Oh, not they're not!

   (SHE *burns more bills.)*
MAX: *(Off)*   I'm telling you, our kid is gonna have everything. Everything money can buy.
MAXIE: You mustn't be so extravagant.
MAX: *(Off)*   Why not?
MAXIE: Well, you know how money is. It can burn a hole right through your pocket.

MAX: *(Off)*   Say listen, I'm gonna buy us a car, a swanky apartment, a yacht!

MAXIE: I hope you haven't bought anything on the lay-away plan.

MAX: *(Off)*   I won't have to! I'm going to pay cash.

MAXIE: Sure, you can wait for a fire sale.

MAX: *(Off)*   I don't need no sale. I'm going to buy you the moon and the stars, babe.

MAXIE: The moon and the stars, huh? That sounds like a bargain. A red hot bargain!

(MAX enters with lather on his face. Wiping his hands with a hand cloth)

MAX: Yes, sir, I'm going to buy you the moon and the star . . .

(HE stops, seeing the burning bills on the floor. HE panics, rushes over and begins to stamp out the fire. MAXIE remains impassive.)

What the hell are you doing, babe?! Have you gone crazy?

(HE gets down on all fours and begins to stamp out the bills with his hand cloth.)

This is nuts! Burning money! What do you mean by burning our money?
(HE puts out the fire.)

MAXIE: It's not *our* money.

MAX: What do you mean, it's not *our* money? Whose is it, if it's not ours?

MAXIE: It belongs to you . . . you and your whore.

MAX: My what?

MAXIE: Your whore. Dorrine. That whore you've got in the show with you. The one that's taken my place.

MAX: Honey, babe, sweetheart, you know that's not true.

MAXIE: Isn't it? Oh, isn't it? God, you look funny down there on all fours. Like a dog. Trying to save your precious whore money.

MAX: *(Standing)*   It's not whore money. It's ours, we earned it.

MAXIE: That's not ours! Ours was the money we made on the road! When we lived together. When we worked together. We'd get out there on that stage and we were like one. One person. And I loved it and you loved it too. But you never let me know. You never let me know you liked the way the act was going, 'cause to you—as long as the act was going okay and went well, and I didn't mess up—as long as you got the laughs and people applauded, then the act worked. But you never got it that I was the other half. I was there, too, you know! You wouldn't have gotten your laughs. It's Max and Maxie. Don't forget! Max and Maxie! Well, this, what you're doing now, it may be Broadway, it may pay a lot of money, but don't forget who paid a lot of dues getting you there . . . I know you. She doesn't know you. She'll never know you. We are the act. You're the comedian. I'm the girl dancer. That's the act.

MAX: I'm the comedian. I make them laugh. That's who they pay to see.

MAXIE: And hoofers are a dime a dozen?

MAX: And hoofers are a dime a dozen . . . babe. I've hustled all my life! All of my life, I've hustled.

MAXIE: Who hasn't?

MAX: I'm not giving this up.

MAXIE: I'm coming back to the act.

MAX: What about the baby?

MAXIE: I'm coming back to the act now!

MAX: Babe . . . be reasonable.

MAXIE: What's unreasonable about it?

MAX: You know what the doctors say.

MAXIE: Fuck the doctors!

MAX: Babe, the neighbors.

MAXIE: Fuck the neighbors!

MAX: That's right, fuck everybody!

MAXIE: No, not everybody. I don't fuck you.

MAX: No.

MAXIE: Not since being pregnant. But I don't suppose that matters to you. I suppose you no longer find me desirable because you've got your whore.

MAX: Maxie . . . you are my wife . . . my beloved wife . . . I love you . . . I desire you. I don't sleep with anyone else.

MAXIE: Make love to me.

(SHE *spreads herself out on the bed, seductively.*)

MAX: Huh?

MAXIE: Make love to me. Don't you find me attractive?

MAX: Well, sure, of course I do.

(SHE *begins to raise her skirt as she lies on the bed.*)

MAXIE: Don't you miss me?

MAX: I miss you, more than I can say

MAXIE: It was good with us once, wasn't it?

MAX: Babe . . .

MAXIE: Don't talk.

(MAX crawls on the bed, lies on top of her. Begins to kiss, make love to her)

MAX: Oh, babe.
MAXIE: Max.
MAX: Why can't it be like it used to be?
MAXIE: I don't know.
MAX: I love you. I love you.
        (Pause)
MAXIE: That's the first time you've ever said that like you meant it.

(HE begins to make passionate love to her. SHE begins to laugh. HE sits up.)

MAX: What's the matter with you?
        (SHE continues to laugh.)
  What're you laughing at? Are you laughing at me?
        (SHE laughs.)
  What're you laughing at? What're you laughing at?
        (SHE continues to laugh. HE slaps her.)
MAXIE: Don't say you're sorry.
MAX: I'm not sorry.

(Pause. SHE resumes laughing. MAX sits on the end of the bed, his head in his hands.)

SCENE FIVE

(MAX and MAXIE walking along "the way" arm in arm. HE nods to people. The BOY comes up as an autograph seeker.)

BOY: Gee, Mr. Love, could I have an autograph?
MAX: Sure, kid.
        (HE signs the book.)
BOY: Gee, Mr. Love, do something funny.
MAX: Not now, I'm not working.
        (THEY walk on.)
MAXIE: You know what you've become?
MAX: Yeah. Important.
MAXIE: No. you've become like all the others.
        (Lights change to the "present." Rehearsal lights.)
MAX: *(To the BOY)* What the hell are you bringing all this up for?
BOY: What?

MAX: You weren't there!

BOY: I didn't say I was.

MAX: You read a few books. A few magazine articles! But you don't know me! You don't know me! Who the hell do you think you are? I'm Max Love! I'm Max Love!
 (Pause)

BOY: You know, Mr. Love, I wanted to work with you because I admire you, I respect you. And because you grew up with my grand-dad. And everybody told me you were impossible to work with. But you know what you are?

MAX: What?

BOY: You're impossible to work with!
 (The BOY *begins to leave.)*

MAX: And you know what you are? You're a wise-ass kid who thinks he knows everything!

BOY: I don't know anything.

MAX: That's right. You don't know nothing!

BOY: That's right! I was hoping to learn something from you!

MAX: Sit down! Where you going? Sit down! Do your job.

BOY: I can't do my job with someone yelling at me all the time.

MAX: Okay. I won't yell at the second cousin! I won't yell.

BOY: Oh, you'll yell. You say you won't yell, but you'll yell. You're just like my grandfather!

MAX: *(Yelling)* I won't yell! Stay with me.

BOY: Not if you're gonna yell! After all I've spent two years at the Cleveland Playhouse!

MAX: For that you should be yelling. We used to call Cleveland the mistake on the lake.

BOY: *(Yelling)* It still is!

MAX: *(Yelling)* You see? Now you're yelling.

BOY: *(Yelling)* Okay! I'm yelling! I'm frustrated! I idolize you! I've read everything about you! You treat me like shit! That's why I'm yelling! Why are you yelling?!

MAX: Because you don't know anything about Max and Maxie!
 (Pause)

BOY: I know that Max loved Maxie. Otherwise he wouldn't be yelling about her in a rehearsal hall in Miami after all these years. Am I right? I mean did you love her or didn't you?

 (MAX turns his back on the BOY. Lowers his head. Holds the chair. His shoulders jerk as he cries in silence. HE turns and stares at the BOY. MAXIE appears upstage.)

 Mr. Love . . . I'm sorry. I had no right.

MAX: Could we just do the lines?

(THEY *set up to do the lines.*)
BOY: "It was yesterday, you must remember."
MAX: "It wasn't here."
BOY: "Yes, you were here."
MAX: "It wasn't me."
BOY: "You were here."
       (*Pause*)

SCENE SIX

(*The bedroom.* MAXIE *pacing the bedroom floor with the baby crying in her arms.* MAX *enters, flashily dressed.*)

MAX: Babe, great news. The new show, it's going to be great. $5000 a week. I think it'll run for a year. It's going to be such a hit. Babe, do you hear what I'm saying?
MAXIE: I hear.
MAX: How are you today?
MAXIE: Fine.
MAX: How's the baby?
MAXIE: Fine.
MAX: Lemme hold him for a sec.
MAXIE: No.
       (*Pause*)
MAX: Oh, c'mon.
MAXIE: He doesn't like you. He told me so.
       (*Pause*)
MAX: Honey, you know he can't talk yet.
MAXIE: He told me so.
       (*Pause*)
MAX: Let me hold him.
MAXIE: No.

       (HE *goes near her.* SHE *rushes to the window, tries to throw the baby out the window.* HE *stops her.* SHE *goes to the bed. The baby cries.*)

Help me.
MAX: (*Sings to the baby.*)   "Honolulu baby, where'd you get those eyes? And your dark complexion that I idolize."
       (*To the* BOY)
It all happened such a long time ago when I was young. I don't know
. . . It was all so sad . . . My career was all I could think of . . .

I wanted . . . I wanted . . . what was it I wanted . . . I was always reaching . . . reaching . . .

BOY: Well, you had to, to be a star.

MAX: I didn't have to.

BOY: But the book said it all had to do with her mother.

MAX: Yeah, I suppose so. When her mother died she sat there staring at the casket for three days.

BOY: And after that she was never the same.

(The BOY helps MAX change into a tuxedo.)

SCENE SEVEN

(A sparse, institutional room. MAXIE alone. SHE tries to make herself up. SHE is clearly nervous. SHE tries out several "hellos" to an imaginary MAX. This scene is played as if occuring in the present.)

MAX: *(Enters. HE carries a box.)*   Hello Maxie.

MAXIE: *(Blankly)*   Hello Max . . . How are you?

MAX: *(Automatically)*   Talented.   *(Pause)*   So how are they treating you?

MAXIE: I'm fine.

MAX: Good. That's good.

MAXIE: Won't you sit down?

MAX: I can only stay a minute.

MAXIE: What?

MAX: Yeah, I gotta matinee.

MAXIE: You always hated matinees.
      (HE sits. SHE remains standing. HE stands.)

MAX: Aren't you gonna sit?

MAXIE: Sit? Oh, sure.

(THEY both sit opposite each other: HE in a chair by the door, SHE in a chair by the bed.)

MAX: So, how are they treating you?

MAXIE: Fine. I'm fine.

MAX: That's good. I almost forgot. I got a present. Whatta dope.

MAXIE: What is it?

MAX: You'll have to open it to find out.

MAXIE: It's a surprise.

MAX: Yeah, sure, it's a surprise.

    (HE hands her the package.)

MAXIE: What's the occasion. Is it Christmas?

MAX: No, sweetheart. It's August.

    (MAXIE laughing gaily.)

What? What is it?

MAXIE: You haven't called me sweetheart for a long time.

    (MAXIE opens the box. It is a dress. SHE holds it up before her body. SHE studies herself in the mirror.)

MAX: It looks good. The salesgirl said it was a very popular item. Well, do you like it?

MAXIE: Max, I don't want to hurt your feelings. You know, personally, I like anything you give me, but frankly, and we must face this, you have no taste.

MAX: No taste?

MAXIE: You never have had. You never will. No, this will never do for the act. You've married again, haven't you? I've talked it over with mother. It seems best. I've kept up with you over the years. Years? Has it been years? Yes, I suppose it has. How old am I, Max? Am I old now?

MAX: Not old.

MAXIE: I don't like her.

MAX: Who?

MAXIE: Your new wife.

MAX: Well, she likes you.

MAXIE: Does she?

MAX: Yes, of course.

MAXIE: I like being liked.

    (Silence)

I'll be ready to return to the act soon.

MAX: What?

MAXIE: Yes, I've been practicing.

MAX: That's good.

MAXIE: The artistry of one's youth is not the artistry of one's mature years.

MAX: No.

MAXIE: Shall I dance for you?

MAX: Please.

    (SHE dances. Stops abruptly)

MAXIE: Come, we must go.

MAX: Where?

MAXIE: They're waiting for us.

MAX: Who?

MAXIE: Them.

MAX: Them?

MAXIE: Be quiet and you can fool them.
    (Pause)
MAX: Sure.
MAXIE: Be quiet and they'll think you're one of them.
    (Pause)
MAX: I've got to go.
MAXIE: I understand.
MAX: I'll come back soon.
MAXIE: I understand. Not for a long time.
MAX: No.
MAXIE: Yes. You're married now. I understand.
MAX: Maxie.
MAXIE: Call me babe.
MAX: Babe.
MAXIE: I like that. You go now. I'll practice. And when you come back, I'll be able to return to the act.
MAX: If you need anything—
MAXIE: I'll call you.

(HE kisses her and leaves. SHE pauses. Then begins tap dancing)

(Blackout)

SCENE EIGHT

(The rehearsal hall. The BOY and MAX in the middle of the scene. MAX'S face contorted in an image of anguish and regret.)

BOY: "We could go away from here."
MAX: "Good idea."
BOY: "Do you think so?"
MAX: "Far, far away."
BOY: *(Idea)*   "No! I know! Let's hang ourselves."
MAX: "Good idea."
BOY: "How will we do it?"
MAX: "By our necks."
BOY: "No! No! What will we use."
MAX: "Our necks! Our necks!"
BOY: "No! What will we use for rope? Where will we get a rope?"
MAX: "We'll improvise."
    (MAX pulls off his belt. HIS trousers fall to his knees.)
BOY: "Improvisation! Ingenious! You should have been an artist."
MAX: "I was. *(Gestures to the trousers)*   Isn't that obvious? *(Silence)*   Bebe."

BOY: "Yes?"

MAX: "I can't go on like this."

BOY: "Oh yes you will."

MAX: "Maybe it'd been better if we'd never met."

BOY: "No."

MAX: "No." *(Breaking character)* Maybe it'd been better if we'd never met.

BOY: Uh, no, Mr. Love. That's not in the script.

MAX: I'm tired.

BOY: "I'm in form."

MAX: What?

BOY: I'm cueing you.

MAX: I just said, "I'm tired."

BOY: Oh, I thought that was the line.

MAX: Why?

BOY: It's in the script. See.
    (Shows him the script)

MAX: Oh, yeah. Well, I was just saying I was tired. I wasn't acting.

BOY: Oh.

MAX: You can't even tell when I'm acting.

BOY: No.

MAX: Great.

BOY: Well, shall we take a break?

MAX: No, let's stop.

BOY: Stop?

MAX: I don't want to go on.

BOY: Oh.

MAX: Today. *(Coughs)* Someday, I'll die of something. I know I will.

BOY: Are you leaving now?

MAX: No, I'm going to stay and practice.

BOY: I'll stay if you want me to.

MAX: No, I work better alone.

BOY: Okay.

MAX: No, no, no. I'm sorry, you were a help.

BOY: I'm glad.
    (Pause)
Thank you for telling me about your career and your—about Mrs. Love. Did you ever have a partner after—Maxie?

MAX: I only shared the dream once.
    (Pause)

BOY: Well, goodnight.

MAX: Yeah.
    (The BOY gets to the door. Pauses)

BOY: I really love the take you do.

MAX: Which take?

BOY: When your character cries out for humanity. I really believe it. It's a great take.

MAX: What's the matter with all the other takes?

BOY: Goodnight, Mr. Love.

(*BOY exits. MAX alone. HE silently goes over lines. MAXIE appears. HE hears her but doesn't turn.*)

MAXIE: Come. It's time.

MAX: When?

MAXIE: Now. They're here.

MAX: Who?

MAXIE: The others.

MAX: Babe.

MAXIE: Yes.

MAX: I can't come to you.

MAXIE: Then, I'll come to you. Okay?

MAX: Okay.

(*SHE begins tapping softly. HE opens his arms to embrace her. HE cries silently. HE clutches his hands and weeps.*)

(*Blackout*)

END OF PLAY

James McLure, author of *Max and Maxie*
Originally an actor, Jim made his playwriting debut on Broadway in 1979 with his enormously successful one-acts, *Lone Star* and *Laundry and Bourbon*. Since then, these plays have been staged hundreds of times in regional theatres, universities and community theaters across the country. His subsequent plays (*The Day They Shot John Lennon, Thanksgiving, Wild Oats, River Cane, Napolean Night Dreams*) have been produced in major theatres such as the Mark Taper Forum, The McCarter Theatre, The Actors' Theatre of Louisville and The Abbey Theatre, Dublin.

Rachel's Fate
Larry Ketron

Rachel's Fate was first performed as a staged reading in *US West's PrimaFacie II*—A Presentation of New American Plays in the Denver Center Theatre Company's Source Theatre in April of 1986.

RACHEL'S FATE
by Larry Ketron

Directed by Peter Hackett

THE CAST—PRIMAFACIE II

Cliffort .... Jamie Horton
Owen .... Michael X. Martin
Andrea .... Annette Bening
Fugut .... James Aerni

The Denver Center Theatre Company, Donovan Marley, Artistic Director, presented the World Premiere of *Rachel's Fate* in the Source Theatre, as part of the DCTC's 1986-87 season, with the following artists:

Directed by Murphy Guyer
Scenic Design by John Dexter
Costume Design by John Dexter
Lighting Design by Michael W. Vennerstrom
Dramaturg, Peter Hackett
Stage Manager, Paul Jefferson

THE CAST

Cliffort, 38 .... Richard Elmore
Owen, 37 .... Mick Regan
Andrea, 34 .... Lynnda Ferguson
Fugut, 40 .... Stephen Lee Anderson

TIME AND PLACE

Act I: Summer. A highway rest stop in South Carolina
Act II: The next morning

Rachel's Fate

ACT ONE

(Morning. Summer. No liquor is present but it's in the air, all around. Just off an old highway in South Carolina, going east. Tall pines. A rundown picnic table in what used to be a clearing, a highway rest stop. Weeds have overgrown the place. OWEN sitting on end of table, patting ANDREA'S forehead with his handkerchief. ANDREA'S lying on picnic table, trying to nap. She moans softly, arm over her eyes.)

ANDREA: Cliffort?
OWEN: No. It's Owen.
ANDREA: Owen?
OWEN: Yes. It's me Andi.
ANDREA: Where's Cliffort?
OWEN: He went the car to see if he was thirsty.
ANDREA: I heard the ocean.
OWEN: No, we're thirty minutes from the ocean.
ANDREA: I dozed off. I heard the water.

71

OWEN: I don't think so.

ANDREA: Then it must be the smell.

OWEN: I don't think you can smell in your sleep, I don't think you can do that.

ANDREA: Did I go to sleep?

OWEN: I don't know, you dozed off.

ANDREA: All this drinking, you guys, we better think about—

OWEN: There is no safety, Andi, there's none to think about.

(CLIFFORT *enters, bumping into, knocking over a garbage can. He stumbles to the table.* ANDREA *takes her arm away from her eyes to see what's going on.* CLIFFORT *pulls himself together, steadies himself.* ANDREA *shifts on the table, moans a little bit. Then:)*

CLIFFORT: *(To* OWEN*)* You talked me into this, so don't do anything.

ANDREA: Who?

OWEN: Into what?

CLIFFORT: Owen. I should have been on my last trip with you already. Here I am I haven't been. Everytime I go somewhere with you, two girls get murdered.

OWEN: No they don't. Don't always bring it up. This whole trip was designed to get us over that other trip, so now let's—

CLIFFORT: No! This trip was not designed. This trip . . . came about.

OWEN: But it came about because Wendel's dad—

CLIFFORT: —died and left the lot, so is what caused this trip. There was no design. There never is any design which is why things are the condition they are.

*(*ANDREA *groans.)*

OWEN: You take a nap.

ANDREA: Last night was too bumpy. I couldn't sleep.

CLIFFORT: You know the dads of those two?

OWEN: Who?

CLIFFORT: The daddies of the two girls, Owen?

OWEN: I don't want to talk about those two girls!

CLIFFORT: I'm not talkin about the two girls, I'm talkin about the two daddies.

OWEN: What do you mean, do I know them? There's uh, investigation, I met them, didn't I?

CLIFFORT: I have something comin. I have something comin to me by way of somebody.

ANDREA: Who?

OWEN: What's coming to you?

CLIFFORT: I don't know yet. I have a *wish* comin to me.

OWEN: A wish now?

CLIFFORT: What?

OWEN: A wish now?

CLIFFORT: What are you talking about!?

OWEN: Now a wish? You have a wish comin to you now?

CLIFFORT: Not *now*. When I decide. All I have to do is decide.

OWEN: Did you put anything to drink back under the seat?

CLIFFORT: I think I did. I'll go check, I'll be back.

OWEN: I'll come with you.

CLIFFORT: You'll leave her here alone?

ANDREA: I'll be fine.

OWEN: It's broad daylight.

CLIFFORT: So what?

OWEN: Okay, no.

CLIFFORT: So when I come back, you go have something. I'm just gonna check I put it under the seat.

OWEN: Then when you come back.

CLIFFORT: That's all, or maybe a swallow more. You did not lock up the gizmo, for what it's worth.

OWEN: I parked it, didn't I?

CLIFFORT: I said if you *locked* it, Owen.

OWEN: I forgot.

CLIFFORT: Do you still feel funny?

OWEN: I feel a little bit funny.

CLIFFORT: Way you drive you make yourself sick. Don't ask me to drive anymore, it's out of the question.

OWEN: I'll drive.

CLIFFORT: No, not you. Me. The road becomes a live snake, you behind the wheel. That's how come you totaled your Opal. So I drive us on into the ocean. I mean the beach.

OWEN: Good, I can sleep.

CLIFFORT: No. If you go to sleep up there in the front seat with me, you won't wake up.

(ANDREA *is awake. She sits up. She pulls out a cigarette, lights it.*)

CLIFFORT: Put that out.

ANDREA: I'm not inhaling it.

CLIFFORT: Did you tell us this morning you're pregnant?

ANDREA: Yes.

CLIFFORT: Do something with any cigarettes you have.

ANDREA: (*Putting it out*) You can trust me.

CLIFFORT: Are you *sneaking* them too?

ANDREA: No.

CLIFFORT: Are you asking that baby to live in there in your fumes?

ANDREA: I forgot not to smoke!

CLIFFORT: That's impossible. Are you drinking?

ANDREA: No.

CLIFFORT: Are you sneaking drinks like this one and me?

OWEN: She said no.

CLIFFORT: You don't drink wine, Andrea?

ANDREA: No!

CLIFFORT: If I found a bottle under the seat got lipstick on it?

ANDREA: It wouldn't be mine.

CLIFFORT: Either way, but be honest.

ANDREA: No! If you don't believe me, Cliffort, I just can't stand this suspicion!

CLIFFORT: Look at me. No, are Owen and me, am I being good about it and him?

ANDREA: Uh-huh.

CLIFFORT: We're not either of us drinking or smoking *around* you.

ANDREA: You don't have to do that.

OWEN: Cliffort . . .?

CLIFFORT: If the child is colic, somebody's going to have to rub those cigarettes in somebody's face.

OWEN: Lay off her.

ANDREA: No, because I haven't!

CLIFFORT: Look at me. If the kid is six but can't learn a problem? And don't tell me Einstein couldn't tie his shoes!

ANDREA: If I were smoking, would I smoke in front of you? *(Pause)*

CLIFFORT: I wish it were a long time ago. You could do anything without knowing, it was fine. But these days it better not be a small baby because the doctor told you.

ANDREA: Stop scaring me! You're not my husband or anything. You're not my boyfriend or anything. It's not your baby or anything, stop scarin me or something. (ANDREA *pulls a banana from a dirty canvas bag, peels it, starts eating.)*

CLIFFORT: What are you eating?

CLIFFORT: *(She ignores him. To* OWEN*)*   Last week, you didn't eat yours, what happened to it?

OWEN: I'm gonna go have a touch.

CLIFFORT: So go! Stop taking about it.

        (OWEN exits, mumbling.)

CLIFFORT: Andrea? Look at . . . Elley ate two banana splits at once. Not a good sign. So you tell Owen what to do.

ANDREA: No.

CLIFFORT: Then he won't tell her at all.

ANDREA: He better face her!

CLIFFORT: He can't face her!

ANDREA: Doesn't he have any backbone?

CLIFFORT: Marriage means if Owen goes out, he has to come back. Does that sound like a description of Owen? No. What about the other women who also exist to be done things to? Maybe you can tell Owen *no* to them, I can't.

ANDREA: He asked Elley to marry him.

CLIFFORT: That was a reaction to the deaths of those girls, he jumped to Elley. Which is very different.

ANDREA: Maybe so, but he asked her.

CLIFFORT: You're like talking to someone who won't give an inch!

ANDREA: No!

CLIFFORT: He was out of his mind when he said he'd marry somebody!

ANDREA: He took her away from her *children*, Cliffort!

CLIFFORT: They were vandals! And they weren't her children, they were the other guy's, her step-things. And nasty vandals.

ANDREA: But he had led her to believe!

CLIFFORT: A man gets with a woman, he says things.

ANDREA: She, this will destroy her for a long time.

CLIFFORT: Are you saying she won't survive?

ANDREA: Of course she will.

CLIFFORT: Because suicide doesn't happen, a woman doesn't take her own life.

    (OWEN returns.)

CLIFFORT: *(To OWEN)* Where did you go?

OWEN: Just over the machine to have a slug.

CLIFFORT: Is it okay with you now if I go over the machine and have the same slug?

OWEN: It's okay with me.

ANDREA: You two stop not drinking and not smoking in front of me!

CLIFFORT: No!

ANDREA: It's driving me crazy!

CLIFFORT: I said no! Not around you!

ANDREA: This running back and forth, this drinking, running off, drink, drink, drink, it's driving me, it's making me dizzy! Or I don't know if you know it—but all you do is drink.

CLIFFORT: Everybody drinks.

ANDREA: No, it's gotten so bad. It always *was* bad, sure but, not like this!

OWEN: We're on vacation.

CLIFFORT: Leave me alone, Andi! Stop clawing at me like a bird! Let me enjoy my vacation. I'm not drunk, is that what you think? I know what drunk is and I'm not it.

ANDREA: Yeah.

CLIFFORT: Yeah, yeah, yeah!   *(Pause, then to* OWEN*)*   I asked
  her the Elley thing, she said no, I can't help you.   (CLIFFORT
  exits.)
OWEN: You won't, huh?
ANDREA: No. Elley'll get over it. For everybody there is somebody, then for everybody there is somebody *else.* I'm beginning to
  think especially you.

> (ANDREA *begins spreading out the skimpy picnic she brought.*
> OWEN *is distracted by something off somewhere.)*

ANDREA: What do you see?
OWEN: Mmmnnn . . .?
ANDREA: You know who had it for you?
OWEN: Who?
ANDREA: Gloria.
OWEN: Gloria had it for *me*? She was the most, I mean, she was so
  sweet.
ANDREA: Once I got a letter from her, a picture this place she built
  herself, just a shack in the mountains, this brook running by outside,
  then her dogs and cats. She always had the wilderness in her, nature,
  you know? Gloria always had it in her blood.

> (OWEN *still looking off from time to time.* ANDREA *glances
> off when he does, trying to see what he's looking at.)*

OWEN: Elley sits down, she eats two banana splits. There's something impure about that. I betcha Gloria never had ice cream her
  life. There was something pure about Gloria.
ANDREA: She was fond of you.
OWEN: I could almost use something to drink again. It must be the
  heat or something. I swear, the more you drink the more you have
  to have sometimes. They do that on purpose.
ANDREA: Who?
OWEN: No, according to Cliffort they make drinks that *give* you a
  thirst. Who makes water? The earth makes water, not trying to
  cheat you but satisfy you. Who makes *other* drinks? They *give* you
  a thirst, you keep coming back for more, he's right.
ANDREA: Owen . . . you're almost as old as, say, Cliffort—how
  can you drink so much, eat and sleep so little, drive yourself so hard,
  still stay in shape and look so good?
OWEN: Me? I don't know, but I swear, I been young all my life.
ANDREA: You look . . . look at you.
OWEN: I just haven't quite crashed yet, Andi. I 'spect it's comin,
  don't you?

> (OWEN *starts off toward whatever has been distracting him as*

CLIFFORT *returns, exhaling smoke, kicks a garbage can, over-turns it, staggers around it.)*

ANDREA: *(To* OWEN*)* What is it you see over there?
CLIFFORT: Are you wandering off?
OWEN: I saw something over there.
CLIFFORT: What?
OWEN: I'm gonna wander over there.
CLIFFORT: So you *are* wandering off, just like I said if you were. We'll be heading off to the beach before . . . ah . . .

*(*OWEN *wanders off.* ANDREA *has spread out a meager pic-nic, some bread and cheese, so on.)*

ANDREA: Do you know what Wendel is gonna do with the lot, do you know?
CLIFFORT: No.
ANDREA: He's gonna sell it.
CLIFFORT: No he's not.
ANDREA: I'm afraid so. Doesn't it break your heart?
CLIFFORT: Sell it to who?
ANDREA: Best offer.
CLIFFORT: But his dad gave it to him in a will of his!
ANDREA: It's the kind of thing fathers would love to leave for us, but they don't.
CLIFFORT: Except in this case they did. He left Wendel something to have, assuming he would protect it. It's a relay race, Andrea, which if Wendel drops the stick!
ANDREA: He wants the money.
CLIFFORT: What do *you* want?
ANDREA: I want the land.
CLIFFORT: I'm with you.
ANDREA: I don't know what I'd do with it, what Wendel and I would do with it, but, even if it just set there, so what, it's set there till now. It would be a place to go, it would be there.
CLIFFORT: You don't have to explain to me. You take what's in-herited by you only to reduce it down, that's a dangerous path to stagger on. Wendel doesn't have his thumbs on the future.
ANDREA: *(Meaning her baby)* He sees this as his future, right here.
CLIFFORT: So what about *it?*
ANDREA: What about it?
CLIFFORT: Where's his ocean lot on Bailey Beach gonna be? Let me . . . would Wendel sell the lot to me?
ANDREA: You? You don't have any money.

CLIFFORT: Wouldn't he give me a break on it?

ANDREA: He wants every penny he can get, you know Wendel.

CLIFFORT: Are you aware Owen's family money?

ANDREA: If there is any it's not his.

CLIFFORT: But his uncle we work for at the glass factory?

ANDREA: He might have money, I don't know.

CLIFFORT: Might have *money*? Thanksgiving they baste a turkey in *gold* over there!

ANDREA: Why would Owen's uncle give you money to—

CLIFFORT: Don't give up out of hand! What's happened to you?

ANDREA: What?

CLIFFORT: You never used to give up out of hand. You used to be, a breath of life in you.

ANDREA: Ask Owen if his uncle would—

CLIFFORT: Forget about Owen. Forget about his uncle too. I'm askin you if somethin has happened to you.

ANDREA: Yes.

CLIFFORT: What?

ANDREA: Wendel has, no, I've *let* Wendel . . . he's taken the air out of me, Cliff.

CLIFFORT: Well that pretty much breaks my heart. What can I, is there something I can do?

ANDREA (Lynnda Ferguson) and CLIFFORT (Richard Elmore) at the picnic site.

Photo Credit: Ted Trainor

ANDREA: What? Do what?

CLIFFORT: I'm your closest, I mean, aren't I your closest—

ANDREA: Yes.

CLIFFORT: He's taken the—

ANDREA: Air out of me.

CLIFFORT: You mean you don't, or you no longer feel the, the, the . . . what you're supposed to?

ANDREA: Maybe I never did.

CLIFFORT: What are you gonna do?

ANDREA: I don't know yet.

CLIFFORT: You leave, that's all. You leave him. Can't you leave him?

ANDREA: That would be so hard. So complicated. My head gets thick when I think about it, or but . . . my legs don't move, they simply refuse. *(Then)* I'd like to see you have the lot, but there's really no way, is there?

CLIFFORT: Yes! I have a secret source!

ANDREA: Who?

CLIFFORT: Secret, I said, a secret source for plenty a money.

ANDREA: You really could come up with, or, at least make Wendel an offer?

CLIFFORT: I get the lot, it's good as yours, you know that!

ANDREA: What would you do with the lot if you had it?

CLIFFORT: When I have it! When I have it! Move down here and live on it!

ANDREA: In what?

CLIFFORT: I'll build something.

ANDREA: I just don't know where you think all this money is gonna come from. Why, the taxes alone would kill ya.

CLIFFORT: Some people have to fight for what they want, okay?

ANDREA: I don't think you're in any shape to fight.

CLIFFORT: Oh, no? I might fool you. I've always wanted to live in a house on my own land on the ocean just like everybody else in the world. I could get a job down here. South Carolina hires men to work in jobs, I assume. At night I build my house on my lot on the beach, build it through my bare hands. You wanna come visit, please do. Don't bring Wendel, that's all I ask.

ANDREA: You can't bring your dad, he'd never make it. You sure can't leave your dad back home, he's got nobody else.

CLIFFORT: Don't be like one of those people who throws a wrench into something.

ANDREA: I'm trying to be, no, I'm suggesting you be practical instead of foolish.

CLIFFORT: No! Selling your lot to somebody to *destroy* it, that's foolish. I'm being practical when I say give it to me.

ANDREA: Why would somebody automatically destroy it, Cliffort?

CLIFFORT: Because that's what people automatically do, stupid. They build some lousy motel on it with tacky little rooms, hair in the bathroom.

ANDREA: I don't know.

CLIFFORT: No, you *don't* know, that's why I'm tellin you. Just because my dad is bedridden, I'll toss his bed in the back, I'll drive him to the beach in bed. Just because the old guy is dying, he doesn't want to hold me back.

ANDREA: Take it up with Wendel.

CLIFFORT: You bet I will!

ANDREA: Will you take it up with him?

CLIFFORT: Yes! Do you blame me for introducing you to Wendel?

ANDREA: No.

CLIFFORT: Are you sure?

ANDREA: I don't blame you . . . much.

CLIFFORT: Why did you marry Wendel, I forget?

ANDREA: I don't know . . . I just didn't want to make him mad.

CLIFFORT: Look how he acts. The trip is planned, everybody's ready, he's locked himself in his workshop with a bunch of tree stumps he's dug up.

ANDREA: Don't you know why he didn't come?

CLIFFORT: Why?

ANDREA: Today is the day my daughter was born. You know that.

CLIFFORT: No, I didn't.

ANDREA: Cliffort.

CLIFFORT: I forgot! Okay, today's her birthday. Maybe, yes, maybe I knew that somewhere in my mind somewhere.

ANDREA: Wendel forgot, then it came up. He always hates me on the day she was born.

CLIFFORT: How old is your daughter today, wherever she is?

ANDREA: Seventeen.

CLIFFORT: Seventeen. You were sixteen. Years before I introduced you to Wendel.

ANDREA: It doesn't matter. One day every year he hates me. But I chose to come ahead with you today because—

CLIFFORT: You wanted to get away from him. That's why. Because you wanted to get away from Wendel. I don't blame you.

ANDREA: *(She squeezes both his hands, her eyes closed.)*   My old friend . . . my good old friend . . .

CLIFFORT: *(Pulling away from her)*   It's practice, that's all. Your legs won't take you away from him? This trip is some practice for you. Wendel. He's too sick in the head to be a father.

(ANDREA sits on downstage bench, pulls up her shirt, exposing her belly to the sun.)

CLIFFORT: What are you trying to, roast it alive? Andi? Look at me.

ANDREA: No, I'm not trying to roast anybody alive.

CLIFFORT: Who's the first woman swims the English Channel?

ANDREA: Gertrude Ederle.

CLIFFORT: Maybe *your* kid will do something, who knows? I mean if somebody gives it a chance.

(OWEN enters with two pieces of fried chicken. He's eating one, hands the other to ANDREA.)

CLIFFORT: You came back eating chicken to me?

OWEN: There's some girls other side over there.

CLIFFORT: Who?

OWEN: Two.

(OWEN takes his shirt off, bathes in the sun through the following. His body has not gone to hell.)

CLIFFORT: You were invited to join them?

OWEN: They almost begged me.

CLIFFORT: They get chicken and we get, uh . . . *(Referring to the meager spread)*   mouse food?

ANDREA: This big fight with Wendel, so everything got messed up. I had made lots of good sandwiches, but they got thrown at him or against the walls.

CLIFFORT: *(To ANDREA)*   No, it wasn't a personal attack on you.

OWEN: They're eating outside their Camaro. They got potato salad, ham, baked beans, they got—

CLIFFORT: Shut up. Haven't we seen in our pasts when we talk to girls?

ANDREA: If you're going to fool around with girls down here, I don't want to listen to it! What am I supposed to say to Elley when she asks me questions. It's mean of you to put me in a position.

CLIFFORT: *(To OWEN)*   Shut up in front of Andrea, whoever you meet.

ANDREA: I'll just go to the car.

CLIFFORT: You don't have to go to the—

ANDREA: No, I'll just wait in the car till you guys are ready to go to the beach. Are we going to the beach or not? Bring the picnic things when you—

CLIFFORT: Don't go sit in the old hot—!

ANDREA: I'm not going to listen to anymore Elley, I'm not!

CLIFFORT: *(To OWEN)*   Shut up about Elley!

OWEN: I didn't!

CLIFFORT: Andrea, look at me. I don't want you sitting in the
Morris Minor in this heat. *(ANDREA sits on bench. Pause)* I
don't know, girls leaving themselves open to other people, offering
their chicken. *(To OWEN)* Andrea's right, you have too many
women.

ANDREA: No, that's none of my, all I said was Elley.

CLIFFORT: No, he's like everybody else, he wastes them. He tosses
women around like a boat. Remember: waste not because of whatever
that expression is. And always remember Chestnut Falls.

OWEN: Forget Chestnut Falls.

CLIFFORT: If Rachel had stayed in our room in Chestnut Falls
instead of going back to the bar—

OWEN: *(Overlapping)* They'd be alive today.

CLIFFORT: That's all I'm saying too! They had stayed with us that
night, we wouldn't have *killed* them, I can almost guarantee you that.

OWEN: That yours left made mine leave, why did they leave us?

CLIFFORT: If they weren't dead you could ask her, couldn't you?

OWEN: I'm asking *you* for the two thousand times!

CLIFFORT: Shut up for once in your life!

ANDREA: You wanna tell *me* why the girl left or what happened?

CLIFFORT: No!

ANDREA: If you blame yourself you—

CLIFFORT: It wasn't all *my* fault!

OWEN: Who blames you for any of anything?

CLIFFORT: *(To OWEN)* You know in Chestnut I got all clean,
we went out? You know I took all kinda showers? Whose idea we
find the nearest bar?

OWEN: It was both ours idea.

CLIFFORT: Just so somebody reminds you it wasn't all my fault.

ANDREA: I don't think it was anybody's—

CLIFFORT: *(To ANDREA)* Shut up, you weren't there, you don't
know what happened.

ANDREA: Well when you get ready to feel like too get it off your—

OWEN: So we're in our room though. You got dressed, you were
polishing your shoes.

CLIFFORT: Then what'd I do?

OWEN: Uh . . .

CLIFFORT: I took another shower. If you're gonna tell it, tell it.

OWEN: I can't tell it, I don't know, you won't tell me.

CLIFFORT: You *act* like you're telling it! *(Then)* All right. After
I cleaned up again, I got dressed, that's all.

OWEN: You got dressed.

CLIFFORT: But I don't look good.

OWEN: You always look good.

CLIFFORT: *You* looked good. I don't look so good.

ANDREA: You have good bones, good skin. Clothes hang on you right.

CLIFFORT: Clothes hang on me right?

OWEN: A lot of the time they do.

ANDREA: You know they do. Women always, huh, you know they do.

CLIFFORT: Women?

ANDREA: I don't have to tell you they do.

CLIFFORT: That was true up until this particular night.

ANDREA: What was it?

CLIFFORT: My face is funny, my eyes, under my eyes. My eyes are . . . withdrawing.

OWEN: Huh?

ANDREA: Doing what?

CLIFFORT: Pulling . . . pulling back into my gourd. I remember looking down at my shoes—one is shiny, the other one won't shine up. Things are awful, they're awful.

OWEN: Cliff. . . I didn't know you were havin all these problems.

CLIFFORT: So I take one more shower.

OWEN: You were laughing, you said, "one more shower for the road."

CLIFFORT: I was not laughing! I had stopped laughing and I haven't laughed since, so shut up, you don't know!

ANDREA: So you . . .

CLIFFORT: What?

ANDREA: So you . . .

CLIFFORT: Oh. *(To OWEN)* We had spotted these two earlier by the pool, you remember? They're in our motel. Then we see them at the bar.

OWEN: So we all leave the bar.

CLIFFORT: *(To ANDREA)* I don't even feel like girls anymore that night, but Owen is a team of horses when it comes to them.

ANDREA: I don't, you don't owe me any, you don't have to . . . anything.

CLIFFORT: But you're so, you've, we've never told you about some of our . . . ah, what do you call em . . . exploits.

ANDREA: I don't care.

CLIFFORT: I think you do care because you—

ANDREA: I don't care!

CLIFFORT: Because you care about us! Or you care about *me.*

OWEN: *(To ANDREA)* Also you care about me, don't you?

CLIFFORT: So don't create lies. So we have these girls by this time.

OWEN: So we all leave the bar, we go out. Or, I mean, we go back to the motel rooms.

CLIFFORT: So . . . now it's Rachel and me alone in this room. We

are talking with each other, me from the plastic chair while she sits
there, call it the edge of the bed.

ANDREA: You, that quickly, went from the bar to the motel rooms,
that fast?

CLIFFORT: Yes, no, no, yes, but—look, you're married and fuddy-
duddy so you don't even *know* anymore how things can happen
quickly if—

ANDREA: No, don't start preaching to me about how to—

CLIFFORT: You asked me!

ANDREA: Okay!

CLIFFORT: That's all! *(Then)* Now I've lost my thought train.

OWEN: So Rachel's in a chair, you're sitting, on the bed.

CLIFFORT: Huh?

OWEN: You're sitting on the bed, the plastic—

CLIFFORT: No! *I* was in the chair—she the bed, she the bed! I am
explaining the glass process, how you start with limestone, the cool-
ing down without crystalizing, the furnaces we . . . But before I
bore her to tears I start turning red a little bit.

(And the LIGHTS slowly begin to turn RED)

ANDREA: You start turning red?

CLIFFORT: A little bit. I should be comfortable with her but I'm
not. After all, *they* picked *us* up.

ANDREA: They picked you up?

CLIFFORT: They beat *us* to picking *them* up. We made ourselves
available, they took advantage an opportunity we made.

ANDREA: I don't get you talking about this turning—

CLIFFORT: I'm only saying it happened while I sit there with her
with her whisper voice of hers.

OWEN: What are you nervous about?

CLIFFORT: Didn't I say already?

OWEN: Are you hot?

CLIFFORT: No I'm not hot! I'm nervous! I'm red in the face and it
feels like all over, and besides, I'm dripping wet! I'm soaking wet
with her! And I am so embarrassed, so embarrassed, so, so ashamed.
She says to me quietly, would you like to take a shower?

(ANDREA is patting his forehead with a yellow bandana.)

ANDREA: *(Softly, just as RACHEL must have said it)* Would you
like to take a shower?

CLIFFORT: It threw me, I was so embarrassed. I couldn't move
except to squirm now because my seat is wet.

ANDREA: And so you've turned red.

CLIFFORT: It's something profuse, if you had been there, you, it
was profusely doing it, fire engine red.

ANDREA: Had you been drinking? *(Pause. CLIFFORT, OWEN*

just look at her. By now the whole stage is a RED glow.)   So you
go back to the shower, you take a—
CLIFFORT: No.
ANDREA: Then what did you do?
CLIFFORT: I wanted her out.
OWEN: How could you want her out?
CLIFFORT: I wanted her out of my room!
OWEN: Rachel was so much. Not someone you want out of your room.
CLIFFORT: I was burning red!   *(ANDREA has pulled a towel out
    of the canvas bag, she's wiping CLIFFORT with it in the red light;
    slow, sensual, inside his shirt, around his neck.)*   And the water
    coming from these, I don't know, these glands of mine, the water
    is gasoline! I, I, I, just don't . . .
ANDREA: Oh.
CLIFFORT: Not "oh" because she didn't. She went into the you-
    know, comes to me with a towel to dry me off. I can't stand it.
OWEN: So . . .
CLIFFORT: I let my temper get the best of her. *(And he grabs one
    end of the towel, jerks it around ANDREA'S neck, pushes her away.)*
OWEN: At which time she comes to her own room where I am with
    the other one, because—
CLIFFORT: That's all.
OWEN: And asked me to leave.
CLIFFORT: I don't have anything left. Confidence, youth-hood, any-
    thing like the things somebody needs.
OWEN: You're wrong.
CLIFFORT: I'm not wrong, I just told you.
ANDREA: To a lot of people you're very young. You know, *compared*
    to them. Don't feel sorry for yourself. A lot of people would like to
    slug you if they hear you complaining.
OWEN: You just hit a rough place in the road, Cliffort, it was a
    rough place in the road.
CLIFFORT: You're a whole year younger than me, out there totally
    living life on your own terms. But *me*, no, I'm some sink hole caving
    in.
ANDREA: You're exaggerating.
CLIFFORT: I am not! You're *four* years younger than me, so what
    do you know?
ANDREA: You were afraid of her? You thought you were too old
    for her?
CLIFFORT: I'm no longer the kid I was always going to be.
ANDREA: That's the way it works.
CLIFFORT: You don't tell me how it works! I know how it works,
    don't you tell me!
ANDREA: You don't *seem* to know how it works.

CLIFFORT: Well I do! I taught *you* how it works, don't forget. Then you pay me back by getting pregnant at sixteen years old!

ANDREA: Oh, I did that, I did that, I did that, what—it was something I did? Or something? What?

CLIFFORT: No! I'm sorry, I didn't mean to bring that up.

ANDREA: I got pregnant when I was a kid to, what, against you? Is that what you think? Is that what you think? And today is her birthday, wherever she is, so you use it against me in some evil or some way you have?

CLIFFORT: Okay! That's enough! *(Pause. To* OWEN*)* You have to go on without me.

OWEN: What do you mean?

CLIFFORT: I mean I no longer exist so when it comes to what we've always done together, you have to go on without me.

OWEN: We're a team.

CLIFFORT: We *were* a team, now you have to go on without me, more pleasure to you.

ANDREA: So that's how you two got out of the picture. Then the two girls went back out, got picked up again, this time by the monster, by the maniac.

CLIFFORT: That's all.

(Suddenly, the lights change back to bright sunshine.)

ANDREA: And you blame yourself, Cliffort?

CLIFFORT: I didn't say that—don't put psychological aspects in your head.

ANDREA: How was anybody to know about a madman?

CLIFFORT: You have to count on there being a madman! They proliferate! Early man in Mesopotamia someplace left that as a . . . as a . . . as a . . . huh? Is it going to be improved on? That's up to you.

ANDREA: What's up to me?

CLIFFORT: Don't bury your head in the sand because I got news for you, the tide comes in. Whatever happened to Mesopotamia, anyhow?

ANDREA: It's Iraq.

CLIFFORT: It figures. *(ANDREA rises, starts off.* OWEN *has put his shirt back on.)* The jalopy's locked up, okay?

ANDREA: I'm not going to the wreck, okay?

CLIFFORT: Okay, where are you going?

ANDREA: I'm going to the bathroom, okay?

CLIFFORT: All right. We'll wait, we won't leave without you.

ANDREA: Okay. *(ANDREA goes off.)*

CLIFFORT: All I was saying was I wish the girls at Chestnut Falls hadn't been seventeen years old. Even though they looked much older, at least to be sufficient.

OWEN: Let's talk about something else.

CLIFFORT: Plus at a resort by themselves.

OWEN: I'm going to rent a float at the beach, so don't expect me out of the water for hours on end, don't expect me. And I don't expect to be alone.

CLIFFORT: Not that if they had been eighteen we would feel any better about—

OWEN: No! Can't you hear me! No!

CLIFFORT: Say these girls out here fried up this chicken. Who are *we*? It's like, how do you know who a stranger is? He's someone comes, takes something alive, destroys it.

OWEN: Not everybody in the world's a murderer.

CLIFFORT: My point is they are! Look, Owen, I know you're gonna run across girls the next few days, they come to you, you always draw them like glue, do what you want. But people are buffalo killers, then they leave the carcass to rot. I know you wouldn't throw two girls off a motel roof, but they don't know that. So watch yourself.

OWEN: I set it up those two out there. I set it up, we got these couple dates when we all get to the beach.

CLIFFORT: Now we got these couple dates on our hands?

OWEN: I couldn't help it.

CLIFFORT: You never could. Is mine pretty?

OWEN: I think you'll find her to be pretty, yes.

CLIFFORT: Because you know how I like them.

OWEN: I told them we're from Montana, so . . .

CLIFFORT: Who's from Montana? *Us*?

OWEN: We're from Big Sky Country now, so . . .

CLIFFORT: You told them we're from Montana?

OWEN: We're from Billings, Montana now, so . . .

CLIFFORT: What's a matter with you?

OWEN: I don't know.

CLIFFORT: What do we do in Billings, Montana, me and you?

OWEN: Cattle.

CLIFFORT: You ever branded a cow in your life?

OWEN: No.

CLIFFORT: Do you think we can keep that from them?

OWEN: I don't know.

CLIFFORT: What about our license plate? It doesn't say any place even *near* Montana?

OWEN: We bought the car in Tennessee from a man.

CLIFFORT: Oh, we did?

OWEN: It was on sale.

CLIFFORT: Aren't you proud of who you are and where you're from?

OWEN: I don't know if I am, maybe not, I don't know.

CLIFFORT: Why do you have to hide behind something all of a sudden? *(OWEN shrugs.)* You must not be yourself. Who are you?

OWEN: I'm from Montana, see, get it?

CLIFFORT: Is this a game you play now?

OWEN: Yes.

CLIFFORT: Because when we used to meet girls, one thing we was, we were honest. We might have been despicable to a certain degree, but we were honest. Now we don't even have *that*? Look, I don't want somebody pimping for me.

OWEN: Then you don't have to go.

CLIFFORT: I didn't say that! *(Then)* I haven't been on a date since Chestnut Falls.

OWEN: Me either except Elley, so that's why it's time.

CLIFFORT: Two months. No girls, no women, you name it, no nothin. Eight weeks a that, drive somebody wild. Even depress you. *(Then)* What color hair does mine have?

OWEN: Blonde.

CLIFFORT: Natural?

OWEN: Uh . . .

CLIFFORT: How come you get the other one?

OWEN: I thought you'd want the blonde, we can switch.

CLIFFORT: Just don't go cramming one down my throat before the other one's the one I want.

OWEN: I didn't say that.

CLIFFORT: What are the ages on these two?

OWEN: Plenty old enough, don't worry about it.

CLIFFORT: They're not *too* old, are they? Well, I have to know something more about her. This is not the old days when anybody would do.

OWEN: I only talked to them couple minutes. I gave them my own famous recipe for my own fried chicken where you keep adding flour as it's cooking.

CLIFFORT: Your fried chicken, bah . . . I don't want to be with some girl, then she feels about something the way I don't, not anymore. That used to be challenging—they don't agree with you, you make them pay for it. But I've become selective. So carry that a step further—we are the selected species, but look at us.

OWEN: Huh?

CLIFFORT: I'm only saying I hope the Chestnut Falls incident has affected you, that you've learned.

OWEN: I'm sick of you bringing that up! Sick, sick of it! Stop bringing it up! Bring up something else.

CLIFFORT: There's two beautiful young women would love to forget all about it, too, but they're dead! Dead, Owen.

OWEN: Well *I* didn't do it!

CLIFFORT: *I* didn't do it either, but the fact remains!

   (Pause)

OWEN: The hair on her arms was *down* like you were looking at a swan, I swear it was. If you brushed her arm you brushed a swan, I swear.

CLIFFORT: Both of them. I ever tell you what mine said to me by the motel pool that night before it happened?

OWEN: What did she say?

CLIFFORT: What, by the pool?

OWEN: That night.

CLIFFORT: She says to me—We are ninety-seven per cent water. Because we are all protoplasm which is ninety-seven per cent water. She was a *high school* student. High school students today, I swear, they look like they're in *college.* She sat there kicking her white feet in the water. Those legs. Where's the nearest bottle?

OWEN: Under the seat.

CLIFFORT: Under the seat of the Morris Minor? Anything left in anything?

OWEN: There must be a little in a couple of em.

CLIFFORT: Cause I just had the horrible thought of not being drunk enough. *(ANDREA returns with two cans of Coca-Cola, sets them on picnic table.)* What?

ANDREA: What?

CLIFFORT: This is what?

ANDREA: Twenty mile stretch a highway, used to be nine service stations. Now this guy over there is the only one left and barely makin it. Did we even know about the *interstate* to the beach?

CLIFFORT: We came the old way on purpose. I knew this highway had died in disgrace. We're payin, uh, that thing, homage, to it. *(OWEN slowly reaches for one of the Cokes. Carefully)* Owen . . . no, Owen. Not in front of Andrea.

OWEN: It's Coke.

CLIFFORT: Not in *front* of her. We are a example, don't you see?

OWEN: *We* are a example?

CLIFFORT: Don't you see?

ANDREA: Cliffort . . . it's Coca-Cola.

CLIFFORT: No it isn't.

ANDREA: What?

CLIFFORT: It's what he plans to put *in* the Coca-Cola.

ANDREA: Oh, *in* the Coca-Cola.

CLIFFORT: You have to know how his mind works. We're not gonna drink in *front* of you. Who was that temperance lady, whatcha call it?

ANDREA: Look, I've begged you to stop sneaking out to the—

CLIFFORT: No, but her name.

ANDREA: Carry Nation.

CLIFFORT: That's all—we are tempering in *front* of you.

ANDREA: Give me the keys to the—

CLIFFORT: I don't want you sitting in the—
ANDREA: Give me the keys! *(CLIFFORT hands them over. Refer-
ring to the picnic spread)* Bring these things with you—
CLIFFORT: We're coming. *(ANDREA exits. CLIFFORT and
OWEN light up cigarettes. Now OWEN takes two giant styrofoam
cups out of the canvas bag, takes a flask out of his jacket, pours a
thick red drink into each cup, hands one to CLIFFORT.)* You've
been hiding Bloody Marys in your jacket since we left this morning?
OWEN: I was afraid some emergency might happen.
CLIFFORT: You made these up at home?
OWEN: I followed my famous recipe.

       *(CLIFFORT takes a drink from the cup, thinks about what he's
    just tasted. Then)*

CLIFFORT: See if you can follow this: You have a container of your
    favorite beverage. You sip it. But you don't sip it. You take enormous
    slugs of it. But besides a pig, you're careless too, you kick it over.
    You pick it up, it's empty. In disgust you break the bottle. Now you
    cry. Because the drink once in your hand, now it's gone. Now I
    appear before you. Why do I?
OWEN: I don't know.
CLIFFORT: Because we all drink from the same bottle, we're all
    members of the same whatever-it-is. I want a sip of the beverage.
    But what do I see? Broken glass all around, you hanging your head
    in despair.
OWEN: I don't exactly, I'm afraid I don't—
CLIFFORT: Stop. There are only two people—those who clean,
    those who litter. So do something with all this crap, let's go to the
    beach. I'd like to see the ocean one more time before I die and these
    women you come across. That so-called phone booth over the station
    over there, does it work?
OWEN: I don't know.
CLIFFORT: Because I never told you this, you want me to tell you?
OWEN: *(A deep breath, then)* No. But I guess go ahead.
CLIFFORT: After the investigation, one night, who comes to me?
    Both daddies come to my door. Drove up in one of their crates.
OWEN: Who, those poor ol country boys come to you?
CLIFFORT: So they come in. They shake my hand off. Each of them,
    they get very close to me. They offer me the world on the end of
    some stick.
OWEN: They offer you the—
CLIFFORT: World, Owen. On a string. Or money. Or anything they
    can do for me. They aren't very well-off, true. But that's their prob-
    lem they have to be poor, I can't help that.

OWEN: How come you never tell me this?

CLIFFORT: If a genie came to you, you rubbed her out of some receptacle, would you blab it?

OWEN: To *me*, I would, if I was my best friend.

CLIFFORT: I told you I had a wish comin to me. They felt so inadequate. That they had not provided safety . . . that they let this happen to their girls. They want to give to me.

OWEN: They come to you cause you fingered the guy?

CLIFFORT: I did more than finger the guy.

OWEN: But they don't know that.

CLIFFORT: They found out.

OWEN: How?

CLIFFORT: The cop.

OWEN: They went the cop first?

CLIFFORT: He told them me.

OWEN: This is not talk should get around. The cop knows, I know, the daddies know, fine. Maybe the mothers know, but it better stop. Otherwise you wake up some afternoon to an inquest of what you did.

CLIFFORT: Nobody else is gonna know. Don't break out in somebody's rash.

OWEN: Don't ever take anything from the daddies.

CLIFFORT: They owe me.

OWEN: They don't owe you!

CLIFFORT: They *feel* they do because owed their girls!

OWEN: You don't want them to owe you! You took the daughter.

CLIFFORT: What does that mean?

OWEN: You had the, the, the thrill of the daughter. To enjoy, to feel them around, to talk to her, to feel her around. So you had payment in that. That was your reward, her touch of her. They were our reward, their faces on those bodies with those fragrances and all that softness. Their being with us. How could you ever want any more than that?

CLIFFORT: You miss the point.

OWEN: *You* miss the point!

CLIFFORT: I do not miss the point, Owen, you do! You miss the point! Those fathers wish to repay me! Wish to with a wish!

OWEN: You were paid in advance!

CLIFFORT: Those two girls are dead!

OWEN: Quit saying it! Stop saying it!

CLIFFORT: "Paid in advance," you make me sick!

OWEN: You make *me* sick! That you would take from the fathers.

CLIFFORT: That's the scheme of things, Owen! THAT-IS-THE-SCHEME-OF-THE-THINGS! You know this lot belongs to Wendel and Andrea? Wendel's selling it. I'm gonna make those two daddies come up with the dough to buy Wendel's lot on the beach, give it to me.

OWEN: Ah, come on . . .! You're crazy!

CLIFFORT: That's irrelevant.

OWEN: If you go to them, leave me out of it!

CLIFFORT: You're not *in* it!

OWEN: Leave me out!

CLIFFORT: I'm gonna call those daddies, maybe they want to join me, look over Wendel's lot.

OWEN: No, you're not.

CLIFFORT: Let em know I've zeroed in on this wish I want. No, I won't call Fugut. I won't call Rachel's daddy, Fugut, I'll call Alhammer, the other one. Fugut, he gives me the willies. I hate some guy who you can't tell what he's thinking. I'll negotiate the other one.

OWEN: You, you, you know something?

CLIFFORT: No.

OWEN: You really start to do something to my stomach. You know that?

CLIFFORT: That's too bad.

OWEN: It sure is.

CLIFFORT: Then, all right! *(Coming off a sip of his drink)* Don't *ever* put Tabasco sauce in a drink of mine—it takes up space!

(CURTAIN)

END OF ACT ONE

ACT TWO

(The next morning. The picnic site is burned to hell, black and charred. A thick gray sky hangs over the black wood and burnt weeds. The picnic table still stands, barely stands, burned black. It has been raining. OWEN half asleep on the table, a road map sort of in his hand, dragging on the ground. ANDREA and CLIF-FORT, face to face. CLIFFORT shaking her.)

CLIFFORT: Get ahold of yourself. Pull yourself to—get ahold of yourself. Your pupils are funny. What have you had?

ANDREA: A substance, I'm sorry.

CLIFFORT: Go over the gas station, get some coffees.

ANDREA: Tell me, Cliffort.

CLIFFORT: Go get some before it rains again. Then we've got to get to the beach, I've got to meet somebody at the Pavilion.

ANDREA: *Meet* somebody? Who?

CLIFFORT: Don't worry about it.

ANDREA: Tell me why you came to me last night.

CLIFFORT: I can't. I was drawn to you. I can't explain it.

ANDREA: Do you want to destroy me? Completely? Confuse me too?

CLIFFORT: No!

ANDREA: With you lying next to me last night I could only think about being sixteen years old one August, deep in that foxhole we all dug, twisted together on a blanket on the clay that was almost mud, me and you. Do you remember that afternoon? You do, don't you.

CLIFFORT: *(Almost screaming)* Coffee. . .! *(ANDREA exits with a slight limp.)* Wake up! I said wake up! *(OWEN comes around, sits up.)*

OWEN: Ohhhh . . . what happened?

CLIFFORT: You don't even know what happened, do you?

OWEN: No.

CLIFFORT: Do you know who I am?

OWEN: No.

CLIFFORT: You *better* know!

OWEN: What happened?

CLIFFORT: You passed out behind the wheel!

OWEN: I did?

CLIFFORT: Of course you did. It's typical.

OWEN: You, weren't you in the *back* seat?

CLIFFORT: Yes. I woke up in time to save our lives.

OWEN: Where's, uh . . . where's, uh . . .

CLIFFORT: Andrea, stupid. She's the only thing saved our lives.

OWEN: Huh? I thought you did.

CLIFFORT: Of course I did, but not before she went berserk in the front seat, woke me up. Didn't you hear her laughing?

OWEN: No.

CLIFFORT: Well she was. Laughing like she'd gone berserk or something. Laughing like it was the last laugh and she was having it.

OWEN: I was following the Camaro . . .

CLIFFORT: Those two are *berserk*, those two girls.

OWEN: Where's Andrea?

CLIFFORT: I told you!

OWEN: Oh. Where?

CLIFFORT: She swallowed something, she took some killer . . . substance.

OWEN: She dead?

CLIFFORT: Yeah, okay, *dead*—you'd like that, wouldn't ya?

OWEN: No.

(CLIFFORT *kicks at the bench, chipping away little pieces. Black dust filters through the air.* CLIFFORT *and* OWEN *look at each other. Pause*)

CLIFFORT: I can't believe what did this. We left here yesterday, was it fine?

OWEN: I don't remember it like this, no.

CLIFFORT: I don't know. People bent on destruction of Mother Earth, whoever she is.

OWEN: Then sometimes you're a kid, though, you take a magnifying glass you got?

CLIFFORT: What?

OWEN: Hold it into the sun, focus it on a crumpled up cigarette pack or something, heat it up, catch it on fire. Or boys used to do it to a big red ant they caught in a jar.

CLIFFORT: Who?

OWEN: Neighbors' kids.

CLIFFORT: You think somebody was here with a magnifying glass torturing an ant and by accident burned down half the state?

OWEN: No.

CLIFFORT: There's too much *deliberate* meanness, it far outweighs any accident. I know this much: lightning does not strike. Mother Earth does not do this to *herself*. She may do, she may do . . . pruning.

OWEN: Pruning.

CLIFFORT: She may do *that*. But this . . .!

OWEN: Arson.

CLIFFORT: No, like Andrea. She may have a *sip* of something, but not destroy herself, her child either one. She may put a capsule in her bloodstream. But not . . . what am I trying to say?

OWEN: *Excess or—*

CLIFFORT: The extreme, yes, that's right, that's all. *(ANDREA returns, still limping. She comes over with two styrofoam cups, sets one in front of CLIFFORT.)* What'd the man over the gas station say, this disaster?

ANDREA: *(Interrupting on "gas station say")* This disaster? Tourists.

CLIFFORT: Exactly. That may be the best example of mankind we have today. What is *that?*

ANDREA: Coffee.

CLIFFORT: No.

ANDREA: You *asked* for coffee!

CLIFFORT: That's impossible!

OWEN: *(With a road map)* On the way home when we get into North Carolina, we could get off 23 and go find Gloria.

CLIFFORT: *(To OWEN)* What are you talking about?

OWEN: I was dreaming about Gloria, don't you remember her? She left for the wild, moved up in the mountians . . . *(pointing on the map)* . . . up in here somewhere north of Blowing Rock.

CLIFFORT: Stop talking other women in front of Andrea! Talk about Elley or not at all!

ANDREA: I don't care anymore. It doesn't matter.

CLIFFORT: *(To OWEN)* You happy now?

OWEN: I want to find Gloria.

CLIFFORT: Gloria left the mountains, must be long time ago.

OWEN: How do *you* know?

CLIFFORT: Because I ran into her in town.

ANDREA: When?

CLIFFORT: Must be long time ago.

ANDREA: *(Interrupting on "long time ago")* A long time ago?

CLIFFORT: I bought her a meal. Okay, I even took her home, okay? She had this wicked ol pick up truck full of domestic animals, I think, and a mountain goat.

ANDREA: *(Interrupting on "a mountain goat")* And a mountain goat?

OWEN: You took her home with you? Where was I?

CLIFFORT: I don't know where you are every second. What am I, my brother's thing?

ANDREA: Gloria was fond of me.

CLIFFORT: She said she was. But she doesn't have it for you anymore.

OWEN: She told you that? You talked about me?

CLIFFORT: I don't remember. She left before the sun come up. Disappeared.

ANDREA: Where to?

CLIFFORT: Not where to—when you disappear, that means you vanish. Gloria vanished.

ANDREA: I was, we were very close. There was a time we were almost the same person, me and Gloria. No, before she left for the mountains. I can't believe she came back to town, never even called or looked me up.

CLIFFORT: Don't be surprised, she was very different.

ANDREA: How?

CLIFFORT: She was . . . shorter.

OWEN: Shorter?

CLIFFORT: I don't know, she was bent over.

ANDREA: Hard work, see, you carry your own water, grow your own food, away from everything, enough hard winters . . .

CLIFFORT: Frankly she wasn't too sexy anymore.

OWEN: Where was she going?

CLIFFORT: Why?

OWEN: I'd like to find her.

CLIFFORT: Why?

OWEN: I've been thinking I like the *idea* of her.

ANDREA: Why had Gloria left? Did she say why she had come down from the mountains?

CLIFFORT: *People* did it. They started closing in on her. They poured things in her water. They trampled through her vegetables. They broke into her shack and tied her up, took a hatchet to the place.

ANDREA: In God's name why?

CLIFFORT: I don't know! It doesn't sound like *carelessness*, does it? It's just something people do.

ANDREA: And you never mentioned this to anybody.

CLIFFORT: I musta been trying to forget it or put it out of my, maybe I didn't want to believe it.

OWEN: I want to find her.

ANDREA: So you can ask *her* to marry you too?

CLIFFORT: Can't you leave any woman alive alone?

OWEN: She was pure.

CLIFFORT: That was a long time ago. She doesn't have it for you anymore, Owen.

OWEN: We'll see about that.

CLIFFORT: She doesn't have it for any of us anymore, Owen, or some liar claims he's some big Montana sky man.

ANDREA: Why'd you tell those girls that anyway?

OWEN: I didn't want, no, because if they could recognize us.

CLIFFORT: Us who did what?

OWEN: Were involved in that thing.

CLIFFORT/ANDREA: Chestnut Falls?

CLIFFORT: Recognize us? How could they recognize us? What are you, some paranoid schizo with brain trouble? I've got news for you—when you meet new girls, don't hide in Billings, Montana.

OWEN: It happened to me, too, ya know?

ANDREA: What did?

OWEN: That night! *One* of the girls killed was with *me*, ya know?

CLIFFORT: Of course I know.

OWEN: That's all.

CLIFFORT: I don't think it *is* all.

OWEN: What are you a swami now?

CLIFFORT: What?

OWEN: A SWAMI NOW!?

CLIFFORT: No.

OWEN: What do you think *I* did?

ANDREA: Tell us what you did, Owen.

CLIFFORT: You went off!

OWEN: Where'd I go?

CLIFFORT: I don't know!

OWEN: You're gonna tell it, tell it! I come back to our room, you're on the bed, your hands behind your head.

CLIFFORT: So? You can't talk to me, I'm a stiff, you went out.

OWEN: Go ahead, tell it.

CLIFFORT: I can't tell it, I don't know!

ANDREA: Where, Owen?

CLIFFORT: You went out.

OWEN: You've known me, what, since we rode tricycles?

CLIFFORT: Six and a half, seven . . .

OWEN: Am I the kind a guy takes, no, takes no for, no, I mean in this case, an answer?

CLIFFORT: No.

OWEN: Well haven't you thought about that?

CLIFFORT: What?

OWEN: I went *back* to her.

ANDREA: Alhammer's daughter?

OWEN: Me and her had to, or no, she asked me to leave because yours came back, you had thrown her out or something.

ANDREA: *(Interrupting from "you had thrown")*   You had kicked her out that room.

CLIFFORT: I had asked her to leave, yes, take those—

OWEN: Legs like a white bird she had or something.

CLIFFORT: That's all.

OWEN: I don't, I haven't gotten where I am by taking no, no, no, no-no. *(Pause)* We, me and Alhammer's daughter had been having a good time. We liked each other. So what am I gonna do?
     (Pause)

ANDREA: Return to her.

OWEN: Yes.

CLIFFORT: Are you telling me something, Owen? Are you, no, are you *saying* something to me?

OWEN: Don't get ahead of me.

CLIFFORT: I'm not ahead of you, I'm, I don't know where you are.

OWEN: I went back to her!

ANDREA: Where?

OWEN: They were on their way out again, I said, look, honey, please? So I took her aside, she went aside with me over the edge of the woods and we got to talkin or makin out.

CLIFFORT: What do you mean—making out?

OWEN: Just on the ground behind some trees.

ANDREA: Where's Rachel?

CLIFFORT: Right, where's mine, the other one? Where's Rachel?

ANDREA: *(Interrupting)* Where's Rachel, Owen?

OWEN: She's waitin.

CLIFFORT: Where?

OWEN: Over there someplace.

ANDREA: *(On top of Owen's line)* You mean just over there somewhere?

CLIFFORT: Waiting it out?

OWEN: I guess so.

CLIFFORT: But I don't understand what this has got to do with, no, why you feel or whatever you're saying . . .

ANDREA: *(Interrupting from "you feel or whatever")* Why can't you get to what you're saying?

OWEN: He came out of the woods right there, then. The guy who was going to kill them in a little while. He came out of the woods like some nasty animal. I heard him walk out, crackin on dead leaves. He started talkin to Rachel.

CLIFFORT: Then what happened?

OWEN: I said I better get back to my friend.

ANDREA: Who, Cliffort?

CLIFFORT: Who, me?

OWEN: I said I better get back to you.

CLIFFORT: They didn't want to go with you, though.

OWEN: No.

ANDREA: They didn't want to get back to Cliffort.

OWEN: Rachel thought, you know, you treated her badly.

CLIFFORT: So she decided to stay with a guy who was—

ANDREA: Going to kill them in a few minutes?

OWEN: Yes. They took him back up to their room.

(Suddenly FUGUT is standing among some burned rubble. His

shoulders are slumped, hands behind his back. CLIFFORT *spots him.)*

CLIFFORT: Fugut? Come mere. Come over here.
   (FUGUT comes over.)
FUGUT: Well . . . I found ja'll.
CLIFFORT: We were supposed to meet you at the beach, the Pavilion. How'd you find us, Fugut?
FUGUT: I's a whizzin by lookin at everything all burned down over here, I spotted your little Morris Minor Car.
ANDREA: *(Interrupting from "I spotted you little")* He saw that mustard-colored Morris Minor.
CLIFFORT: I appreciate you showed up, Fugut.
FUGUT: Told you anytime, anywheres.
CLIFFORT: Yes you did.
OWEN: Fugut.
FUGUT: Hello, Owen.
OWEN: Made it, huh?
FUGUT: Sure I made it.
OWEN: Drove through the night?
FUGUT: I don't mind a night ride.
OWEN: Come on Cliffort's whim, huh?
CLIFFORT: Don't annoy me, Owen, or Fugut either one.
FUGUT: I'd a been here sooner if I hadn't had to wait till I got off work. They're layin off at the plant, so I hate to rile em up any.
OWEN: I thought you had a farm.
FUGUT: It's gone bad on me.
CLIFFORT: Come on, Fugut, you drove all night as it was, can't ask for more than that. This is Andrea here, friend of ours.
ANDREA: *(Interrupting on "Andrea here")* I'm Andrea, hi.
FUGUT: How ya do?
ANDREA: What are you, what are you doing here, Mr. Fugut?
OWEN: Andrea, you don't wanna get—
CLIFFORT: Come at my request, Andi, that's all. I called him yesterday, phoned him up.
FUGUT: Alhammer wanted to come, too, when I told him I was comin.
CLIFFORT: I called Alhammer first, Fugut, to tell ya the truth.
FUGUT: Yeah, I know ya did. They don't know what he's got. He's lost eighty-two pound in three weeks.
CLIFFORT: He better stay in bed.
FUGUT: What did you want, Cliffort, from us?
CLIFFORT: Fugut . . . I don't like to take people up on their offers cause they never mean anything they say, anyway.
FUGUT: I know it.

CLIFFORT: But I'm about to take you up on yours cause it's too good to pass up.

ANDREA: What offer? What's going on?

OWEN: Andi—

CLIFFORT: Andi, this is a conversation here, if you don't mind? Can ya hold on for five lousy seconds?

FUGUT: What can I do for ya?

CLIFFORT: Do you know why we're staying at this dump motel a few miles back, thirty minutes from the beach? Staying those match-box cottages?

FUGUT: No.

CLIFFORT: There's no vacancies anywheres else. It's so crowded down at the beach, it's overrun.

FUGUT: Pop'lar, ain't it?

CLIFFORT: Yes, but it's more than popular, it's . . . it's what's happenin to the world we supposedly love.

FUGUT: *(A little puzzled)* What's happenin to it?

CLIFFORT: We are destroyin it, now aren't we? It got me to thinkin, what if somebody had him a piece of prime property that nobody could destroy. Am I making myself clear?

FUGUT: Well, uh,—

CLIFFORT: *(To* FUGUT*)* Hey. How's, uh, help me out—your wife?

FUGUT: Katherine? She's all right.

CLIFFORT: She's good?

FUGUT: Could I impose upon you again?

CLIFFORT: For what?

FUGUT: To tell me again.

CLIFFORT: The night again? I told you plenty of times.

FUGUT: But could I impose upon you?

CLIFFORT: No, it was, I happened to look in their window from outside.

FUGUT: Oh, I know, but that was because you felt—

CLIFFORT: Well, sure, because I just felt the fella was the wrong kind.

FUGUT: To be with Rachel and—

CLIFFORT: To be with Rachel and the Alhammer girl. So sure, that's all. You know how you get something inside you, it starts eating away at your guts?

FUGUT: Tell me.

CLIFFORT: No, but I peep in, he's dancing with Rachel, the radio, you know, soft, just dancing, I'm peepin in. I thought they must be, or no, everything must be all right.

FUGUT: Tell me.

CLIFFORT: No, but look, if I *had* had anything to go on, ya see?

FUGUT: But you glanced in the window instead of just knockin.

CLIFFORT: That was an accident.

FUGUT: Didn't he even have the drapes pulled shut?

CLIFFORT: Of course he did, but those cheap-ass drapes don't fit together.

FUGUT: But you're looking at them dancin', what's the expression on Rachel's face?

CLIFFORT: Come on, Fugut . . .!

FUGUT: No, I just mean—

CLIFFORT: Your daughter danced with no expression.

FUGUT: And where was Alhammer's daughter?

CLIFFORT: Bouncing up and down on the bed like a trampoline.

FUGUT: And laughin, you said?

CLIFFORT: Look, these kids get away from home, use the bed for a spring board, that's not unusual, Fugut, that's what narcotics are for, things like that.

ANDREA: And you saw him give them drugs, didn't you?

FUGUT: *(Interrupting from "give them drugs")* And you saw him give them drugs, didn't you, and they took these drugs.

CLIFFORT: Say, Fugut, you aren't thirsty, are you?

FUGUT: This sun can get hot quick, can't it?

CLIFFORT: It can if you let it.

FUGUT: Ya' all want to go get some breakfast?

CLIFFORT: I don't know, are you *hungry* or *thirsty*?

FUGUT: I don't care.

CLIFFORT: I'm funny anymore. I like to have about a six-pack a tall boys to get my eyes open. Then breakfast tastes good.

FUGUT: I'll drink a beer with ya.

CLIFFORT: I don't have any beer, I guess, is part of my point. All I could muster this mornin was some vodka from some Bloody Marys I think we had. All those fancy drinks, bah . . .

FUGUT: Why don't I drive down, get us a six-pack of beer?

CLIFFORT: You don't mind?

FUGUT: I don't mind a'tall.

CLIFFORT: Get a case.

FUGUT: You want me to pick up a case?

CLIFFORT: This sun is so hot. What we'll do, we'll take some beer, drive into the ocean again, you know, the beach.

FUGUT: That sounds fine.

CLIFFORT: I know a place I want to take you.

FUGUT: Where's 'at?

CLIFFORT: On the beach, a lot on the beach, thirty minutes from here.

FUGUT: I brought some old bathin suit had prob'ly fifteen years. Wife made me bring it. Lord, I bet my legs, white as a ghost.

ANDREA: *(Interrupting)* White as a ghost?

CLIFFORT: Then you flop on your towel this place, I'll do the talking, how's that sound?

FUGUT: Fine.

CLIFFORT: Did ya think to bring a towel, Fugut? *(FUGUT stares at him.)* Cause I think you're gonna like this place. Nothin special, but . . .

FUGUT: But it's close to the water?

CLIFFORT: It's *on* the water. You can go back and forth like a amphibian does. Bake for awhile, then go in and baste yourself. Come out again and roast. You know what it is? Man walked outa the ocean, what—maybe a billion years ago? That's the reason we flock to the ocean, we just wanna go home. I know what you're thinkin—*What* home? Whose keepin house?

ANDREA: *(To CLIFFORT)* I don't know, what are you asking him? Are you asking Mr. Fugut . . .? Wait a minute, this is your "secret source" you were talking about?

FUGUT: *(To ANDREA)* Do you know what he did for me?

CLIFFORT: No! She doesn't know.

(And the lights slowly begin to turn BLUE)

ANDREA: He identified the man.

FUGUT: He gave positive i.d. on the guy. That's what he did. Then he did the other thing.

CLIFFORT: Shhhh . . .! About that, you don't mind?

FUGUT: I'm sorry.

CLIFFORT: No, because they could annihilate me.

FUGUT: Oh, I wouldn't do anything to—

CLIFFORT: Then don't. Fugut.

FUGUT: Well you confirmed the guy was the guy.

CLIFFORT: Leave it at that.

ANDREA: What's the other thing you did, Cliff? There's somethin you can't say with me around? I know everything.

CLIFFORT: No, you *think* you know everything, but you don't.

ANDREA: *(To FUGUT)* What happened?

CLIFFORT: Shut up Fugut! Is this how you repay me, I help you out?

ANDREA: What happened, Owen?

CLIFFORT: You don't need to know.

ANDREA: I bet I *do* know.

OWEN: Tell her, Cliffort.

ANDREA: I imagine I know, Cliffort.

CLIFFORT: You don't know.

ANDREA: What happened on the roof?

OWEN: Everything was dark and blue.

CLIFFORT: No! Not *you*, me! Three-thirty in the mornin. Some cop in a suit taps on the door, takes me and Owen across the way,

round the balcony, over the girls' room again. We go in the yellow
door. He asks us were we out earlier, these two chicks. Yes, but
then they went out, some other guy. I could identify the guy if I
saw him again, because I had seen him with them. *(Slight pause)*
Lookin around, overturned lamp in the room. Bedcovers torn apart,
knotted up, used for ropes. Pillowcase for gags in the mouth . . .
Bad smell in this room, too. Now another cop comes in the room
bringin the guy. He was the guy. The odor was even him. Cop says
to me and Owen, We're goin back up the roof, you wanna come?
We're standin now on the rooftop, the four of us. *(OWEN hops up
on the rickety picnic table, looks down on the scene.)* Other cop
down below beside the dumpster. He's lookin around. Nobody
around. Cop up here says to this killer, Did you kill them before you
brought them up here? Or'd the fall kill em? He laughs a little bit
out loud and it echoes.

    (SOUND EFFECT—a man's laughter over mountaintops)
Then it comes *over* me. Or the state of mind I'm in, I feel as despicable
as him. And bein as low a lowlife as he is, I can do what he did. And
he knows it. He realizes it. So he stops laughin. See, he thought me
and Owen be his insurance—cop wouldn't do anything to him, me
and Owen there. But he sees in my face that there's some of him in
me now. So he starts jerkin his head around to figure out what to
do. Because the outrage, the outrage that has overcome us all at
this moment! So I jump into his skin! *(And CLIFFORT jumps up
onto the table, grabs OWEN by the front of his shirt.)* And I slap
him! I slap, slap, slap him. And off the roof he goes. *(And CLIF-
FORT throws OWEN to the ground. Then)* No, no, he didn't fall
to his death or jump to his death or die trying to escape, no, no.

    (LIGHTS suddenly return to normal. Pause)

ANDREA: Nobody in the whole state ever thought otherwise.

CLIFFORT: No, but ever'body thought—

ANDREA: Ever'body thought the cop. Almost ever'body.

FUGUT: I'm gonna go get us 'at beer.

CLIFFORT: Go . . .! Will ya? Can't you see somebody's thirsty?

FUGUT: I'll be back.

CLIFFORT: That's all.

FUGUT: You two be lookin for dates down *here* next, won't ya? You
two sumpin', ain't ya?

    *(FUGUT exits. ANDREA follows him off, still limping
slightly.)*

CLIFFORT: What'd he mean by that? Sometimes he gives me the
willies, that Fugut. I tried Alhammer first, but he's dyin on me.
Sick and dyin from it. Andrea doesn't feel well either.

OWEN: She's sick.

CLIFFORT: I know it. It makes me sick too, when she is. I wonder what that is?

OWEN: You didn't ask Fugut yet to finance your land deal.

CLIFFORT: No I didn't. You got to set these patsies up.

OWEN: Oh.

CLIFFORT: You can lead a horse but he has to be thirsty first. I just about got him exactly where I want him to slaughter him like a lamb. *(Then)* What'd you two do last night?

OWEN: Pavilion.

CLIFFORT: Did you dance?

OWEN: I don't dance.

CLIFFORT: You don't bust broncos either but you *say* you do. Big Sky Country . . .

OWEN: No, we just drank. Watched ever'body. Went down and played Skee Ball.

CLIFFORT: Win anything?

OWEN: Little pink tiger.

CLIFFORT: What, a Teddybear or something?

OWEN: No, a lion.

CLIFFORT: I don't think that's how you impress a hotshot architect, do you?

OWEN: What are you talkin about?

CLIFFORT: No, I can't see her being easily impressed, that's all.

OWEN: What architect?

CLIFFORT: They're architects, didn't she tell you?

OWEN: They're not architects.

CLIFFORT: What?

OWEN: Skin divers.

CLIFFORT: Huh?

OWEN: Frogwomen.

CLIFFORT: *Frogwomen?*

OWEN: That's what *mine* said.

CLIFFORT: Frog *what?*

OWEN: They salvage things.

CLIFFORT: Sure they do. Put two plus two together for once, will ya? Somebody's on to somebody.

OWEN: What'd you two do?

CLIFFORT: I might have done something stupid last night.

OWEN: What?

CLIFFORT: When I was together with her, I wasn't comfortable. I went red on her like I was the cape to some bull somewhere.

OWEN: Stupid.

CLIFFORT: That's not the stupid thing I did, okay? I tell her she better go home, I drove her home, I came back here. I went to Andrea.

Photo Credit: Ted Trainor

OWEN (Mick Regan) getting ready for the beach.

OWEN: You . . .? Went to Andrea?

CLIFFORT: Yes.

OWEN: Did you sleep with her?

CLIFFORT: Yes, in a literal, uh . . . I slept *there* with her in her cabin. That's all.

OWEN: But you didn't come-on to her.

CLIFFORT: What? I wouldn't have to come-on to Andrea. You would be talking, drinking, you would . . . You see, Owen, Andrea and I are like two . . . or I mean but if . . . things went wrong between us once, see?

OWEN: Yeah . . .

CLIFFORT: She was so . . . and I was . . . I mean it was a long time ago. I guess it was all my . . . but that doesn't mean you don't have . . . when she touches you, it's like no other touch in the . . . No, it's like, or when *I* touch her. Or we *hold* each other. Does that make any sense?

OWEN: Sure. *(Beat)* Why was it stupid?

(ANDREA *comes on, limping, bringing a bottle of wine, offers it to* CLIFFORT. HE *takes a slug, passes it to* OWEN.)

CLIFFORT: Are you feelin better from whatever just about made you die?

ANDREA: Yes.

CLIFFORT: What happened to your foot?

ANDREA: Cut it.

CLIFFORT: On what?

ANDREA: Last night, or . . . it's nothin.   (*To* OWEN)   You didn't come home.

OWEN: No.

CLIFFORT: (*To* ANDREA)   How do *you* know?

ANDREA: Because I sat out on my little porch outside Number 7 and waited for him to come home to go swimming.

CLIFFORT: That dump we're stayin's got no pool.

ANDREA: No, the ocean.

CLIFFORT: What?

ANDREA: I thought Owen might go with me.

OWEN: Last night I had a date.

ANDREA: I know. I waited, then I took the car and went.

OWEN: Alone?

ANDREA: Yeah, I just went.

CLIFFORT: Wait a minute.

ANDREA: I took the keys, I drove. It's only thirty minutes.

CLIFFORT: When?

ANDREA: After you went to sleep.

CLIFFORT: You drove back to the ocean alone last night, you went in?

ANDREA: Yes, I did.

CLIFFORT: Did you go out too far for your own good?

ANDREA: No.

CLIFFORT: Of course you did. I'm very upset with you.

ANDREA: Don't be.

CLIFFORT: Over your head? Don't lie to me.

ANDREA: No.

CLIFFORT: That's a lie, right there.

OWEN: If she says she didn't go in over—

CLIFFORT: Everybody lies to you, it's a way of life. (*To* ANDREA)   How did you cut your foot?

ANDREA: No.

CLIFFORT: Look at me! Because you're over your head with *two* people now, you know, you're lugging around some fetus, too! What, you cut your foot on a piece of what?

ANDREA: Shell.

CLIFFORT: Glass.

ANDREA: No.

CLIFFORT: Trash.

ANDREA: I stepped on a piece of a—

CLIFFORT: Don't be naive. Shells are gone. They're all covered over with trash, with broken bottles, with sticky balls of oil. What if I wake up, you're not in the room?

ANDREA: Maybe I am outside waiting for Owen.

CLIFFORT: No, maybe you've gone to the beach, into the water, drowning yourself.

ANDREA: Well that's not what happened, okay?

CLIFFORT: It doesn't matter that it didn't happen.

ANDREA: Oh.

CLIFFORT: It *could* have happened. It was thoughtless of you.

OWEN: You have to let people do what they want to do.

CLIFFORT: No you don't! That's exactly why everything is ruined! I don't want somebody getting their legs ripped off by a—*(To ANDREA)*   What's something feeds at night in the ocean?

ANDREA: Don't worry. I won't get my legs ripped off by a moray eel, then come running to you. Have I ever come running to you? No. Have I ever made you go through what I was going through, even if I was young, going through something, something, something horrible?

CLIFFORT: All I was talking about, I was talking about you being in danger.

ANDREA: Now look, don't confuse me with your girl in Chestnut Falls.

CLIFFORT: You don't have any, Andi . . . look at me. You don't have any right to bring that up.

ANDREA: Just because she left you that night and got—

CLIFFORT: It's always right on the back of your tongue, isn't it?

ANDREA: No, but if you're going to—

CLIFFORT: Oh, yes it is! Waiting there to poison me because there's your *own* seventeen-year-old daughter somewhere, God knows where, you don't even know!

ANDREA: *(Slapping CLIFFORT repeatedly)* You fight dirty! *(Stops slapping)*   How could you bring her up to me when you know I'm, when you know I'm . . . that I wish I had her so much! You *know* that!

(CLIFFORT *takes her hand and with it he slaps his own face, back and forth repeatedly.* ANDREA *pulls away. Pause. Finally)*

CLIFFORT: I was talking about *you* going to the *ocean*.

ANDREA: Yes, I busted out! And tried to forget a few things—about

Wendel, locked up putting clocks inside pieces of redwood trees. Tried to forget about being sixteen in a foxhole with *you*. I went into the water and, I don't know, you're the one who reminded me I used to have something or a breath of life in me, you said.

CLIFFORT: But if something happened to *you*, that would be the end.

ANDREA: The end of *me*, yeah.

CLIFFORT: I'd feel like I let *you* die too. Just like I let—

OWEN: No, no, no . . .

CLIFFORT: Yes, I did!

ANDREA: What? Just like you let what?

CLIFFORT: Just like I let Rachel Fugut die!

OWEN: You didn't let her die, don't be, don't even *say* that!

CLIFFORT: She was *my* responsibility!

OWEN: How many times we have to—!

CLIFFORT: I saw him *slap* her!

ANDREA/OWEN: What?

CLIFFORT: Just as I left their window! Out of the corner of my . . . then I walked down, around, down to the lake. It was late. I watched some men sneak in, dump garbage into the lake from a giant truck. I walked away from that, too.

OWEN: You saw him slap her with—

CLIFFORT: His hand.

(FUGUT *appears as if coming from nowhere. He has a case of beer. He sets it down on the picnic table.*)

OWEN: Hey, Fugut.

FUGUT: Saw who?

CLIFFORT: No, we were . . . not that I *saw* anything.

FUGUT: Somebody slapped somebody?

CLIFFORT: Not that I know of. Can I pay you for this beer you bought?

FUGUT: No.

CLIFFORT: (*To* OWEN) Pay the man.

FUGUT: But who did you see somebody slap her with his hand?

CLIFFORT: Back off, okay! You sneaked in, you heard some fragment of some conversation somewhere, it means little or nothing to you.

FUGUT: You didn't see—

CLIFFORT: No.

FUGUT: Did you?

CLIFFORT: No!

(ANDREA *takes a beer, pops it.*)

ANDREA: (*To* FUGUT) I wanted to do something. So that day outside the courthouse I said, I whispered, "Maybe you don't know me, but I am so affected by your loss, I want to do something if there's something I can do. Can I listen to you talk? Or hold your hand?" I whispered all that, you didn't hear me. But you looked into my eyes, you remember that?

FUGUT: No.

(ANDREA *leans against a burned-up tree.*)

CLIFFORT: Say, Fugut, what are you drivin?

FUGUT: Same ol van a mine.

CLIFFORT: Yeah . . . maybe we could go to this—

OWEN: No. *You.*

CLIFFORT: *(To* OWEN*)* Okay, *me,* you're not in it, okay? *(To* FUGUT*)* Maybe you could drive *me* to this place I want to show you concerning this something.

FUGUT: Why don't you tell me?

CLIFFORT: What? *(Getting a little desperate)* Oh, it's . . . I have this opportunity, Fugut, to get my hands on a choice piece of beachfront property. What do ya think, off hand?

FUGUT: What?

ANDREA: Cliff . . .?

CLIFFORT: Hold it, Andi, would you please?

ANDREA: Don't ask him to—

CLIFFORT: Be quiet a minute, okay? *(To* FUGUT*)* Could you . . . help me out here, what am I trying to say?

OWEN: I don't think I've ever in my life seen—

CLIFFORT: *(To* OWEN*)* Wait a minute—would you do me a big, would you mind driving back to our motel for me?

OWEN: For what?

CLIFFORT: I was goin myself, but that's okay, you go for me. Tell the owner a that rat trap I lost two quarters in the ice machine last night.

OWEN: Oh, you lost two quar—

CLIFFORT: Owen! Go to the office! Take her with you this time, I mean it!

ANDREA: We're staying. We're going to listen to what you say to Mr. Fugut. I want to know who you are, if I've ever known you in my life.

CLIFFORT: Then, okay! Then okay, stay! You can think what you want to, but I've got something to handle here.

ANDREA: You handle it, Cliff.

(Pause)

CLIFFORT: I don't know, have you ever been interested in ocean-front property?

FUGUT: You mean interested in buyin some?

CLIFFORT: Sure.

FUGUT: To give to somebody else?

CLIFFORT: Well . . . in this case, yes.

FUGUT: You want me to buy you a piece of land?

CLIFFORT: Look, I'm only talking about a loan.

FUGUT: A loan?

CLIFFORT: Until I could pay you back.

FUGUT: How much would it cost?

CLIFFORT: The lot? I don't know.

FUGUT: When will you know?

CLIFFORT: I can find out.

FUGUT: When?

CLIFFORT: As soon as I ask somebody.

FUGUT: If you had the land, then what?

CLIFFORT: I build a house on it. See, improve it, right away. That's
what you have to do—you get something, you improve it.

FUGUT: But . . .

CLIFFORT: I originally hoped, or no, the plan was Alhammer would
half it with you.

FUGUT: No, he's got medical—

CLIFFORT: No, his medical bills must be out the window.
Fugut . . . ?

FUGUT: I don't know.

CLIFFORT: (To ANDREA and OWEN)   I asked you two not to
be here. So if anything, all I could do was warn you.

FUGUT: How much you been drinkin the night my daughter was
killed?

CLIFFORT/OWEN/ANDREA: Huh?

CLIFFORT: We were on vacation.

FUGUT: I just thought . . .

CLIFFORT: What? What did you think?

FUGUT: Had you been drinkin steady?

CLIFFORT: *Had* I been drinkin steady? Yes. *Had* been. After your
daughter left me, went off, there was time in there between when
I saw her again.

FUGUT: You sobered up?

CLIFFORT: Who's tellin this story?

FUGUT: I'm just askin you.

CLIFFORT: I can't . . . are you saying this matters to some impth
degree, Fugut? For the life of me, I don't know what you're trying
to say.

FUGUT: Did you see the man who killed my daughter slap my daughter?

ANDREA: Tell him, Cliffort. Stop shaking inside and all over and
tell him.

CLIFFORT: (To ANDREA)   Shut up! How many times do I have

to be rude, Andrea! Shut your mouth! Fugut . . . have you ever
caught something in the periphery of your, no, out of the side? But
you don't *know* if you saw it?

FUGUT: Did you see him slap her but you were too drunk to do
anything about it?

CLIFFORT: I said you don't *know* if you saw it!

FUGUT: You could have prevented her—

CLIFFORT: Fugut, how have you turned things around on the tables
on me? You came here because—why did you even come here?

FUGUT: You identified the man who threw my daughter off a motel
roof and then you—

CLIFFORT: No!

FUGUT: What was *beginning* to happen, *going* to happen?

CLIFFORT: I said "This is not my scene!" You know that expression
from your youth! It was not my scene, him striking her! *I* had every
intention of treating her *gently*, she walked out on that!

FUGUT: You had gone back to her room to—

CLIFFORT: See if I could re-interest her, yes!

FUGUT: Still drinkin?

CLIFFORT: That's *my* right, isn't it?! What are you now, I'm sorry,
some forensic expert, measure my footprints?

FUGUT: I wish you hadn't looked in that window. Had just knocked
on the door.

CLIFFORT: There's no reason Rachel woulda had me back!

FUGUT: Or I wish he had seen *you* when you looked in that window.
If he knew he had been *seen* slapping her. If he know someone had
seen him slap her, that mighta cooled him off. I think he woulda
backed off, that's what I think.

CLIFFORT: I was drunk! Yes, drunk! Okay! True, true, true! But
the last thing you think, I don't care how drunk you are, the very
last thing you think is that somethin so precious as she was will
die! *(He kicks over the picnic table and bench. Long pause)* I
went back, crawled in, couldn't sleep. I hadn't slept a wink, cop
knocks on the door. I took action, I killed the guy. I took, I killed
the guy. But I took . . . too late.

ANDREA: My old friend.

FUGUT: There was always somethin . . .

CLIFFORT: What?

FUGUT: Missin to me. About ever'thing. I guess that was it. I guess
I always thought . . . *somebody* could have done *somethin.*

CLIFFORT: Me.

FUGUT: Now she's just part of the earth, just part of the earth.
Ain't she.

CLIFFORT: I wish to all that's Holy there was somethin I could—

FUGUT: Naw, there's really nothin.

CLIFFORT: You created, you raised this, this, this, this . . . girl. And we allowed . . .

FUGUT: *We* . . . allowed?

CLIFFORT: You know *you* felt inadequate, too. That you hadn't provided safety. None of us had.

FUGUT: Rachel said they's spendin the night Alhammer's house. Alhammer's girl told the Alhammers same about my house. It was my day off and it was in the afternoon and my van been cuttin out on me so I'm puttin me in a new set of plugs, then come on inside and Rachel's in the kitchen with her mother. She had her little grip packed up, Rachel did, goin over to spend the night with her friend, Alhammer's daughter. I said, Rachel, you come over here and give me a big hug. And she sees my hands all oily and greasy ready to grab her tight and she pushes me away and giggles and I play act like I'm a monster then, gonna get her good with these dirty hands I got and I chase her slow around the kitchen with her yelpin and her mother a-sittin there shakin her head at us and laughin. Then Rachel escaped me, went to the screendoor and threw me a kiss and blew it at me and left. They went to Chestnut Falls, see what they could get into, I guess. *(Pause)* Reckon I oughta get home.

CLIFFORT: I wish . . .

FUGUT: What?

CLIFFORT: No, did you tell me I had a wish?

FUGUT: Once I did.

CLIFFORT: That's all, so I . . . *(Pause)* I wish you'd drive carefully.

FUGUT: I will. *(Starts off, stops)* Don't be too hard on yourself.

(FUGUT *exits.* CLIFFORT *picks up a can of beer from the case, looks it over, sets it down.)*

CLIFFORT: Owen, all your life you've had too much of everything. *You* are the result of that. It's quite a sight. *(To* ANDREA*)* Name somebody who had nothin.

ANDREA: Who?

CLIFFORT: Or no, very little of anything but got by. Somebody who didn't waste everything he got his hands on including his own human body or anything else he came in contact with.

ANDREA: Let's see, I can't uh . . .

CLIFFORT: From one of those classes you always take.

ANDREA: Yeah, no, uh . . .

CLIFFORT: How about that guy, uh—

ANDREA: Thoreau.

CLIFFORT: How's your foot?

ANDREA: It's okay.

CLIFFORT: Good.

ANDREA: It's red and puffy, it's—

CLIFFORT: Infected.

OWEN: *(OWEN has been staring at all that beer.)*   I'm goin to the car.

CLIFFORT: Don't get behind the wheel. *I'll* drive us home.

OWEN: I'm sober.

CLIFFORT: Me too. Wait a minute, Owen.

> *(ANDREA has sat up on the table, rubbing the bottom of her injured foot. The heavy clouds have been gradually clearing. The sun is shining through, hot and bright.)*

CLIFFORT: How sore is that?

ANDREA: I should live.

CLIFFORT: *(Takes out handkerchief; to* OWEN*)*   Prove to me you can walk. Run get some hot water on this.

ANDREA: Thanks, Owen.

> *(OWEN exits with handkerchief.* CLIFFORT *starts removing bandage from* ANDREA'S *foot.)*

ANDREA: Sometime just before dawn I was there on my back. You were asleep beside me. It occurred to me that if Wendel got his throat caught in one of his power saws, it wouldn't be the worst thing that ever happened. Not that I wish anybody ill.

CLIFFORT: No, listen, sometimes I think *I* could take better care of you than Wendel does, so—*(Then)*   Not that you can't take care of yourself, but in the sense that every one of us needs to look out for the whole.

ANDREA: I understand that. To look out for the whole. Wendel cuts down trees, cuts them into slices to put clocks in them. There's something, Owen's right, there's something not pure about that. I think "pure" is a word somebody should use more often.

CLIFFORT: I agree. In fact I faked it to pretend I was upset Wendel didn't come with us on this trip.

ANDREA: The pure truth is I was hoping he was in the garage sawing through a vital organ. Or at least a vein.

CLIFFORT: You wanna wish you child doesn't have a father?

ANDREA: *(Staring* CLIFFORT *in the eye)*   Our daughter, wherever she is—could we find her and look her in the eye?

CLIFFORT: You signed a thing you never would try to find her.

ANDREA: You didn't sign nothing. Did you?

CLIFFORT: No. I didn't. *(Then)*   Many, or, uh—years ago that day when the doctor asked you if you wanted to see your baby but you said no?

ANDREA: Say *our* baby. Yours and mine.

CLIFFORT: Well, you know, our baby. I was standing outside your room.

ANDREA: You were?

CLIFFORT: Yeah. I was there.

ANDREA: You were there?

CLIFFORT: Yeah. Then this doctor comes out so I said I would like to see her. He nodded and took me to her. I thought at least one of us should see her.

ANDREA: When I was, say, sixteen, maybe you used me. But last night . . . say, over the years, you haven't fallen in love with me, have you?

CLIFFORT: I haven't fallen in love with *you*. I've fallen in love with who and what you *are*.

ANDREA: With . . .

CLIFFORT: Who and what you *are*.

ANDREA: Who and what I . . .

CLIFFORT: Am. And what you represent to me.

ANDREA: Woman?

CLIFFORT: More than woman.

ANDREA: Mother.

CLIFFORT: More than woman and mother. Life and earth and, please, if, you know . . . another chance.

(OWEN *returns with the wet cloth, hands it to* CLIFFORT *who is at* ANDREA'S *feet. He washes her foot, holds it gently, then kisses it.* ANDREA *stares* CLIFFORT *in the eye.* OWEN *looks on. The sun is burning brightly.*)

(CURTAIN)

END OF PLAY

Larry Ketron, author of *Rachel's Fate*

Mr. Ketron is from Tennessee and lives in Manhattan. He was awarded a Guggenheim Fellowship for playwriting in 1984. Some of his many plays include *Fresh Horses, The Hitch-Hikers, Asian Shade, Ghosts of the Loyal Oaks,* and *The Trading Post,* all originally produced by the WPA Theatre in New York City. Other plays: *Cowboy Pictures, Augusta, Patrick Henry Lake Liquors, Quail Southwest, Rib Cage,* have been presented by Playwrights Horizons and the Manhattan Theatre Club, also in New York City.

Shooting Stars
Molly Newman

Shooting Stars was first performed as a staged reading in *US West's PrimaFacie II*—A Presentation of New American Plays, in the Denver Center Theatre Company's Source Theatre in April of 1986.

SHOOTING STARS
by Molly Newman

Directed by Randal Myler

THE CAST—PRIMAFACIE II

Butch	Anna Miller
Tammy	Wendy Lawless
Wilma	Barta Heiner
Birdie	Coleen Hubbard
Gay	Paula Gruskiewicz
Shelby	Leslie Hendrix
Cassius	James H. (Buddy) Zimmer
Charlene	C.J. Keith

The Denver Center Theatre Company, Donovan Marley, Artistic Director, presented the World Premiere of *Shooting Stars* in the Stage Theatre, as part of the DCTC's 1986-87 season, with the following artists:

Directed by Randal Myler
Scenic Design by Richard L. Hay
Costume Design by Janet S. Morris
Lighting Design by Wendy Heffner
Sound Design by Benton Delinger
Stage Manager, Paul Jefferson

THE CAST

Gay, the center, very tall, early 20's	Nancy Houfek
Butch, a guard, early 20's	Anna Miller
Tammy, the rookie guard, late teens	Wendy Lawless
Wilma, a forward, mid-20's	Lynnda Ferguson
Birdie, a guard, mid-30's	Sandra Ellis Lafferty
Shelby, a forward, early to mid-20's	Leslie Hendrix
Charlene, the assistant coach, a forward, early to mid-30's	Caitlin O'Connell
Cassius, the owner/coach, a large man in his late 50's	Archie Smith

TIME: Christmas week, 1962.

PLACE: A men's locker room in an old, run-down high school gymnasium in a small mid-western town. Christmas music and "girl group" rock and roll songs of the period are heard.

Shooting Stars

ACT ONE

*(A men's locker room in an old, run down high school gym-
nasium in a small midwestern town. Old dented lockers line the
walls, and exposed pipes run along the ceiling. There is one toilet
stall next to a rust-stained men's urinal, and a sink. There are
several wooden benches, and perhaps a training table. Stage left
is the entrance to a hallway which leads to the gym office, and
beyond that, outdoors. The gym/basketball court is also accessible
from this hallway. Stage right is the entrance to the showers, and
up center there are double doors leading directly to the gym (these
double doors are not opened until the last moments of the play.)
The clock on the wall reads 4:00. This is a place that will always
smell of dirty socks.)*

*(As the lights come up, GAY enters. SHE carries a bag of basket-
balls, a red bucket marked "FIRE," a huge butterfly net, and an
athletic bag. SHE looks around briefly, puts down her things,
and begins unpacking. BUTCH and TAMMY enter. THEY, too,*

*carry athletic bags, and various athletic and "gag" parapher-
nalia—sparkly top hats and canes, etc. BUTCH is animatedly
telling* TAMMY *a shaggy dog story.)*

BUTCH: So Elizabeth Taylor says, "Hi, Bill, how ya doin?" and he
turns to the guy and says, "I told ya. My name's Bill Williams, I'm
from Dallas, Texas. I know everybody and everybody knows me."
So this guy doesn't see Bill for awhile, and then he goes to New
York City for the Macy's Thanksgiving Day Parade and he's standin'
there and who walks up but ol' Bill Williams and he says, "Howdy
friend, my name's Bill Williams, I'm from Houston, Texas . . ."
TAMMY: I thought it was Dallas, Texas.
BUTCH: Okay Dallas, Texas. "I know everybody and everybody
knows me." So the guy says, "C'mon Bill, I don't believe you know
everybody." Right then Roy Rogers comes ridin' by in the parade
and the guy says, "I bet you don't know *him*." Well, Bill gives a
little whistle and Roy looks over and says, "Bill Williams! How are
ya, buddy?" and ol' Trigger, he sorta hunkers down and gives Bill
a little bow. And Bill says to the guy, "See? My name's Bill Williams,
I'm from Houston, Texas, I know everybody and everybody knows
me." So a coupla months go by and the guy's in Washington D.C.,
listening to President Kennedy give a speech and who sits down
next to him but Bill Williams, and he says to the guy, "Howdy
Pardner, I'm here to tell you, my name's Bill Williams, I'm from
Houston, Texas, I know everybody and everybody knows me."

(By this time WILMA, BIRDIE *and* GAY *have trickled into
the locker room.* SHELBY *enters during* BUTCH'S *last line.)*

SHELBY: Aaaaaaagh! Bill Williams! No! No! Not again!
TAMMY: I haven't heard it yet.
BUTCH: So right about that time, President Kennedy finishes up
his speech and says . . .
SHELBY: *(Backing out the door)* I can't take this.
BUTCH: . . . "I'd like to take this opportunity to recognize my good
friend Bill Williams." So ol' Bill stands up and everybody claps and
Bill says to the guy, "My name's Bill Williams, I'm from Houston,
Texas. I know everybody and everybody knows me." Well, this guy
just can't hardly believe it, you know . . .

*(*WILMA *and* BIRDIE *have taken off their coats and almost
simultaneously open lockers to hang them up.* BOTH *react with
disgust.)*

WILMA: GAAAAA!

BIRDIE: Sheeeez!

WILMA: You got what I got?

BIRDIE: I don't know, what've you got?

WILMA: *(Swinging the locker door wide to expose a pin-up of a half-naked woman)* Boobies.

BIRDIE: I got worse. Can't you smell it? *(SHE goes to the corner to fetch a mop, which she uses to carefully hook a jock strap from within the locker. SHE handles it as if it were radioactive. As SHE heads out the door with it, CASSIUS enters followed by CHARLENE, and BIRDIE almost hits him in the face with it.)*

CASSIUS: Judas priest! What are you doing?

BIRDIE: Sorry Cassius. I was just trying to dispose of this . . . thing.

CASSIUS: You didn't touch it, did you?

BIRDIE: Heck no, Cassius.

CASSIUS: Go ahead on. Get it outta here. But next time, you call a custodian to take care of that kind of thing. That's nothin' for ladies to be concerned with.

BIRDIE: Yessir.

WILMA: Gay, you have got it?

GAY: I gave it to Charlene.

WILMA: Charlene, have you got it?

CHARLENE: What?

(WILMA swings the locker door wide again to show CHARLENE the girlie picture.)

WILMA: Elvis.

CHARLENE: Oh. . . yeah. *(SHE leafs through her clipboard and hands WILMA an 8x10 glossy of Elvis Presley. It has a piece of athletic tape at the top and WILMA unceremoniously slaps it over the girlie picture. SHELBY enters carrying a newspaper.)*

CASSIUS: All right, ladies. Game time is 7:30, so you've got plenty of time to relax. Do your nails, fix your hair or whatever, but stick around close. I got some business to take care of, and I'll pick up your dinner, but I want you to be ready for a short practice when I get back. As usual, Charlene'll be "Little Cassius" while I'm gone. Give her the same respect you'd give me, and mind what she says. Okay, Little Cassius, they're all yours. Bye bye girls.

TAMMY: *(et al)* Bye bye, Cassius.

BUTCH: So anyway, this guy is just shocked, you know . . .

CHARLENE: Listen up! We'll check into the motel after the game. Your room assignmets are as follows: Gay and Butch, Wilma and Birdie, and Shelby, Tammy and I will triple up. Bed check will be at 11 o'clock. I'll give you your car seat assignments in the morning. Starting line-up tonight will be as usual. Shelby, I have a note here for you that Cassius wants you to stop passing off to Wilma so much—she's scoring more than her share of points. Pass off to some of your other teammates and let them get their shots too. That goes for you too, Wilma. Birdie and Gay, you two will sell programs . . . try to do a little better than Wilma and Shelby did last night. Butch, you're on latrine duty . . . and Tammy, you're on laundry—the machines are next to the gym office down the hall. Okay, that's it.

Assistant Coach, CHARLENE (Caitlin O'Connell), gives orders to her teammates.

BIRDIE: Wait, I'm almost done with the story . . .

TAMMY: But Charlene said I . . .

BUTCH: I'm almost done, I'm almost done.

GAY: Go ahead, you two, I'll take your turn, Tammy.

CHARLENE: I don't care, long as it gets done.

TAMMY: Thanks, Gay. *(GAY gathers up the laundry bags and detergent and exits.)* Okay, so this guy can't hardly believe it . . .

SHELBY: Hey, ya'll! Lookit! I got my picture in the paper.

TAMMY: Oooooooo! Lemme see!

SHELBY: Wilma too. See? Right there.

WILMA: Where is that, Owensboro?

SHELBY: Yeah, they musta sent somebody down there. Oooo, there's a big write-up too. "Holiday Basketball treat for the Whole Family!" Here in basketball country, fans are used to seeing their favorite game in many shapes and forms, but tonight at the Tiger gym, when Cassius Birdwell's Indiana Shooting Stars meet the Northside Men's Faculty team, fans will be seeing basketball in a new, shapely form indeed. The Shooting Stars are a septet of girl basketball players who travel 250 days out of the year, playing and often beating, mens' teams around the country. But don't expect to see the rule book followed when the Shooting Stars play. These lady hoopsters play a brand of basketball that's a mixture of clowning around with their opponents and the audience, razzle-dazzle ball handling displays, and jokes that'll have you rolling in the aisles."

(BUTCH, WILMA *and* BIRDIE *join in on the last phrase—they've heard it all before.* SHELBY *and* WILMA *continue reading.*)

BUTCH: So anyway, this guy goes to Rome, see, and he's walking around the Vatican, and who does he run into but Bill Williams. And Bill says, "Well, hello friend, my name's Bill Williams, I'm from Dallas, Texas. I know everybody, and everybody knows me." And the guy says, "Bill, you sure do seem to know a lot of people, but there's one person I bet you don't know. I bet you don't know the Pope."

WILMA: Listen to this . . . "Wilma Simmons is the star of the team." This guy obviously knows what he's talking about. "With her deadeye shooting and cool head under pressure, she regularly racks up over 25 points a game. But for straight good looks, Shelby Tanner is the sweetheart of the team." Looks like you got yourself an admirer, Shellshock.

SHELBY: Lemme see that.

BUTCH: So he says, "I bet you don't know the Pope." So Bill says, "Look here, I want you to stand right under that balcony there and look up, and see if I don't come out with the Pope himself. Just like I said, my name's Bill Williams, I'm from Dallas, Texas, I know everybody and everybody knows me."

SHELBY: Look out . . .

BUTCH: Now what?

WILMA: Uh-ohhh . . .

SHELBY: Listen to this. "Included in the Northside High Faculty line-up tonight are two former local basketball greats: six-foot-one Varsity Coach Tom Allen, and Driver's Education teacher and former Northside forward, Steve 'The Spear' Harold . . ."

CHARLENE: Shelby!

TAMMY: The Spear?! The Spear! What does that mean?

BUTCH: Oh, great.

TAMMY: The Spear? Char-lene?

CHARLENE: Maybe it means he's skinny . . .

WILMA: Or tall . . .

CHARLENE: . . . maybe he's got a pointy head!

TAMMY: Charlene!

CHARLENE: Calm down, Tammy, it'll be fine.

SHELBY: Just look at it this way, Tam, when you go to dribble between his legs, you won't even have to bend over!

TAMMY: Ohhhhhhhh . . .

CHARLENE: Shelby! Now Tammy, look into my eyes. Do I look afraid?

TAMMY: No.

CHARLENE: And look at Birdie, how does she look?

TAMMY: Birdie? Nice.

CHARLENE: Does she look afraid?

TAMMY: No.

CHARLENE: You know why?

TAMMY: No.

CHARLENE: Because Birdie and I have been doing this for longer than either one of us cares to think about. And we know how to handle ourselves, and we know how to handle guys named "Spear." We know that it's teamwork that gets the job done, and the thing we Shooting Stars do best is play as a team. Okay?

TAMMY: *(Not totally convinced)* Okay.

CHARLENE: Okay.

WILMA: She's right, Tammy.

SHELBY: Yeah, Tammy, it even says here—"The Shooting Stars can give any men's team a run for their money—solid outside shooting, precise passing, and when all else fails, a secret weapon named Bertha 'Birdie' Dickerson. Every team needs a muscleman" . . . um . . . ohboy . . .

BIRDIE: What?

SHELBY: Nuthin . . .

BIRDIE: C'mon, what's it say?

SHELBY: Nothing. It doesn't say anything. *(Throwing the newspaper toward* WILMA*)* Here, Wilm!

WILMA: Don't give it to me.

BIRDIE: *(Snatching it)* Lemme see. "Every team needs a muscleman and Dickerson fits the bill. She's a real heavyweight who walks, talks, and plays like a man." Damn. Thanks a lot, Shelby.

SHELBY: *I* didn't say it!

WILMA: Shel-by . . .

SHELBY: I'm sorry!

BUTCH: *SO!* The guy says, "I bet you don't know the pope." And Bill says, "Yes I do. I'll go up there and you can see me talking to

him." So, the guy stands around for awhile and sure enough two
people come out onto the balcony. But it's kinda far off and he can't
see too good. So he grabs this guy who happens to be walkin' by
and he says, "S'cuse me, but I can't see too good, is that the Pope
standin' up there?" And the guy looks up and says, "I don't know
who that guy in his pajamas is, but the other guy looks just like Bill
Williams from Houston, Texas!"

(BUTCH *is convulsed by this.* SHE *roars at her joke.* TAMMY
laughs good naturedly, although she's not sure she got it.)

SHELBY: Thank God that's over.
   (GAY enters carrying the detergent.)
GAY: What's so funny?
WILMA: *(Pointing at* BUTCH*)*   Don't you dare . . .
CHARLENE   *(To* GAY*)*   Bill Williams.
BIRDIE: Shelby's real funny, aren't you, Shelby?
SHELBY: Aw, Birdie, I'm sorry. I didn't mean to laugh. I couldn't
   help it.
BIRDIE: Yeah . . .
WILMA: C'mon now, don't let that get to ya.
SHELBY: Heck, Birdie, those jerks are always writing stupid stuff
   like that. No kidding. Last year some newspaper guy said I looked
   like a dog.
BIRDIE: Really?
SHELBY: Yeah, he said I looked like a cross between an Irish Setter
   and a Poodle.
BIRDIE: No joke?
SHELBY: Yeah, so I bit him.

(At once, SHELBY *and* WILMA *jump together and side by
side do a unison rendition of Woody Woodpecker's signature
laugh.)*

SHELBY AND WILMA: HaHaHaHaHa HaHaHaHaHa HaHaHa-
HaHa hahahahahahahah . . .
CHARLENE: Okay, okay, knock it off, you two. Gimme that
   paper.   *(SHE throws it away.)*   You know what Cassius would say
   if he caught you readin' that stuff.
SHELBY AND WILMA: "Bad for morale."
CHARLENE: Yeah, and he's right too. We should learn. First you
   got Tammy upset and now look what you did.
BIRDIE: I'm all right. I was just steamed 'cause my sister was think-
   ing about coming to the game tonight. Her and her husband live

about fifty miles from here and I don't want 'em reading that trash in the paper, you know?

TAMMY: I bet they don't even read the paper.

GAY: That's great Birdie. When are they coming?

BIRDIE: I don't know. I'm s'posed to call 'em. They got a new baby I haven't even seen yet. I got him a little toy for Christmas and everything. Ya'll wanna see it?

GAY: *(et al)* Sure, Birdie.

(BIRDIE *produces a little wind-up bear that plays the cymbals.*)

BIRDIE: Look, you wind him up and he claps his little hands together. They had a little boy—you think he'll like it? It's not really a doll or anything so I thought it'd be okay.

TAMMY: Ohhhh, I used to have one of these. Oh God, it's so *cute.* Can I see it?

BIRDIE: You sure it's okay for a boy baby?

GAY: Oh sure. I bet he really likes it.

BIRDIE: I hope so. I didn't know what to get.

GAY: It's perfect Birdie. Now go and call 'em and tell 'em you're here. They're probably dyin' to hear from you. There's a phone in the gym office. Go on.

BIRDIE: I guess I should. *(SHE exits.)*

TAMMY: *(Still playing with the bear)*   God, have you ever seen anything so cute?

BUTCH: I'm hungry.

CHARLENE: Just hold your horses. Cassius'll be back soon with dinner.

TAMMY: I got half a Twinkie in my case.

BUTCH: I'll buy it from ya.

TAMMY: Okay.

BUTCH: How much you want for it?

TAMMY: I don't know.

BUTCH: How much was it?

TAMMY: Twelve cents.

BUTCH: For the whole thing?

TAMMY: Yeah.

BUTCH: It's half a Twinkie, or half a pack of Twinkies?

TAMMY: Oh it's a whole Twinkie—I didn't touch it or anything.

BUTCH: So it's one whole half a pack of Twinkies.

TAMMY: It's one whole Twinkie.

BUTCH: Half of two Twinkies, right?

TAMMY: Right.

BUTCH: So, would ya take a nickel?

TAMMY: It would be six cents, wouldn't it?

BUTCH: Well, yeah, but it's not like it's brand new.

TAMMY: That's true.

SHELBY: Tammy . . . I'll give you a dime for it.

TAMMY: A dime? Sure, okay.

BUTCH: Wait a second.

SHELBY: Too late. We struck a deal.

BUTCH: Tammy . . .

SHELBY: Sorry, Butch.

BUTCH: Awww, sheez.

SHELBY: You really want it, Butch? I'll sell it to ya.

BUTCH: I'll give you eleven cents.

SHELBY: Cost you a quarter.

BUTCH: Forget it.

SHELBY: Okay. You want a bite, Wilm?

WILMA: I don't know. Do I get half of a whole bite or a whole half a bite?

SHELBY: You can have two halves of a whole bite of the . . . moist . . . yellow . . . cake . . . filled with . . . luscious . . . white . . . cream.

WILMA: Mmmmmmmm . . .

SHELBY: Mmmmmmmm . . .

BUTCH: Gimme that.

SHELBY: Where's my quarter.

BUTCH: Here . . . take it . . . buncha jerks.

WILMA AND SHELBY: HaHaHaHaHa HaHaHaHaHa hahahahahah.

CHARLENE: Honestly, it's like kindy-garten in here. I can't even hear myself think.

WILMA: Oh, Charlene, we're just trying to kill some time.

CHARLENE: Can't ya'll think of something more useful to do than tease one another?

SHELBY: Why? It's fun.

CHARLENE: I, for one, am going to work on my spinning techniques. Anybody wanna join me?

WILMA: Char, you been spinning balls on your fingers and toes every halftime for nine years. How in the world can you get any better at it?

CHARLENE: Cassius wants me to learn how to spin one on my nose.

TAMMY: Oooo—that'd be neat, Charlene.

GAY: Doesn't it hurt?

CHARLENE: A little. But Cassius thinks it'll be worth it.

WILMA: Can you do it yet?

CHARLENE: Not yet. But Cassius thinks I can. Tammy, you wanna practice with me?

TAMMY: Oh, no thanks, Char. I got a movie magazine I wanna look at.

CHARLENE: How 'bout you, Gay? I could show you some new tricks.

GAY: Naw, not right now . . . thanks.

CHARLENE: Okay. . . (SHE *exits, spinning a ball on her finger.)*

SHELBY: You know what she's gonna look like with that ball on her nose?

GAY: What?

SHELBY: *(Doing an imitation of a seal)* HONK HONK, HONK HONK. Just pray she doesn't learn how to do it.

TAMMY: She will.

WILMA: Charlene can do anything.

SHELBY: Don't say that. If she learns how to do it, Cassius'll have us all out there doin' it, lookin' like a bunch of fools. I swear, sometimes I think he stays up nights tryin' to think up new ways for us to look stupid.

WILMA: If it sells tickets, Cassius will think of it.

SHELBY: Just once, I'd like to play a game where nobody laughed at us.

WILMA: Yeah . . .

BUTCH: *(Getting undressed)* I think I'll take a shower.

WILMA: Another one? God, Butch, you take more showers than anybody I ever heard of. Nobody's that dirty.

BUTCH: I can't help it. I sweat a lot. It's hereditary.

SHELBY: Wilm, will you Dippity-Do my hair?

WILMA: I don't know. I should do my nails. Cassius'll kill me if he does an inspection.

TAMMY: I'll do your hair Shelby.

SHELBY: You want to?

TAMMY: Oh yeah, I love to do hair . . . other people's hair. Always have. I just love to comb it and brush it and play with it. The longer the better. My little sister has two Barbie dolls and I even used to do their hair. I just love it. I just comb it and brush it and comb it and brush it . . .

SHELBY: Mmmmmm . . . feels good.

TAMMY: You know, I used to have hair clear down to my butt.

WILMA: Why'd you cut it off?

TAMMY: Cassius told me to when he recruited me. Said it would get in the way. I just cried and cried.

BUTCH: I knew a girl in high school who had hair like that. She had to move it so she wouldn't sit on it. I hated her guts.

TAMMY: Why?

BUTCH: Cuz she was a priss. She was in my same grade in school, and she drove me crazy. Her mother let her wear a garter belt and hose in the sixth grade. She thought she was God's Gift. We were friends for a while, but then I couldn't stand her anymore. She was

a twirler in high school. She used to stand out in her front yard and
practice her baton, and I'd be in our driveway shootin' baskets. She
had room in her backyard to practice, but she had to do it out in the
front yard so everybody could see her. She ended up gettin' second
runner-up in the Miss Arkansas Pageant and I ended up an Indiana
Shooting Star.

TAMMY: My brother dated a girl once who was up for Miss Memphis,
but she didn't get it.

BUTCH: *(Down to her bra and underpants now)*   God, it was sicken-
ing. A bunch of us drove up to the pageant in Little Rock to make
fun of her. You shoulda seen her prancin' around on stage. The only
reason she won the swimsuit competition was 'cuz she had so much
hair, nobody could tell what she looked like underneath. I shoulda
entered. I could do that stuff.

*(BUTCH mimics a contestant in a swimsuit competition. On
tiptoes as if in high heels, she minces forward and poses.)*

BUTCH: *(In a sultry beauty contestant voice)*   My dream is to become a stewardess so I can meet peoples of all the world. Then I
would like to settle down and raise a Christian family while pursuing
my ongoing interest in cosmetology. I would also like to work to
institute twirling as an Olympic event, to promote understanding
between the peoples of all the world. Thank you and God bless.

WILMA: No wait—here's Butch: "My dream is to stop hunger in the
peoples of the world by providing Twinkies to all needy families.
For my talent I will now sweat a lot and take a shower.

SHELBY: And now Ladies and Gentlemen, for the award that all
these girls have voted on themselves—the Miss Congeniality Award.
Now all our contestants have got to know one another during the
pageant week and even though they're all smiling and holding hands
now, we all know that in their hearts, they truly hate each other.
So now our Miss Congeniality Award for 1962 goes to the only contestant who did *not* vote for herself, Miss Tennessee, Tammy Lynn
Dwyer! Come on around here, Tammy, and say something to the
folks at home.

TAMMY: *(Sincerely touched by this.)*   Gosh, I don't know what to say.
What should I say, Wilma?

WILMA: Thank somebody.

TAMMY: I'd like to, um, thank Mama and Daddy for raisin' me, and,
um, Cassius for makin' me a Shooting Star, and Charlene and Shelby
and Wilma, and Butch and Birdie and Gay for bein' my friends and
helpin' me do better all the time. Thank you very much. That's all
I could think of. was that Okay?

GAY: Thanks, Tammy, that was real sweet.

SHELBY: Yeah, that was real good, Tammy.

TAMMY: I didn't really know what to say.

WILMA: Shelby really was a beauty queen once. Weren't you, Shelb?

BUTCH: Yeah, Shelby got voted Miss Conceited 1961.

SHELBY: It was just a stupid little local beauty contest. I was Miss January at the Boat Show in my hometown.

BUTCH: Boat Show?! In Kansas? The biggest body of water ya'll got in Kansas is a galvanized washtub.

SHELBY: We got lakes. Anyway, I didn't win.

BUTCH: The Primp Queen didn't win? As much as you work on your looks, you shoulda won for sheer determination. Didn't you even get Most Improved?

SHELBY: The girl that won had big cleavage.

TAMMY: That's important.

WILMA: Why is that, Tam?

TAMMY: Men like 'em.

WILMA: Zat true, Butch?

BUTCH: Well, I don't like to brag . . . but you know what they say—the bigger they are . . .

SHELBY: The more they sweat.

(BIRDIE *enters.*)

GAY: What'd your sister say, Birdie? Is she comin'?

BIRDIE: Naw, she can't. Her baby's got cholera or somethin'.

WILMA: Cholera?!

BIRDIE: Yeah, somethin' like that—makes him all crabby or somethin' so they can't leave him.

WILMA: Cholera?. . .chol. . .colic. . .you sure it wasn't colic?

BIRDIE: Cholera, colic, I don't know. Anyway, they can't come.

GAY: Oh, Birdie, I'm sorry. You must be pretty disappointed.

BIRDIE: Aw, it doesn't matter. It's just that it's Christmas and everything.

BUTCH: I'm gonna take my shower. Tammy, lemme borrow your shower cap.

TAMMY: (*Putting the finishing touches on* SHELBY'S *hair*) It's over there in my grip.

(BUTCH *finds it and puts it on; it's one of those pink lacy jobs with four tiers, for bouffant hairstyles.*)

BUTCH: I always wanted to be tall.

TAMMY: Don't get it wet, okay?

BUTCH: Tammy . . . it's a shower cap.

TAMMY: I know, but I just got it, and I haven't even got to wear it yet.

BUTCH: And it's so important to look one's best in the shower.

(SHE does a Loretta Young walk offstage to the shower room.)

TAMMY: There we go, all Dippity-Dooed and done.

SHELBY: Now you promise I'll look like Jackie Kennedy?

CHARLENE: *(Entering)*   Mail call! And there's a box for Miss Dwyer.

TAMMY: For me?

ALL IN UNISON: Care Package!

TAMMY: Ooooo! Maybe something for Christmas!

CHARLENE: Here Tanner—pass it out.   *(SHE takes her own letters and sits down.)*

SHELBY: *(Going through the bundle of mail)*   Gay . . . Butch . . . Bertha . . . Gay . . . Wilma . . . Me . . . Tammy . . . TWO more for Gay.

ALL IN UNISON: *(Except for Charlene)*   RAY-MOND!!

SHELBY: Birdie, and . . . whoa . . .

GAY: What?

SHELBY: Holy Smokes. Wilma . . .

WILMA: What?

SHELBY: Are you expecting a letter from the Basketball Hall of Fame?

WILMA: What?

SHELBY: Look.

WILMA: For me?

SHELBY: No joke, Wilm—look.

WILMA: God.

SHELBY: Open it.

WILMA: Okay, okay.

SHELBY: What's it say?

(WILMA reads from the letter—slack jawed. All eyes are on her. She continues reading, no expression. She finally looks up and collapses backward, arms outstretched, onto the bench, and screams. TAMMY screams too.)

SHELBY: Wilma . . . what?   *(WILMA hands SHELBY the letter unable to speak.)*   "Dear Miss Simmons . . . it is with great pleasure . . . because of your outstanding career . . . great, exceptional talent . . . chosen to have your jersey hang in the Basketball Hall of Fame!"

(SHELBY screams, then everyone but CHARLENE screams.)

BIRDIE: Wow, Wilma.

TAMMY: You're famous and I know you!
GAY: Congratulations, Wilma.

(BUTCH comes tearing out of the shower wrapped in a towel and soaking wet.)

BUTCH: Whassamatter whassamatter?
TAMMY: Butch!
BUTCH: What?
TAMMY: Wilma's in the Hall of Fame!
(BUTCH screams, then all except CHARLENE scream again.)
SHELBY: I can't believe it. I can't believe it. Wilma, you're immortalized! Wilma! God! Say something!
WILMA: *(After a pause)*   . . . I'd like to thank my mama and daddy for raisin' me . . .
SHELBY: Wilma!
WILMA: I'm flabbergasted . . .
SHELBY: So am I. I can't believe they didn't pick me.
WILMA: Shelby . . .
SHELBY: I'm kidding!
BIRDIE: We're all real happy for ya', Wilm.
BUTCH: *(Taking off her shower cap and putting it on WILMA'S head)*   Here, Champ, you'll be needing this.
WILMA: What's this for?
TAMMY: It's your crown.
BUTCH: Naw, it's to keep her head from gettin' too big.
WILMA: Thanks, Butch.
TAMMY: This is just great—isn't it great, Charlene?
CHARLENE: *(Who has been standing apart from the celebration)* It sure is. Really, Wilma, congratulations. It's something we can all be proud of.
WILMA: Char . . . I . . . feel bad. They coulda picked you just as easy. You've been playin' a lot longer than I have. I don't know why they picked me.
CHARLENE: 'Cause you're a great player. Name one other girl who's a better player than you.
TAMMY: You've scored more points than anybody, Charlene—that's just as good.
CHARLENE: Wilma'll break my record easy in a few years. No, they were right to pick you, Wilm.
WILMA: Thanks, Char.
SHELBY: Number 22 goes down in history.
TAMMY: *(Finally getting her package open)*   Oh, look—fruitcake!
BUTCH: I love fruitcake.
TAMMY: Mama makes it every year for Christmas. Here, Wilma, you cut it and we'll celebrate.

WILMA: Okay. Thanks.

CHARLENE: No fruitcake.

WILMA: Why not?

CHARLENE: Cassius is on his way with dinner. You shouldn't be filling up on sweets.

BUTCH: Oh, c'mon, he won't care. And it looks so good.

WILMA: It's okay, we'll celebrate when he gets here.

TAMMY: Oh it is good. It's not the cakey kind of fruitcake, it's the moist kind. Some people like the cakey kind, but our family doesn't. It's too dry. We like the moist kind. Bubber, my little brother, he doesn't like fruitcake at all. He says he won't eat fruit that's blue or purple or green, even if it *is* in a cake. Plus he hates nuts. He always picks all the nuts out of brownies and cookies, so even if he liked the fruit part, he'd pick all the nuts out. So he just doesn't eat any fruitcake at all. Some people are funny like that, but I figure that just leaves more for me. Course, I'm kinda funny about the cakey kind of fruitcake. If it's dry, I just know I won't like it. Mama usually makes Christmas cookies too, you know, for Bubber, since he doesn't like fruitcake. She makes star shapes, and bell shapes and ones shaped like Santa with red and green sprinkles. It was always my job to put on the sprinkles and, you know, those little silver balls. What do you call those little silver balls?

SHELBY: Tammy, let me guess. Is this your first Christmas away from home? *(TAMMY nods.)*

(CASSIUS bursts through the door, carrying sacks of food. BUTCH runs to grab her clothes and ducks into the shower room.)

CASSIUS: Make a circle, make a circle, Ladies. I have brought your training table. Chock full of the best nutrition and all six food groups.

BUTCH: Finally.

CASSIUS: Impatience is not becoming in a lady, Butch.

BUTCH: Sorry.

(CHARLENE gets up unsteadily to join the circle.)

CASSIUS: Charlene, is your knee giving you trouble again?

CHARLENE: It's fine.

CASSIUS: Hurry up Butch, the circle is waiting.

(BUTCH runs out buttoning her shirt and completes the circle. THEY all join hands and CASSIUS gives the blessing.)

CASSIUS: We thank thee, O Lord, for this, Thy bounty, which we are about to receive. Thank you too, Lord, for these seven lovely children who are with me today. Lord, please grant me the strength and the patience necessary to teach and guide these girls in the correct way. We ask this in Jesus' name. Amen.

ALL: Amen.

CASSIUS: Charlene, please pass everyone a carton of milk. Charlene, Wilma and Shelby all get steak sandwiches and french fries for strength. Birdie and Gay, for you I have tuna fish to promote good vision. Tammy, you're having egg salad for shiny hair and smooth skin, and Butch gets a chef salad for good digestion.

BUTCH: Thanks, Cassius.

(ALL *thank Cassius.*)

TAMMY: (*After taking a big bite*) Cassius, Wilma . . .

CASSIUS: Chew your food properly, Tammy . . . very good. Now swallow. All right, Tammy, what would you like to say?

TAMMY: Tell him, Wilma.

SHELBY: Wilma has just the best news.

WILMA: Well, Cassius, you're not going to believe this, but I got a letter today, forwarded from my mother, saying that I have been chosen to have my jersey hang . . .

CASSIUS AND WILMA: . . . in the Basketball Hall of Fame.

WILMA: Yes! You knew?

CASSIUS: I knew. I got a letter yesterday.

SHELBY: Why didn't you say something?

CASSIUS: Everything in its own time. Congratulations, Wilma.

WILMA: (*Hugging him*) Oh, Cassius. Thank you.

CASSIUS: Come here and sit by me. (*Stroking her hair*) I'm just so proud of you I could bust. But then I'm proud of *all* of my team. You know, I'm kinda sad that each and every one of you couldn't have been included in this recognition.

WILMA: He's right. You all deserve it.

CASSIUS: That's very generous of you, Wilma. And you're right—everyone in this room deserves it. But you were the one they named "The Best." How does that make you feel?

WILMA: Well, good . . . but . . . I don't know . . . kinda funny, I guess.

CASSIUS: Kinda funny, huh? Like it makes you want to laugh?

WILMA: Well, no. Like I feel good, but, you know, kinda embarrassed.

CASSIUS: I understand. You know that your team has put you in the position to win this award.

WILMA: Definitely.

CASSIUS: You know that you couldn't have done it without them.

WILMA: No way.

CASSIUS: But Wilma, you've got to get used to the idea that you're the one that's gonna get all the credit and all the attention. There's gonna be photographers, and publicity people and interviewers, and they're gonna surround you and leave the rest of us out. So listen,

everybody, we all might as well get used to it now . . . from here
on out, Wilma's the best and the rest of ya'll are . . . well, second
rate.

WILMA: Cassius! C'mon . . . don't say that!

CASSIUS: Why not? That's the way everybody's gonna see it.

WILMA: I'll tell 'em different. When I get interviewed, I'll tell 'em
how we're a team, and this award's for all of us.

CASSIUS: I think that's real nice . . . I really do. But fact is, they're
gonna say that you're just bein' humble. No, I think this is somethin'
we all just better get used to. I sure do hate it that people'll be
thinkin' that any of my girls are second rate. You know, I think
you're all the best.

SHELBY: Wilma'll tell 'em, won't you, Wilm?

CASSIUS: I'm sure she'll try, Shelby. I don't think it'll do no good,
though.

WILMA: Cassius, I don't know what to do—I don't want people
thinking that I'm better than everybody else . . .

CASSIUS: It's a shame, isn't it? I can't think of no way around it,
though . . .

WILMA: I s'pose I could turn it down . . .

SHELBY, TAMMY, BIRDIE, GAY: No! Wilma, don't do that!
NO!   *(Etc.)*

CASSIUS: Wilma, you are too much. Have you ever heard of anything so generous and sweet? C'mere girl. I just love you and respect
you so much for offering to do that. I'm just so touched. You have
brought a tear to my eye, girl. I just never seen anything so . . .
righteous. This is one of the proudest moments in my life.   *(Giving
her a hug)*

WILMA: Wha. . . . . ?

CASSIUS: I am overcome. Girls, there is a sacrifice bein' made here
for each and everyone of you. I'm just so proud of you, Wilma. Now,
you tell me, do you want me to write the letter, or would you like
to do it yourself? I think it would be best if it came from you. Don't
you think? Tell you what? I'll help you write it, and then you can
sign your name to it. We'll do it together.

WILMA: I don't know . . .

CASSIUS: Or you can write it yourself. That'd be fine if you'd rather.

WILMA: . . . I . . . um . . . Excuse me.   (SHE *rushes out the
door.)*

SHELBY: Wilma!   *(Starting to go after her)*

CHARLENE: Sit down, Tanner.

CASSIUS: Do you all see the sacrifice that is being made here today?
I hope you are all impressed with what Wilma is fixin' to do.

SHELBY: I wish she wouldn't.

CASSIUS: Oh no, don't you take that away from her. She's a hero.

That's what she is. And we can all be proud and learn something from her. *(Picking up his cup)* Here's to Wilma! Let's see some smiles here! Okay. Let's not say anything more about it. This'll be our little secret, just like Wilma wants it. Okay, let's finish up our dinner and clear it away. Tammy?

TAMMY: I'm not so hungry right now.

BUTCH: I'll finish it.

CASSIUS: Just leave it, Butch. Tammy can finish it later. C'mon, let's clean up here. We got some work to do. C'mon now, hop, hop. Everybody make some space. I wanna work on a couple of new plays while we got some time. C'mon now! It's time to get back to work!

SHELBY: Cassius, I wanna go talk to Wilma.

CASSIUS: Just leave her be. I imagine she'd like to be alone right now.

SHELBY: I just want to make sure she's okay.

CASSIUS: Shelby, Wilma has just possibly saved this team from a blow that might have destroyed it. She was smart enough to realize that jealousy and envy can destroy the spirit of teamwork that holds this basketball institution together. She may have just saved you from yourselves. I don't think she needs you to babysit her right now. Okay? Now let's just forget about it, and get back to work. Gay and Butch, front and center, the rest of you listen to what we're doin' here. All right now, I think there's been a lull in our comedy right after we do the bunny hop out-of-bounds play and before we do the on-the-shoulders dunk shot, so I came up with a new little thing that I think'll be funny. Okay, Butch, you got the ball and you just brought it down beyond mid-court. Okay, I want you to hang back a little bit like you're waiting for a play to set up, and everybody else run on down around the lane. Now Butch, you just stand back there dribbling the ball, and let your man come right up on ya'. Kinda taunt him a little bit. Then I want you to line your shoulders up squarallel to the basket, and look up over him like you're gonna try to take a shot from there. That'll get him all excited. Now Gay, that'll be your signal. You give your man a fake, Birdie'll set up the screen and you'll run up quietly behind Butch's man, and while he's wavin' his arms and everything, I want you to just ever so gently but quickly pull his pants down! *(The girls exchange glances.)* Whatsamatter? This is gonna be hilarious! Now Gay, don't pull 'em down all the way, just a couple of inches, so you got his attention, but we don't get arrested. *(Giggling from the girls, HE is winning them over.)*   O.K. Butch, as soon as he drops his arms to catch his britches, you take off around him and try to get your lay up or pass it off to Shelby. I think they'll all be so surprised, we'll catch 'em all sleepin'. Okay, you think you can do it?

GAY AND BUTCH: Sure.

CASSIUS: Run through it a couple times later on, and when you
think you've got it, we'll put it in. Charlene, hand me that bag over
there. Tammy, this is gonna be a great little gag for you. Now
Charlene, sometime near the end of the first half, I want you to call
a time out. Everybody comes on over to the bench, only I want you
to huddle up a little farther out onto the floor, so that everybody
can see you real good. O.K., you all know how sweaty Butch gets
during a game, so when Butch huddles up with everybody, I want
you all to start to notice and kinda make out like she's, you know,
startin' to smell. *(THEY all giggle at this.)* Kinda fan the air or
hold your nose and everybody kinda back off from her . . . Butch'll
be actin' real aggravated and mad, so Tammy, you go over to the
bench and underneath of it, in this bag, will be *this.* *(HE pulls out
an enormous fluffy powderpuff, about a yard in diameter.)* And
while Butch is lookin' off somewhere else . . .
TAMMY: I know, I know! Let me! *(SHE takes the powderpuff and
sort of dabs BUTCH with it.)*
CASSIUS: No, Tammy, hit her with it.
TAMMY: Hard?
CASSIUS: Hard.
    (SHE does. SHE is overcome with giggles.)
TAMMY: Does it hurt?
BUTCH: Naa . . .
    (SHE smacks BUTCH again, giggling and enjoying it.)
TAMMY: Hey, Gay!
GAY: What?

    *(SHE smacks GAY. SHE runs around smacking everybody
    with it, gleefully. WILMA enters.)*

TAMMY: Wilma! Look! *(SHE runs over and smacks WILMA with
it, full force.)*
WILMA: Tammy! *(Wrenching the powderpuff out of her hands)*
TAMMY: *(After a long silence)* I'm . . . sorry . . . Wilma. I . . .
CASSIUS: Wilma, we were just goin' over a new gag. Tammy just
got carried away. Tammy, put it away now.
WILMA: Cassius, I need to talk to you . . .
CASSIUS: Of course you do. I'll make some time for you later. Right
now I need to go out and hang some posters around town. If we
don't sell tickets, we don't have a team, do we? You and I can sit
down later and do what has to be done. You can count on it. I'll be
back soon. Ya'll get your hair done and whatnot, and I'll be back.
While I'm gone, I don't want any of you bothering Wilma about our
previous conversation. That's just over now, and we don't need anymore discussion. All right, Girls . . . bye bye. *(HE exits.)*
    (There is a long strained silence.)

TAMMY: Ya'll want any fruitcake?

(THEY *all shake their heads.*)

TAMMY: I'm sorry I hit you, Wilma.

WILMA: It's okay.

TAMMY: MMMMmmmm . . . smells like Christmas.

BUTCH: Maybe I'll have just a little.

TAMMY: Merry Christmas, Butch.

BUTCH: Thanks.

TAMMY: Just a couple more days now.

CHARLENE: Yep.

TAMMY: If I was home tonight . . . all of us kids'd be out caroling. We'd go to the old folks home, and the preacher's house . . . *(Singing)* WE WISH YOU A MERRY CHRISTMAS, WE WISH YOU A MERRY CHRISTMAS, WE WISH YOU A MERRY CHRISTMAS AND A HAPPY NEW YEAR! *(A long silence)* But, this is just as good . . . we got each other.

SHELBY: Yep.

TAMMY: We'll have a great Christmas.

GAY: Sure.

BUTCH: Yeah, who would want to trade in all this for stuffed turkey and buckeye pudding, mashed potatoes and sweet potatoe pie?

SHELBY: Butch is only sentimental when it comes to her stomach.

BUTCH: Oh yeah?

SHELBY: Yeah.

BUTCH: I got Christmas spirit.

SHELBY: Okay. Let's hear it.

BIRDIE: Shelby, please don't ask Butch to sing.

BUTCH: Why not?

BIRDIE: It makes my ears run.

BUTCH: I didn't want to sing anyway.   *(Putting on her coat)*

CHARLENE: Where do you think you're going?

BUTCH: I got something to prove to Shelby.

SHELBY: You want me to step outside with ya?

BUTCH: That won't be necessary.

CHARLENE: Don't go far.

BUTCH: I'll be back in ten.   *(SHE exits.)*

BIRDIE: What was that all about?

SHELBY: Search me. She probably went out for a smoke.

TAMMY: Oh no, she quit!

CHARLENE: I better not catch her smoking. Cassius warned her, once more and she'd get suspended for a week.

SHELBY: That doesn't sound too bad, then she'd get to go home for Christmas.

CHARLENE: Don't be smart, Tanner.

SHELBY: *(Sarcastic)*   I wasn't, Miss Treadwell.

TAMMY: Anybody want me to do their hair?   *(No response)*   Birdie, let me do your hair. I could do it so cute.

BIRDIE: That's okay.

TAMMY: Oh c'mon. I could make it look real cute. See, no offense, but you don't really wear it right for your face shape. What you need is bangs to cover up your forhead.

BIRDIE: It's too wavy.

TAMMY: No, I could tape them down with Scotch tape to keep 'em straight, or I could iron 'em.

BIRDIE: I don't think so.

(During this WILMA *and* SHELBY *have been talking earnestly under their breath.)*

CHARLENE: What are you two talking about?

SHELBY: Nothing.

CHARLENE: Then knock it off.

SHELBY: We're done anyway.

CHARLENE: Good.

SHELBY: I'm going to go sit by my friend Gay now. Is that okay, "Little Cassius?"

CHARLENE: I couldn't care less.

BIRDIE: Gay's writin' a letter.

SHELBY: I *wonder* who to.

TAMMY, SHELBY, BIRDIE, WILMA: RAY-mond!!

GAY: No, I'm not.

SHELBY: *(In a husky, romantic voice)*   Raymond darling, I love you, I need you, I'd do anything for you, but please . . . don't ask me to touch it.

WILMA: Shelby!

SHELBY: *(Mimicking Raymond in a deep voice)*   Please Gay, my darling, you're torturing me—please touch it. *(Mimicking* GAY *again)*   But it's so ugly . . . it's so red . . . it's so *angry*! . . . but then again, there's something about it . . .

TAMMY: Shelby!

SHELBY: I wouldn't mind touching one, but it's been so long since anybody asked.

GAY: God, Shelby.

SHELBY: I know, you and Raymond have a spiritual relationship.

WILMA: It's kinda hard to have anything else through the mail.

SHELBY: Yeah, I'd settle for a romantic love letter right now. How 'bout reading us another hot one, Gay? C'mon, don't be stingy. It's been weeks since you've read one to us. You and Raymond aren't on the rocks, are ya'?

GAY: No . . .

WILMA: Yeah, Gay, you've been holding out on us.

TAMMY: I'd love to hear one.

SHELBY: Read us a juicy one, please?

GAY: Don't, ya'll. I can't.

CHARLENE: If she doesn't want to—leave her alone.

SHELBY: But Gay, you know how we *live* for Raymond's letters.

WILMA: Remember that poem he wrote?

TAMMY: Ohhhh, he's so dreamy . . .

SHELBY: *(Feigning illness, staggering toward* GAY*)*   Gay, you can't do this to us. I can't go on. I can't play tonight. Just one little letter for all us poor, lonely, tired, lonely, pathetic, lonely girls. *(*SHE *collapses from the strain.)*

GAY: C'mon Shelby. It's kinda private, you know, personal.

SHELBY: Oh sure, I understand. You don't wanna get too personal with people you take a shower with every day.

GAY: Believe me, you wouldn't be interested.

WILMA: I'd be interested.

TAMMY   *(Reverently)*   Me too.

BIRDIE: I think she wants to.

SHELBY: Don't be shy. We're all friends here. C'mon, Gay. Pretty please.

GAY: Ya'll are too much.   *(*THEY *all look at her expectantly.)* Okay, okay.   *(*SHE *begins to read slowly and tentatively)*   . . . "Dear Baby . . . Oh Sweetheart, I miss you so. It seems like years since I have held you tight in my arms, and even more years until I will see you again. Every night I lie awake and dream of you. I dream of your long, lovely legs, and the way you look in a sweater, and about your little tiny waist, and how I would like to wrap my arms around it and squeeze and squeeze and never let go. I can't believe I let you talk me into this basketball thing—I should never have let you go so far away. Now, all I can do is pretend to have you near me, late at night, in the dark," dot, dot, dot. "Oh baby, please come home soon. I have been true-blue to you and never dated out, but I don't know how much longer I can hold on. I miss you like crazy. Passionately, Raymond."

BIRDIE: Boy, he's deep.

SHELBY: *(Reverently)*   Raymond never lets me down. Is there more?

GAY: *(After a pause)*   "P.S. I can't stop thinking about playing house with you. I even picked out your Christmas present yesterday. Just say the word, and I'll go buy it for you. They say that good things come in small packages—that applies to everything but you . . ha ha. Anyway, the present I have picked out for you comes in a little black velvet box. Please say yes."   *(*THEY *all gasp.)*   Don't scream!   *(*THEY *stifle little teeny screams.)*   Don't ya'll.

WILMA: What's the matter? This is great!

TAMMY: You are so lucky.

GAY: You don't understand. I can't marry him.

WILMA: Why in the world not?

SHELBY: Yeah. Why not?

GAY: Well, not right away, anyway. That's the problem, see. You know Raymond's got a lot of pent up passion . . .

SHELBY: I know . . .

WILMA: Tell him you'll marry him in the spring. That's not so long to wait.

GAY: I can't. I've still got almost two years left on my contract.

TAMMY: Cassius'll let you out of it.

GAY: Huh uhhh. I went right to Cassius last week, when Raymond first asked me. I went to him and told him the whole story. He didn't like it one bit. You know, "a contract's a contract." He turned all kinda red in the face, and that little vein, you know, right here in his forehead, it started throbbin'.

TAMMY: Uh oh . . .

GAY: He said he can't go to the grocery store and just buy himself a new center. He don't find girls as tall as me too often. He said the team needs me, and he couldn't let me go. So . . . that was that.

SHELBY: Cassius strikes again . . .

CHARLENE: Hey!

SHELBY: Just like him to stand in the way of true love . . .

CHARLENE: Watch your mouth.

SHELBY: You know I'm right. He doesn't care about anybody but himself. He's just an old b . . .

CHARLENE: Tanner! You're looking at a ten dollar fine. Now sit down. And shut up.

SHELBY: You can't make me shut up. He's wrong and you know it.

GAY: Shelby, don't. Maybe he's right. I did sign a contract.

SHELBY: The old goat . . . he's just jealous 'cause nobody ever wanted to marry him.

CHARLENE: Make it twenty. (SHE *exits.*)

SHELBY: Witch!

TAMMY: Shelby, don't!

BIRDIE: Calm down, Shel . . . this is gonna get real bad for you.

SHELBY: I don't care . . .

GAY: Please Shelby, don't say anything more. I shouldn't even have told you. This is turnin' into a big mess.

SHELBY: Okay, okay.

(BUTCH *bursts through the door carrying a Christmas tree, singing:*)

BUTCH: O Christmas Tree! O Christmas Tree!   *(No one responds.)*
What's the matter with everybody? Look, a real tree—how's this for
Christmas spirit?
BIRDIE: Great, Butch.
TAMMY: *(Gleefully)*   A tree! A tree! Where'd it come from?
BUTCH: *(Mimicing* TAMMY*)*   A forest!
TAMMY: You cut it down yourself!?
BUTCH: Naw, I bought it from some Boy Scouts up the street.
WILMA: Good job, Butch.
BUTCH: Did I interrupt a funeral or something here?
SHELBY: No, everything's fine.
BUTCH: Where's Charlene?
SHELBY: Doin' some laps on her broom.
TAMMY: Oh it's so pretty, Butch. Thank you.
WILMA: Here, put it down over here.
BUTCH: Yeah, it's not so bad, is it?
BIRDIE: Butch, it's a great tree and all, but don't it look a little bare?
BUTCH: Well, what'd you expect? Tinsel and ornaments?
SHELBY: We'll just have to use our heads and come up with some-
thing to dress it up. Wait. I know. I've got this great pair of ear-
rings.   *(SHE rummages through her locker, finds them, and hangs
them on the tree.)*   There!
      (THEY all regard it skeptically.)
SHELBY: Well it's a start.
BIRDIE: *(Retrieving the toy bear from before)*   Here, he can stand
underneath!
TAMMY: Oh yes!
SHELBY: I got it!   *(She rushes to the toilet stall and emerges with
a roll of toilet paper held high.)*   Tee Pee!
WILMA: Isn't that sort of sacreligious or something?
BIRDIE: Yeah, Shelby, I think it is.
SHELBY: Well, you think of something.
TAMMY: If we had scissors and paper, we could cut out snowflakes.
BIRDIE: I know! I know!   *(SHE rummages through her locker.)*
Here!   *(SHE has two cans of shaving cream, one of which SHE
hands to* TAMMY*.)*
TAMMY: Shaving cream?
BIRDIE: Sure, snow! Watch.   *(SHE squirts a dab onto a bough.)*
TAMMY: Can I try?
BIRDIE: Go ahead.

      *(BIRDIE tosses the can to SHELBY who squirts some on too.
SHELBY starts singing "Deck the Halls" to a jazzy beat and they
all join in, snapping their fingers. At this cue, they break into
two lines, as if doing their pre-game warm-up. A girl from each*

line runs up, "shoots" some shaving cream onto the tree and then "passes" the can to the next girl in line. The passes are under the leg and behind the back and fancy hook shots to give us the idea of a fancy ball-handling display. At the last "fa la la la la," TAMMY jumps on BIRDIE'S shoulders and slam dunks the last blob onto the tip of the tree. They all collapse laughing, clapping and cheering for themselves.)

WILMA: It's beautiful!

SHELBY: It's gorgeous!

BUTCH: It's menthol.

(From offstage, the sound of jingling bells is heard.)

BIRDIE: What the heck?

(The jingling continues, and suddenly the door swings open and Cassius appears dressed in a Santa Claus suit with a pack on his back.)

CASSIUS: Ho Ho Ho, girls and girls, Merry Christmas!

(TAMMY, BIRDIE, BUTCH and GAY swarm toward him. CHARLENE enters. WILMA and SHELBY exchange glances. TAMMY is shrieking.)

TAMMY: Santa!

CASSIUS: Ho HO HO, little girls. *(Spying the tree, dropping the Santa voice for a moment)*   What the hell is *that*?

TAMMY: It's our menthol Christmas tree! What's in the bag, Santa? What'd you bring us?

CASSIUS: Where'd it come from?   *(BUTCH raises her hand.)* Cute idea.

CASSIUS: All right. All right. Sit down. I've got some pree-liminary Christmas gifts here in my pack for everyone of my little girls. Let's see, here's one for Tammy.

TAMMY: Thank you, Santa.

CASSIUS: And a little something for Birdie . . .

BIRDIE: Thank you, Cassius.

CASSIUS: And here is Shelby's . . .

SHELBY: Thanks.

CASSIUS: You're welcome. And let's see . . . Charlene . . . and one for Butch . . . and Gay . . . and here's one for Wilma.

(THEY all get their presents and begin opening them.)

TAMMY: Oh, bath oil . . . thank you. I love it.

ALL: Ooooo!

SHELBY: *(Opening a hairbrush)*   Thanks, Cassius.

TAMMY: What'd you get, Bird?

BIRDIE: All different kinds of makeup stuff.

TAMMY: Oooo. Lemme see.

BIRDIE: Thanks, Cassius.

CASSIUS: And I want you to use it too. I want all you girls to show
  Birdie the proper techniques for applying makeup.

TAMMY: Sure, Birdie, I'll help you.

CHARLENE: Mmmmm, perfume. That was very sweet of you, Cassius.

GAY: What a neat pen and pencil set, thank you.

BUTCH: A Lady Schick electric razor . . .

CASSIUS: To keep those legs smooth and feminine.

BUTCH: Thanks.

BIRDIE: What'd you get, Wilm?

WILMA: Pink stationery. I like it a lot. Thanks.

CASSIUS: You are all very welcome. Is it hot in here or what?

CHARLENE: Maybe it's the beard.

CASSIUS: Oh . . . yeah. Will you little elves mind if Santa takes
  off his beard? Whew!

TAMMY: Can I sit on your lap, Santa?

CASSIUS: Why, sure! What are you wishing for, little girl?

TAMMY: A better jump shot!

CASSIUS: Ho Ho HO! Just the right answer! You are a good little
  girl! Get up now, Sweetie, you're gettin' heavy. God, I'm hot! This
  suit is hot. Now why is it Shelby is the only one who has fixed her
  hair? I thought I told you all to get that done.

GAY: Oh, Cassius, we got time.

CASSIUS: You aren't sassin' me, are you?

GAY: No, 'course not.

CASSIUS: Everybody, go on and put away your presents. I need
  some air. On second thought, you all go wait outside. I gotta use
  the facilities. Hurry up now. Git! Get rid of those long faces. I love
  you girls. C'mere, Gay . . . give me a hug. Go on, scat!

TAMMY: I love my bath oil, Santa!

CASSIUS: And I love you!

> (CASSIUS *waits until they leave, then, loosening his collar,
> enters the toilet stall. All we see are his feet and the Santa pants
> around his ankles. There is silence for a time—then the door bursts
> open and, as a prank,* WILMA, BUTCH *and* SHELBY, *laughing
> quietly, shove* TAMMY *through the door, and lock it behind her.*
> TAMMY *pushes and pulls at the door to free herself.* SHE *turns
> and sees* CASSIUS' *feet under the stall and covers her eyes, pres-
> sing against the door with her body.* SHE *whispers into the crack
> in the door.)*

TAMMY: C'mon ya'll, let me out, please!

> (We hear muffled laughter from the other side of the door.)

Oh God, ya'll, please, this isn't funny.

(No movement at the door. More laughter.)
Cassius, I'm so sorry to disturb you, but the girls, they accidentally locked me in here. They won't let me out, Cassius. I'm sorry.
(No response)
If you tell them, they'll let me out and you can finish. . . . Cassius?
(TAMMY walks slowly toward the stall.)
Are you okay?
(No response)
Cassius say something.
(SHE walks to the stall and knocks on the door softly.)
Cassius?
(No response)
This isn't funny. Say something. Cassius?
(SHE runs across the room to the locked door.)
Ya'll Open up! Something's wrong. Cassius is sick or something!
(Banging on the door) I mean it, now! Open up!

(No response from outside. SHE slowly turns and walks toward the stall. SHE is terrified, but she knows what she has to do. SHE approaches the stall, and stands leaning on the wall.)

Cassius? Cassius, here I come . . .

(Slowly SHE slides her body down the wall of the stall until SHE can lower her head and look under it. As SHE looks under, SHE screams.)

Blackout.

END OF ACT ONE

ACT TWO

*(The team, except for Charlene, is assembled in the locker room.
The clock on the wall reads 6:55. The mood in the locker room is
very somber.)*

BIRDIE: *(After a pause)* It's good he was so happy . . .

GAY: Yeah.

BUTCH: He really was, wasn't he?

WILMA: Yeah.

BIRDIE: So that's good.

GAY: Yeah.

TAMMY: It's a blessing really.

SHELBY: What do you mean?

TAMMY: I mean that he was so happy.

SHELBY: Oh. Yeah.

BUTCH: How do they know it was his heart?

WILMA: I don't know. That's what the guy said.

BIRDIE: I heard him say "heart attack."

BUTCH: But how can they tell?

BIRDIE: He told the other guy something about "ticker . . . bad
ticker."

TAMMY: Bad ticker.

BIRDIE: Uh huh.

BUTCH: I wonder how they know for sure.

TAMMY: When I was little, I had a dog named Ticker. *(Starting
to cry)*

WILMA: Tammy . . . don't start again . . .

TAMMY: He was a little dachshund, and you know how they have
real long toenails. When he'd walk across the kitchen floor, he'd go
tick, tick, tick, tick . . . so we called him Ticker!!

GAY: Tammy, honey, don't . . .

BUTCH: Tammy, don't start crying again . . . I mean it . . . I can't
take it.

TAMMY: *(As to her dog)* Bad Ticker . . .

GAY: Shhhh. Don't cry.

TAMMY: I can't help it.

WILMA: Yes you can. C'mon now. We all have to be brave now, for
Cassius.

GAY: Dry your eyes. No more crying.

BIRDIE: I'm all cried out.

SHELBY: I think we better get ahold of ourselves and figure out
what we should do next.

BUTCH: Let's wait and see what Charlene says.

TAMMY: Where'd she go?

GAY: She's calling Booneville, to tell J.D., Cassius' brother.

BIRDIE: Poor thing.

SHELBY: I guess this is the end of the Shooting Stars.

GAY: We don't know that for sure.

SHELBY: No . . . it's all over.

BUTCH: You think so?

BIRDIE: Maybe J.D.'ll want to take over for Cassius.

WILMA: He's got the hardware store . . . I doubt he'll wanna give that up.

SHELBY: I'm tellin' ya'll, we're history.

GAY: Don't give up, everybody.

BUTCH: That would just kill Cassius . . . Oh God . . . I'm sorry.
   (CHARLENE enters.)

WILMA: Did ya get through to J.D.?

CHARLENE: That was the hardest thing I ever did in my life.

BIRDIE: How did he take it?

CHARLENE: Pretty good. He said Cassius has had heart trouble for years. He thought we knew.

WILMA: I never had any idea. Did you know about it?

CHARLENE: He never told me a thing. I'm sure he didn't want to worry us.

GAY: Isn't that just like him?

TAMMY: Poor Cassius.

SHELBY: Did he say he was gonna make the arrangements?

CHARLENE: He said he was gonna try to catch a bus tonight and get here sometime tomorrow. I'm supposed to wait for him here, but he said to tell you all to go ahead and go on home.

SHELBY: I knew it.

CHARLENE: He said for us to gather all the equipment and stuff together and put it in the DeSoto, and he'll drive Cassius back to Booneville in it.

TAMMY: (After a horrified pause) In the station wagon? (Starting to cry again)

BIRDIE: Tammy . . .

GAY: Honey . . . J.D.'s gonna take Cassius back to Indiana.

TAMMY: In the station wagon?

GAY: Uh huh . . .

TAMMY: Sitting up?

CHARLENE: Tammy . . . they'll fold the seats down and put him in the back . . .

TAMMY: Brrrrr . . .

SHELBY: Tammy, are you okay?

TAMMY: (Wide eyed) I just had a picture of Cassius . . . lyin' in the back of the Desoto . . . with all the equipment around him . . .

GAY: Sweetheart . . . he'll be in a casket.

TAMMY: Oh . . . that's good.

GAY: Tammy, honey, are you gonna be all right? Do you want to lie down?

TAMMY: No! . . . I don't wanna lie down. I'm fine.

BIRDIE: Are you sure?

WILMA: Charlene, what about the funeral?

CHARLENE: J.D. said he wished everybody could come but he doesn't have any way of gettin' us all there, so he said he'd understand if we all just went on home.

BIRDIE: I'd feel real bad if I didn't go to his funeral.

TAMMY: I'd go . . . if somebody'd go with me.

GAY: I'll go with you . . . if I can get the money for the trip.

SHELBY: Char, did J.D. say anything about keepin' the team going?

CHARLENE: He said he didn't see how he could. He's got his store and his responsibilities at home, and he just doesn't have the interest in it that Cassius did.

SHELBY: I guess that's it then.

TAMMY: I'm gonna miss you all so much.

BUTCH: I'm gonna miss you too . . .

BIRDIE: Oh, ya'll, don't start crying again. I mean it. This is gonna kill me if I stop and think about it.

GAY: We'll get back together . . . we just have to.

CHARLENE: I wouldn't count on it if I were you.

BIRDIE: Char, do you need help loadin' up the car with all the stuff?

CHARLENE: Yeah, Birdie, thanks. Let's just gather it all together and stack it by the door.

BIRDIE: What all should go?

CHARLENE: Well, let's see, the balls, and the trainer's bag . . . and the powderpuff, and the big whistle and the top hats . . . and the confetti . . . and the big bucket, and the butterfly net, all that stuff . . . and the uniforms.

GAY: The uniforms are still in the dryer.

SHELBY: I'll get 'em. *(SHE starts to exit.)* Why don't you help me, Wilm?

WILMA: Huh?

SHELBY: C'mon. Come help me with the uniforms.

WILMA: Okay . . . *(THEY exit.)*

BUTCH: I guess we ought to call our folks.

CHARLENE: The phone's in the gym office. Who wants to go first?

GAY: Go ahead, Butch.

BUTCH: Oh great. *(SHE exits.)*

CHARLENE: Be sure and reverse the charges.

(THEY all begin gathering up the equipment and piling it next

to the door.)

TAMMY: *(Retrieving the big powderpuff)* This was gonna be so funny . . .

BIRDIE: You did it real good.

TAMMY: Thanks . . . I can't believe it's all over.

BIRDIE: Me neither. Any idea what you're gonna do back in Memphis?

TAMMY: I don't know. My mother always wanted me to go to beauty school. Maybe I'll do that.

BIRDIE: I'll bet you'd be good at that.

TAMMY: Yeah . . . how about you? What are you gonna do?

BIRDIE: I don't know.

TAMMY: Didn't you ever wanna be something else?

BIRDIE: When I was a kid I wanted to be a fireman, but I guess that's stupid.

TAMMY: What about you, Charlene?

CHARLENE: All I ever wanted to do was play basketball. Or be a coach when I couldn't play anymore. I don't wanna do anything else.

GAY: I know what you mean.

CHARLENE: Well, at least you got something to go home to.

GAY: What?

CHARLENE: Raymond. There's nothing to stop you from gettin' married now.

GAY: Yeah, I guess not.

CHARLENE: You gonna have a big wedding?

GAY: I don't know. I guess I haven't given it much thought.

CHARLENE: You gonna have a lotta bridesmaids?

GAY: I don't know.

CHARLENE: I'd sure be pleased to stand up for ya', you know, if you needed somebody.

GAY: That's real nice, Char. Thanks. I'll keep it in mind.

CHARLENE: Like I said . . . If you needed somebody . . .

GAY: Sure.

TAMMY: Me too, Gay.

BIRDIE: Yeah. Me, too.

GAY: O.K.

TAMMY: When Butch is done, you should call Raymond. I'll bet he'll be real happy to hear you're comin' home.

GAY: Yeah.

(SHELBY and WILMA enter. SHELBY is carrying an armload of laundry. WILMA, empty-handed, goes directly to her locker, slips something out from under her blouse and hides it in her locker.)

SHELBY: Here are all the uniforms. *(SHE begins stuffing them into a laundry bag.)*

CHARLENE: Don't just stuff 'em in there . . .

SHELBY: What difference does it make?

CHARLENE: I want everything to be neat and clean and orderly. Here, let me.

SHELBY: I can fold 'em.

CHARLENE: That's okay, I'll do it.

SHELBY: Charlene, I am capable of folding them myself.

CHARLENE: Shelby . . .

SHELBY: I'll do 'em nice and neat, see?

CHARLENE: Stack 'em.

SHELBY: Yes, ma'am.

BUTCH: *(Bursting through door)* Apparently, nobody has bothered to look in the gym lately . . .

WILMA: Why?

BUTCH: . . . There's about a hundred people out there . . . two cheerleader squads . . . half the band . . .

CHARLENE: Oh, my God . . .

BUTCH: . . . and more comin' through the door. Somebody better do something.

CHARLENE: Oh no . . . why didn't somebody tell me what time it was?

TAMMY: It's almost seven.

CHARLENE: Didn't one of you tell somebody what happened?

WILMA: Didn't you tell 'em?

CHARLENE: I was a little busy.

WILMA: So were we.

GAY: We all just forgot . . .

BUTCH: Somebody better get out there and tell 'em.

WILMA: I'll tell 'em.

CHARLENE: Where are you going?

WILMA: What do you mean?

CHARLENE: Well . . . who elected you?

WILMA: Charlene, if you wanna tell 'em, go ahead . . .

CHARLENE: I don't want to . . . I just think it should come from a person in authority.

WILMA: Fine.

CHARLENE: I mean I am the head coach now . . .

SHELBY: Oooooooo—

CHARLENE: But if you're really excited about telling them, go right ahead. I don't care.

WILMA: Look, I was just trying to help. I don't care. Go ahead.

CHARLENE: No really. If you want to, it's fine with me.

WILMA: No, you do it.

CHARLENE: You want me to do it?

WILMA: I don't care.

CHARLENE: I don't care either.

WILMA: Okay, I'll do it.

CHARLENE: Don't do it if you don't want to.

WILMA: Do *you* want to?

CHARLENE: Of course not. I just don't want you to if you don't want to.

GAY: Why don't you both go?

CHARLENE: That's fine with me.

WILMA: Fine.

SHELBY: One of you is gonna have to announce it over the P.A. system.

WILMA: We'll just tell 'em and let them announce it.

CHARLENE: I think it should come from one of us.

BIRDIE: You gonna make a speech?

CHARLENE: I think we should give Cassius a fitting tribute. We can't just say, "Okay, ya'll, everybody go home."

SHELBY: So what're you gonna say?

CHARLENE: I don't know . . . something . . . dignified.

WILMA: Like what?

CHARLENE: I don't know . . . um . . . Ladies and Gentlemen . . .

BUTCH: That's dignified.

CHARLENE: We regret to tell you, that . . . the owner of the Indiana Shooting Stars . . . Mr. Cassius Birdwell is . . .

BIRDIE: Somebody better write this down.

   (GAY does so)

CHARLENE: . . . is . . . passed away.

SHELBY: Is passed away?

CHARLENE: Is . . . what? Dead?

WILMA: Nooo.

TAMMY: Deceased?

BIRDIE: Was deceased a few hours ago . . .

SHELBY: Nooo.

GAY: What was that first part again?

CHARLENE: Ladies and Gentlemen . . .

GAY: I got that.

CHARLENE: We regret to tell you that the owner of the Shooting Stars.

WILMA AND CHARLENE: Mr. Cassius Birdwell . . .

CHARLENE: Is . . .

WILMA: Was struck down by a heart attack . . .

SHELBY: That's good.

WILMA: . . . this evening . . .

CHARLENE: This afternoon . . .

WILMA: Whatever . . .

CHARLENE: . . . and because of this death . . .

GAY: . . . because of this death . . .

SHELBY: That sounds stupid.

CHARLENE: Because of this . . . event . . .

WILMA: Because of this something . . .

SHELBY: Because of this . . .

TAMMY: . . . inconvenience!

WILMA AND SHELBY AND CHARLENE: Nooo.
    (BUTCH exits.)

GAY: How 'bout, "as a result . . ."

CHARLENE: As a result . . .

SHELBY: What?

WILMA: Wait, what are we trying to say?

CHARLENE: As a result, tonight's game is cancelled.

WILMA: I think we should say that he died.

CHARLENE: We already did.

WILMA: No, we didn't.

CHARLENE: You said . . .

WILMA: I said he was struck down by a heart attack. I was trying
  to get around to saying that he passed away.

CHARLENE: Gay, what do we have so far?

WILMA: I don't care . . . I just thought you wanted to do this tribute
  thing.

GAY: Ladies and Gentlemen . . . we regret to . . .

BUTCH: *(Enters running)* Okay, now the whole band is here and
  about a hundred more people and the other team is warming up.

SHELBY: *(Overlapping)* Oh, great.

TAMMY: *(Overlapping)* Quick, you all. "We regret that Cassius
  was struck . . ."

CHARLENE: *(Overlapping)* Shhh, wait, you got me all confused.

WILMA: *(Overlapping)* I think we should just tell 'em and let them
  announce it.

GAY: Can I make a suggestion?

BIRDIE: What, Gay?

GAY: Well, I don't know what ya'll are gonna think of this, but you
  know, we could just go ahead and play.

BUTCH: I don't know . . .

CHARLENE: Let me think about this for a minute.

GAY: It's just an idea.

BIRDIE: I think it's a good idea.

GAY: You do?

BIRDIE: Sure.

CHARLENE: I'm in charge, it's up to me to do the right thing.

SHELBY: Oh boy . . .

CHARLENE: I have to weigh this carefully . . . we don't want to be disrespectful . . . but on the other hand . . .

BUTCH: On the other hand, we're gonna have seven hundred people here in a minute.

BIRDIE: We could vote.

BUTCH: Somebody better decide.

GAY: Yeah, why don't we vote?

CHARLENE: If Cassius were here . . . I think he would want us to go ahead and play.

WILMA: I don't agree.

CHARLENE: I don't care. It's my decision and I say we play.

WILMA: I think it's disrespectful. I vote no.

CHARLENE: Who said anything about voting?

SHELBY: I'm with Wilma.

BUTCH: Me too. I think it would be weird to play.

GAY: I don't think we should disappoint all those people.

BIRDIE: They're all comin' to see us—I don't think we should just send 'em all home.

GAY: I'd like to play one more time . . . for Cassius . . . for old time's sake.

BUTCH: What do you say, Tammy? You don't wanna play, do ya'?

TAMMY: I think we should play . . . but I'm not sure I can.

GAY: You mean you just don't feel up to it?

TAMMY: I just wouldn't feel right . . . We're supposed to be funny, you know with all our tricks and the butterfly net and the big pow- derpuff and pullin' guys' pants down and stuff. I don't think I could do it. I'm just not in a very funny mood right now.

BIRDIE: I know what you mean.

GAY: Yeah, I guess it wouldn't look right.

SHELBY: That's it! That's it! Oh, Tammy, you are a genius.

BUTCH: Tammy's a genius?

SHELBY: I have wanted to do this my whole *life*. This is perfect!

WILMA: What?

SHELBY: What a way to go out. Don't you see?

CHARLENE: What are you talking about?

SHELBY: Ladies, Tammy has given us the perfect compromise. We're gonna play.

WILMA: We are?

SHELBY: Yep. The way I've always wanted to play. Straight *men's* rules. No shenanigans. No gags to slow down the game. We don't have to be funny anymore . . . we just have to be good.

WILMA: . . . And we are good.

SHELBY: This is gonna be great.

TAMMY: What if they fast break?

SHELBY: We can keep up with them.

WILMA: We can do it.

BIRDIE: You know, I wouldn't mind givin' it a try.

SHELBY: I bet we'll slaughter 'em.

GAY: It could be great . . . Charlene, what do ya' think?

CHARLENE: It won't work.

SHELBY: Why not?

CHARLENE: Forget it. It's out of the question.

SHELBY: Why?

CHARLENE: Look, we're not here to beat the home team—we're here to give 'em some entertainment.

SHELBY: I think it'll be very entertaining.

CHARLENE: For you maybe. And I'll tell you something else, I guarantee the other team is not gonna like it one bit.

BUTCH: Maybe she's right—they could get real mad.

BIRDIE: So what? I can get mad right back.

SHELBY: Yeah!

CHARLENE: The crowd'll boo you right off the floor.

GAY: You think so?

BUTCH: Oooo. She's right . . . they could.

CHARLENE: I'm tellin' you, it's a stupid idea.

SHELBY: Why would they boo at us?

BUTCH: Think about it. They came here expectin' us to be clowns. They want us to run around and act like fools.

GAY: I've never been booed at in my life.

BUTCH: Maybe they'll think we're gettin' too big for our britches . . . thinkin' we can play like men.

SHELBY: But we can.

BUTCH: We think we can.

WILMA: You're gettin' worked up over nuthin'.

GAY: I must admit, I'm a little worried about the other team bein' upset with us.

BUTCH: They're gonna get mad.

SHELBY: Why should they get mad? We beat 'em all the time before.

BUTCH: Yeah, but that was playin' silly . . . We beat 'em because we were playin' tricks on 'em . . . crawlin' between their legs, jumpin' on each other's shoulders, puttin' the butterfly net on 'em. We beat 'em bein' silly, playin' our rules. We play straight and we beat 'em, they're gonna be mad.

CHARLENE: And the crowd'll boo at you.

GAY: Maybe we're making a big mistake . . .

CHARLENE: Yeah, why don't you just drop it, Shelby.

SHELBY: Look! Nobody's gonna boo us. And nobody's gonna get mad at us. Why would people get upset with us if we're doing our best? We're good. We're real good. Nobody boos the New York Knickerbockers, do they?

CHARLENE: That's different.

SHELBY: No, it's not. We're the best girl's basketball team in the world, I'll bet. We should act like it. Look, it's worth a try!

WILMA: This is our chance!

SHELBY: We gotta show 'em!

TAMMY: We'll show 'em . . . but they won't be mad at us . . . they'll *like* us. They'll see how good we are and how pretty we are and they'll hoist us up on their shoulders and they'll say we're the best girl's basketball team in America, and we'll travel all over the country . . .

SHELBY: And everyone will respect us because we'll be a real team . . .

WILMA: Playin' real basketball . . .

TAMMY: And we'll go on a world tour, to France and Italy, and the men *there* will like us too . . . and *Life* magazine will take our pictures . . . and we'll be on Ed Sullivan . . . and we'll get to play basketball *every single day.*

SHELBY: Yeah . . .

WILMA: Yeah . . .

BIRDIE: Yeah . . .

TAMMY: Yeah!

BUTCH: Maybe it's not such a bad idea . . . you really think we could be in *Life* magazine?

TAMMY: Why not?

BUTCH: My parents get *Life* magazine!

   (All but CHARLENE explode with excitement.)

SHELBY: Come on, ya'll. Let's give it a try.

GAY: Sounds great, doesn't it?

BUTCH: I s'pose it's worth a try.

CHARLENE: *(Shouting over the din)*   You all take the cake! I never heard anything so stupid in my whole life. Get ahold of yourselves. I got news for ya'. We got us a game to play, and we are gonna play the way we always play and I don't wanna hear another word about it. Or about *Life* magazine! Understand?

TAMMY: But . . .

CHARLENE: I'm gonna go out and talk to the promoter now, and tell him we'll be ready to play in fifteen minutes . . . so I suggest everyone get dressed and ready to go. We've got one last game to play—then ya'll are free to go wherever you want—I couldn't care less. *(SHE exits.)*

WILMA: God! What's with her?

SHELBY: She'll never change.

WILMA: What's eating her, anyway?

GAY: I think she's still upset about Cassius—she was closer to him than any of us were.

TAMMY: Maybe so.

GAY: I'm sure she's just trying to do the right thing.

BUTCH: Why does she have to be so pushy about it?

WILMA: She just won't listen.

SHELBY: Old Bossy, the Cow . . .

TAMMY: I was kinda gettin' excited about playin' the new way.

BIRDIE: Me too.

GAY: Yeah . . .

TAMMY: I don't feel like playin' anymore.

BIRDIE: Me neither.

TAMMY: I wish we'd just called the game off and gone home.

GAY: Tammy . . .

TAMMY: I think I'm depressed.

SHELBY: I'm not playin' unless we play straight. I'm not goin' out there and act like a fool anymore.

WILMA: I don't want to, either.

SHELBY: She can't make us play.

GAY: Ya'll, don't say that. We can't play a whole game without you.

BUTCH: If you two don't play, then Charlene's gonna have to play thirty straight minutes, and there's no way she can do that. She'll keel over.

SHELBY: Let her.

WILMA: Yeah, I might stick around just to watch that.

TAMMY: I don't wanna play, if ya'll don't.

GAY: Tammy . . .

TAMMY: I wanna play the new way . . .

WILMA: What about you, Bird?

BIRDIE: What do we want to be, clowns or ball players?

SHELBY: One thing's for sure, we're never gonna get any respect and we're never gonna go anywhere, except little old small towns like this one, if we play Charlene's way.

BUTCH: What do you think, Gay?

GAY: *(After a pause)* I'll go along with ya'll.

BUTCH: I say we do it our way.

WILMA: It's six against one.

SHELBY: Let's do it.

WILMA: We'll just tell her she's outnumbered.

SHELBY: She can't stop us.

TAMMY: You really think we can beat 'em?

BUTCH: We might.

SHELBY: We're doing something nobody's ever done before.

TAMMY: Oooo! I got goose pimples.

BIRDIE: We better get ready.

SHELBY: Let's go.

GAY: I can't believe we're doin' this.

WILMA: God, I'm shakin'.

(THEY *are very excited. Everyone quickly begins getting ready.*
THEY *begin getting dressed, tape their ankles, or do stretching
exercises. There should be a feeling that they are going through
their nightly pre-game ritual.)*

SHELBY: God, Charlene's gonna have kittens.
WILMA: Let her.
BUTCH: She just got too pushy.
TAMMY: She'll change her mind when the photographers show up.
BIRDIE: Wait a second, ya'll.
GAY: What?
BIRDIE: You're forgettin' something.
SHELBY: What.
BIRDIE: How we gonna get famous and do all that stuff without an
owner? We got no money, we got no car, we got no equipment.
GAY: Oh yeah . . .
BIRDIE: Until we get somebody to take over for Cassius, tonight's
our last game.
BUTCH: Oh yeah . . . we're doomed.
SHELBY: Now wait. Lemme think about this. We need to find a
man to step in and take over.
WILMA: A cute man.
BUTCH: A cute, rich man.
TAMMY: All we need is one cute, rich man to fall in love with us
. . . right away.
SHELBY: Shouldn't be too hard.
WILMA: Sounds like the story of my life.
BIRDIE: Yeah, well, I don't know anybody cute and I don't know
anybody rich and I sure as hell don't know anybody who's in love
with me.
TAMMY: Aw, Birdie . . .
BUTCH: We're doomed.
SHELBY: There's gotta be somebody.
WILMA: C'mon you guys . . . think!
BUTCH: You think if I knew a cute, rich man who was in love with
me—I'd be here?
GAY: She's right.
SHELBY: Wait a minute, Gay.
GAY: What?
SHELBY: What about Raymond?
WILMA AND TAMMY: Yeah!
GAY: What about him?
TAMMY: He could rescue us!

GAY: C'mon, ya'll.

SHELBY: Why not?

GAY: Well, for one thing, he's not rich.

SHELBY: He must have some money set aside. I bet it wouldn't take much to get us goin' again.

BUTCH: Yeah, you could marry him and still play on the team.

TAMMY: Yeah, Gay, it would be perfect!

GAY: I don't think he'd go for it.

TAMMY: Tell him you won't marry him unless he takes over the team.

GAY: I couldn't do that.

TAMMY: C'mon, Gay. Do it, please?

SHELBY: Just call him up and ask him.

WILMA: What could it hurt?

BUTCH: C'mon, Gay.

TAMMY: Don't you wanna go to France?

GAY: Yeah, I do, but . . .

SHELBY: Then call him!

TAMMY: Oh, please!

BUTCH: C'mon!

WILMA AND SHELBY: Please!

GAY: Forget it, ya'll! I mean it!
    (Long pause)

BUTCH: Obviously she wants to keep him all to herself.

SHELBY: I guess so.

WILMA: I s'pose now that Cassius is gone, she's free to quit the team and go on home and get married if she wants.

SHELBY: Looks that way.

GAY: Ya'll, stop talking about me like I'm not here.

BUTCH: Looks like we're doomed.

SHELBY: Yep.

WILMA: No way we can go on without an owner *and* a center.

SHELBY: Nope.

GAY: Look, ya'll, I really want to stay and play . . . more than anything. I just don't think it's fair to make me marry Raymond, just because we need a man to take over the team.

WILMA: I thought you wanted to marry Raymond.

GAY: Well, I thought I did.

SHELBY: You said you did.

WILMA: Yeah, Gay.

GAY: Well, I did when Cassius said I couldn't, but now I'm not so sure. I mean now, if we can work it out, it looks like things might be better. I like the idea about bein' famous, and goin' to France, and playin' professional ball. What the heck I wanna drag around ol' Raymond for?

SHELBY: Old Raymond?

GAY: Well, shoot. You marry him then.

SHELBY: I'm not gonna marry him. Wilma, you marry him.

WILMA: I'm not gonna marry him. I'm gonna catch me a Frenchie.

SHELBY: Tammy, you marry him.

TAMMY: NOOOOOooooo! I'm not gonna marry him. Somebody else marry him!

ALL: NOOOOOOOOooooooo!

WILMA: Looks like we're back where we started.

BUTCH: Yep. We're doomed.

TAMMY: We'll find somebody. We got to.

BUTCH: *(Lighting a cigarette)* Looks to me like we'll all be home for Christmas.

BIRDIE: *(Reacting to the cigarette)* Jeez, Butch, you think that's a good idea?

TAMMY: Butch! You told me you quit!

BUTCH: Well, looks like I started up again.

WILMA: Hey, Butch, c'mon, we got a game to play.

BUTCH: So what?

CHARLENE: *(Bursting through the door, carrying a bank bag)* Look everybody . . . the greatest thing . . . *(Spying the cigarette)* What in the hell?

TAMMY: Uh oh . . .

CHARLENE: I see you're up to your old tricks again, Butch. *(No response from BUTCH)* Put it out. *(No response)* Now.

BUTCH: Why should I?

CHARLENE: Because I said so.

BUTCH: No.

CHARLENE: I'm warning you . . .

BUTCH: Go ahead. What are you gonna do? You got nobody to go tattle to now.

CHARLENE: I'm still in charge and I'm telling you to put it out.

BUTCH: I'm still tougher than you are and I'm telling you "no."

TAMMY: Maybe you oughta put it out, Butch.

CHARLENE: Give it to me . . .

BUTCH: Charlene, I'm gonna smoke this cigarette, and you can't stop me. See?! I smoke, see? I smoke! I smoke! I smoke! I'm a big girl and if I wanna smoke I will! I like it! It feels good! I want to, so I do! It's fun, see? Mmmmm! Smoke! Smoke! Smoke! Love that smoke! Maybe I'll smoke two at once! That would be nice! Mmmmm! *(Takes out another, now has one in each hand)* I'll smoke this one, then I'll smoke that one . . . this one, that one. Mmmmm! Good!

CHARLENE: Are you through?

BUTCH: *(Taking another long drag and exhaling)* Yes.

CHARLENE: Okay, Butch, fine. I was planning on putting you in the starting line-up tonight, but now you are permanently *on the bench.*

TAMMY: No! We need Butch. We can't beat the men without her!

CHARLENE: Too bad.

SHELBY: Hang on a second, Charlene. Who elected you Queen for a Day? I say Butch plays.

WILMA: Me too.

SHELBY: As a matter of fact, I got my own ideas on the starting line-up.

WILMA: Yeah.

SHELBY: Maybe you oughta be the one warming the bench.

CHARLENE: I'll be coaching and playing.

SHELBY: Says who?

CHARLENE: Don't be stupid. Somebody's gotta run this team.

GAY: I'm not so sure there's anything left to run.

SHELBY: Things have changed, Charlene. We all decided. We're not playin' the old way anymore.

CHARLENE: Are you still on that kick?

SHELBY: That's right. We're playin' for real, Charlene. Just like I said.

CHARLENE: Are you all really going along with her on this?

GAY: We just wanna give it a try, Charlene, but we want you to play with us.

TAMMY: C'mon, Charlene. Don't be mad. It'll be fun. We'll beat 'em and then you'll see.

CHARLENE: Birdie, are you going along with this too?

BIRDIE: Well, yeah.

CHARLENE: I can't believe this.

SHELBY: Believe it.

CHARLENE: I got something here that might change your minds.

WILMA: Our minds are already made up.

CHARLENE: C'mere, Birdie . . . take a look at this.   *(BIRDIE walks warily over and peeks into the envelope.)*   You too, Tammy, Gay.

BIRDIE: Wow . . .

TAMMY: What is it?

CHARLENE: Money.

BIRDIE: It's all in twenties . . .

CHARLENE: Three hundred dollars.

GAY: Lemme see!

TAMMY: Where did you get it?

CHARLENE: From the promoter. It's our guarantee for the game tonight. He wanted to give it to Cassius, but I explained that I'm in charge now.

TAMMY: And he just gave it to ya?

CHARLENE: He didn't want to, but I did some pretty fast talkin'.
I told him I was running things and if he didn't give me the money,
we wouldn't play.

BUTCH: Can I see?

CHARLENE: Sure.

BUTCH: You mean this is what we make every night? It's so much!

CHARLENE: This is what Cassius made every night.

GAY: I never dreamed he made so much.

CHARLENE: Me neither.

TAMMY: Can we keep it?

CHARLENE: I'll keep it for us. I can keep the team going with this
money. This'll buy motel rooms and food and bus tickets to the next
game. Then there'll be more money—every night.

GAY: But doesn't Cassius' brother own the team . . . and the money?

CHARLENE: He owns the car and the equipment and the uniforms,
but he doesn't own us. I can cut him in for a couple of hundred until
I pay off the equipment and stuff—he's got no use for all that junk.
I got it all planned out.

SHELBY: And do your big plans include tellin' all of us what to do,
and how to play?

CHARLENE: Look, Shelby, I know what I'm doing.

SHELBY: That money belongs to all of us, Charlene. We're earning
it by playing. We're entitled to it.

CHARLENE: You'll get paid, same as always. And after I pay off
J.D., we'll all get a bigger share.

SHELBY: That's not what I mean. That money's not yours. It belongs
to all of us. We all get to decide what to do with it, and how we're
gonna play.

WILMA: That's right.

GAY: That does seem fair.

BIRDIE: Yeah, Charlene, we still want to play the new way.

TAMMY: Yeah.

SHELBY: If you don't want to go along with us, I think you oughta
hand it over.

CHARLENE: You wouldn't even *have* this money if it weren't for
me. I'm the one who got it! Don't you all see that? You need somebody
to run the team for you. You need me!

WILMA: We don't need you if you won't listen to us.

SHELBY: That's right. Now hand it over, Charlene.

CHARLENE: No! I'm not giving it to you.

SHELBY: C'mon, Charlene.

CHARLENE: NO.

SHELBY: All right. Give it to Birdie. Let her hold onto it, and then
after the game we'll all decide what to do with it. Go ahead, take it,
Birdie. Put it in your locker. (SHE *does*) You can be Treasurer.

GAY: Charlene, it's not personal.

TAMMY: Heck no. This is gonna work out great now. We got money, we got a great future with our new way of playing. We're gonna beat those men and everything's gonna turn out just perfect.

CHARLENE: Count me out.

TAMMY: Oh no! Don't say that!

BIRDIE: Charlene, don't . . .

BUTCH: Char, why are you so dead set against the idea? Don't you even think it's worth a try?

SHELBY: Leave her alone, Butch, if she doesn't want to play, I'm sure she has her reasons. Maybe she's afraid.

CHARLENE: Don't give me that.

SHELBY: Come off it, Charlene. It's no secret you've been slowin' down the last year or two. You're not as young as you used to be, and I think your knee is botherin' you more than you like to admit. You know it's liable to get rough out there playin' straight—goin' head to head with a bunch of men under the boards, fast breakin' up and down the court. You're afraid you can't keep up. Prove me wrong. C'mon, Charlene, give it a shot.

(CHARLENE has begun to pack her things.)

GAY: Char . . . you could still coach . . . We need a coach, don't we, girls? And you could play a little, if you wanted.

WILMA: How can she coach us if she doesn't believe in what we're doin?

TAMMY: She'll come around, won't you, Charlene? You got to. You can't quit now. We've got money now . . . We can go on and keep playing now. You're part of the team. Don't you want to go with us? It wouldn't be the same without you. We need you to be our coach.

WILMA: I don't think we should hold Charlene here against her will . . . If she wants to go, Tammy, I think we should let her.

(During the last speech, strains of the National Anthem are heard from the direction of the gym.)

GAY: Omigosh!

TAMMY: They're starting!

SHELBY: Quick! Get dressed!

BUTCH: Hurry!

BIRDIE: Where are the uniforms?

SHELBY: In the bag! On the table!

(THEY all begin lacing up their shoes, getting undressed, putting on knee pads, etc. TAMMY grabs the uniform bag and begins handing out the uniforms.)

TAMMY: Here's yours, Butch . . . Shelby . . . Here, Birdie,

number 16. Here's mine. Here you go Gay. Charlene, here's yours
. . . please put it on. Oh no! Wilma! Here's your shorts, but your
jersey's not in here. Where is it? Oh no! I can't find it!

WILMA: Tammy. Tammy! It's okay. I got it right here.   *(SHE digs
to the bottom of her locker and pulls it out.)*

TAMMY: Oh good. That scared me . . .

CHARLENE: I wonder what it was doin' in there . . .

WILMA: Oh you do, huh?

CHARLENE: I can guess . . .

WILMA: Oh you're just so damn smart, aren't you, Charlene? Okay,
yeah, I stole it. I snuck down to the laundry room and I swiped it
so I could send it to the Hall of Fame. So arrest me. Call the cops,
Charlene. I'm a thief. I stole my own jersey. And I snuck in here
like a thief and I hid it . . . from you. You know why? 'Cause I was
ashamed. You and Casssius made me ashamed for wantin' something
for myself. But not anymore, Charlene. I did it. And I'm glad I did
it. And I'm glad you found out. 'Cause I want you to get this loud
and clear—my jersey is gonna hang in the Hall of Fame. And you
know what? There's not a damn thing you can do about it.

   *(CHARLENE leans over and takes her athletic bag out of her
locker. She throws it to WILMA.)*

CHARLENE: Catch, Wilma.

WILMA: *(Catching it)*   You're going to have to do better than that,
Charlene.   *(SHE throws it back at CHARLENE, hard.)*

CHARLENE: *(Catching it, pausing for a second, SHE throws it
back to WILMA.)*   Open it.

WILMA: I don't have time for games.

CHARLENE: No games. Open it up.

WILMA: What for?

CHARLENE: I think you might be interested in what's inside.

WILMA: *(Opens it, pulls out a pair of old sneakers)*   You thought
I'd be interested in your smelly shoes?

CHARLENE: Look in the bottom—underneath everything.

   *(WILMA reaches to the bottom of the bag and pulls out CHAR-
LENE'S jersey. It is an old jersey, a different color and style
than the ones they wear now.)*

WILMA: I don't get it. How come you still got this old thing? We
haven't worn this uniform in years.

TAMMY: It's your jersey?

CHARLENE: It was.

WILMA: So?

CHARLENE: I've been carrying it around for a few years. Just in case.

WILMA: Just in case what?

CHARLENE: Wilma . . . I got my letter three years ago.

(There is a long silence as they all take this in.)

GAY: Char . . . why didn't you tell us?

CHARLENE: Cassius made me swear I wouldn't. He didn't want to cause "jealousy" on the team.

WILMA: You musta hated him. Didn't you hate him?

CHARLENE: A lot.

SHELBY: You hated him?

WILMA: Then why?! . . .

CHARLENE: Why what?

SHELBY: Well . . . why'd you act like you loved him?

CHARLENE: Is that what you thought? *(Pause)* I was twenty-nine-years-old when the Hall of Fame letter came. I needed surgery on my knee, and Wilma was about to take over my starting position. Cassius offered me the Assistant Coach job, and I jumped at it. He told me if I could prove myself, he'd eventually make me the Head Coach, and maybe co-owner when he retired. He said he'd "cut me in on a piece of the action." I knew it was either that or get retired. So I did what I was told. I planned on bein' the world's oldest Shootin' Star. What I didn't plan on was Cassius dying . . . just yet.

(THEY all fall silent. WILMA hands CHARLENE her jersey and goes and finishes dressing in silence. We can hear the sound of the crowd starting to cheer and stomp for the game to begin. Finally, WILMA goes to the locker where the envelope full of money has been placed. SHE takes it out, exchanges glances with the other girls, walks over to CHARLENE whose back is turned, and hands her the money bag.)

WILMA: You interested in beatin' the pants off a bunch of men tonight . . . Coach? *(No response. WILMA looks at SHELBY.)*

SHELBY: What's the startin' lineup, Coach?

CHARLENE: *(After a long pause)* Shelby?

SHELBY: *(Jumping up, grabbing a ball)* Yo!

CHARLENE: Butch?

BUTCH: *(Jumping up, grabbing a ball)* Oh, yeah!

CHARLENE: Gay. *(GAY silently jumps up and picks up her ball.)* Birdie.

BIRDIE: *(Jumping up, grabbing a ball)* Yes, ma'am.

CHARLENE: And Wilma. *(WILMA stands up.)* Tammy, you'll be sixth. *(TAMMY jumps up and grabs a ball.)* All right.

(*WILMA steps forward in front of the rest of the team where they have assembled in line.*)

WILMA: I have an announcement to make. It is with great pleasure that I announce to you this evening that our own Charlene Treadwell will be the first Shooting Star to have her jersey hang in the Basketball Hall of Fame . . .

(*THEY all erupt in a hearty scream—a kind of ritual acceptance of CHARLENE. There is general euphoria. THEY are really pumped-up to finally play the game. THEY look resplendent in their flashy uniforms. BUTCH opens the gym doors wide and puts down the doorstops. We can hear crowd noises coming from the direction of the gym. BUTCH steps out into the hall and gives the signal to the offstage M.C. that they are ready. SHE comes back to join the team. All are bouncing and spinning balls.*)

CHARLENE: All right. Real basketball. Huddle up!

(*As an offstage spotlight hits the hall outside the door, we hear the offstage announcer's voice booming through the P.A. system.*)

ANNOUNCER: Ladies and Gentlemen! The INDIANA SHOOTING STARS!!!

(*We hear the crowd cheering. One by one the players run out the door, dribbling their balls toward the gym. WILMA and CHARLENE are the last two to go, and they are momentarily left alone onstage. WILMA picks up a ball and passes it crisply to CHARLENE. Then SHE picks up the last ball, takes a deep breath and heads out of the door. CHARLENE follows her, and as the sound of the cheering crowd increases, the lights fade to black.*)

END OF PLAY

The members of "The Indiana Shooting Stars" pose with Cassius, their coach.

Photo Credit: Ted Trainor

Molly Newman author of *Shooting Stars*

Molly began her playwriting career as co-author of *Quilters*, for which she was nominated for a Tony Award, and a Helen Hayes Award. Her plays have been produced on the mainstages of several regional theatres including The Mark Taper Forum, Actor's Theatre of Louisville, Houston's Alley Theatre, The Kennedy Center, The Denver Center Theatre Company, and the Pittsburgh Public Theatre. She has been awarded two major playwriting grants by the Colorado Council on the Arts and Humanities, and is a founding member, in her fifth year, of the Denver Center Theatre Company's Playwrights Unit. She and her husband Thomas A. Jones reside in Denver.

Koozy's Piece
Frank X. Hogan

Koozy's Piece was first performed as a staged reading in *US West's PrimaFacie III*—A Presentation of New American Plays, at the Denver Center Theatre Company in March of 1987.

KOOZY'S PIECE
by Frank X. Hogan

Directed by Donovan Marley

THE CAST—PRIMAFACIE III

Koozy .... Melinda Deane
Grammie .... Leticia Jaramillo
Tom .... Jim Baker
Krausbe .... Robert Eustace
Case .... James Newcomb
Gloria .... Kay Doubleday

The Denver Center Theatre Company, Donovan Marley, Artistic Director, presented the World Premiere of *Koozy's Piece* in the Space Theatre, as part of the DCTC's 1987-88 season, with the following artists:

Directed by Randal Myler
Scenic Design by Ralph Funicello
Costume Design by Janet S. Morris
Lighting Design by Charles MacLeod
Sound Design by Donald P. Johnson and Steve Stevens
Stage Manager, Christopher C. Ewing

THE CAST

Koozy, a teenager .... Melinda Deane
Grammie, Koozy's grandmother .... Ann Guilbert
Tom, Koozy's father .... Jim Baker
Krausbe, crotchety neighbor .... Guy Raymond
Case, performance artist .... James Newcomb
Gloria, offstage voice .... Johanna Morrison

TIME: Early June

PLACE: A neighborhood in Northwest Denver, near Elitch's World Famous Amusement Park.

Koozy's Piece is for Erin Casey Hogan and is dedicated to Patricia Hogan.

Koozy's Piece

SCENE ONE

(Morning. Early June. Northwest Denver. KOOZY GOR-MAN'S backyard. A brick garage on the edge of the alley. Three-foot wooden/slatted fence separates KOOZY'S yard from neighbor KRAUSBE'S yard. In KOOZY'S yard are a metal table and chairs, sandbox and a tetherball pole. A raked driveway leads into the hilly alley. In darkness a police-band radio squawks in the distance. A dog barks. From Elitch's World Famous Amusement Park a few blocks away comes a rush of roller-coaster screams and the clatter of wheels upon the tracks. Lights fade up. KOOZY sits on a plastic lawnchair, mobile phone in hand. KOOZY'S fifteen, wears black shorts, hightop sneakers—one lemon, the other strawberry—and a white sweatshirt with YES! across the front.)

KOOZY: I know. It is too-cool. I know. I know. I am too-happy. *(Pause)* If he doesn't let me? Walk over to Elitch's. Ride Mister Twister. Stand up at the top of the first hill and snap my neck off.

(Pause) I would too die if I did that. Monica, PEOPLE magazine rated Mister Twister number-one-most-dangerous rollercoaster in the world for like the last five years. Hold on. *(Lights a cigarette)* Uh-huh . . . Uh-huh . . . My poem? I think it's probably more of a lyric. Okay. *(Pause)* "Pain. Ice cubes up my nose, freezing my frontal lobes. Kingsford charcoal mesquite-flavored coals burning white hot holes through my eye sockets. Giant tweezers ripping out the hairs that have so disgustingly begun to grow under The Girl's armpits and in other unmentionable places." *(Pause)* No there's more. *(Pause)* I know it's depressing. I know it's gross. Well, the title is "Pain," remember. Okay . . .

(GRAMMIE enters through back screen door with brown grocery bag, sets it down on the lawn table. She's sixties, wiry, elfin but very fiesty, wears a flaming red wig, baggy slacks that are nearly falling off.)

GRAMMIE: Don't get off.

KOOZY: "Tomato stake pierces my left eardrum and emerges out my right ear . . . with a midget Wall-Mart cashier dangling from stake's end . . . wearing black-Converse hightops, breathing hot dog breath, whispering, Let's have SEX! Let's have dirty SEX. Let's have dirty-gross-superkinky SEX seventeen times in an hour and twenty-six minutes . . ."
(Pause)

GRAMMIE: *(Takes cereal out of bag)* Bran Chex, Sweetie.

KOOZY: *(To Monica)* Really?

GRAMMIE: Fiber.

KOOZY: You do? Oh, Monica, thank you so much. It IS a lyric isn't it? God, I know. I'll DIE if he doesn't let me be one. Okay bye.
(KOOZY hangs up.)

GRAMMIE: You didn't have to do that.

KOOZY: Is Daddy here?

GRAMMIE: He dropped me off and headed for the golf course to squeeze in nine holes before he has to run me to the dentist.

KOOZY: How was the doctor?

GRAMMIE: Good. *(Pulls a tray of flowers from the bag)*

KOOZY: Grammie, what'd he say about how you look so thin?

GRAMMIE: Just that I have that model-ly look.

KOOZY: What'd they do to your hand?

GRAMMIE: Just took a little blood.

KOOZY: From the back of your hand?

GRAMMIE: When you get old and decrepit, Sweetie, they take it wherever they can get it. And speaking of getting any . . . sunburn. I got you some sunscreen . . .

KOOZY: Bain de Soleil. I love it.

GRAMMIE: And I got you something frivolous too. Close your eyes. *(KOOZY does)* Hands out. *(GRAMMIE places a magazine in her hands.)* Open 'em.

KOOZY: "Tiger Beat." Ohhhh, awwwww, thanks so much, Grammie.

GRAMMIE: You wanted "Playgirl."

KOOZY: No, this is really sweet.

GRAMMIE: Your father'd crucify me.

KOOZY: No, I love this. *(Reads)* "What To Do When: You're Crazier Than Boy Crazy!" This is really . . . really . . . really.

GRAMMIE: And these "Letters To Carol" look good. *(Reads)* "Dear Carol, I am fourteen years old and pregnant. I don't know whether I should tell my boyfriend because he might not make love to me anymore."

KOOZY: Grammie!

GRAMMIE: What'd I say?

KOOZY: Nothing. It's just that Daddy is like, besides everything else, he's gone totally berserk about me and sex.

GRAMMIE: That's probably my fault.

KOOZY: Noooo.

GRAMMIE: I raised him on the prudish side, Sweetie.

KOOZY: He's like toasting my brain and crunching it into little crumbs trying to leave this Hansel and Gretel trail from him to me. I swear he's trying to like crawl right inside my brain so he can manipulate everything I do.

GRAMMIE: Well. Maybe this "Cosmo" will perk you up. *(Gives her the "Cosmo")*

KOOZY: Grammie, you are so, so sweet. *(Hugs her)*

GRAMMIE: I know. I'm a dreamboat.

KOOZY: You really are. *(Plays a riff on her electric keyboard, sings:)* Oh-Grammie, Grammie, she's a lifesaver, she's a lifesaver, comes in all flavors, comes in all flavors . . . *(Bangs off-key notes)*

GRAMMIE: Sweetie, what?

KOOZY: Nothing. I'm okay. I'm okay. Really.

GRAMMIE: Well, if you change your mind and decide . . .

KOOZY: Grammie, I'm so miserable.

GRAMMIE: Oh, Sweetie . . . .

KOOZY: But I'm so happy.

GRAMMIE: I know how confusing that can be.

KOOZY: Happier than I've ever-ever been in my entire life.

GRAMMIE: That's wonderful, Sweetie.

KOOZY: Grammie, will you talk to him for me?

GRAMMIE: You'll have to tell me what you . . . .

KOOZY: I want to be a writer/performer, right?

GRAMMIE: Well . . .

KOOZY: Grammie, guess what?
GRAMMIE: All right. Uhhh . . .
KOOZY: I'm a Fresh Virgin!
GRAMMIE: Congratulations. Your father will be so relieved.

(Opens garage door and gets a pair of coveralls, begins putting them over her clothes)

KOOZY: And we're doing a gig on Friday when I'm supposed to be caddying.
GRAMMIE: Fresh Virgins is what?
KOOZY: A performance ensemble.
GRAMMIE: Performance ensemble? That sounds very . . . what's the word?
KOOZY: Inside the moment.
GRAMMIE: Very "inside the moment."
KOOZY: Everything's co-written, co-created, co-performed.
GRAMMIE: That's very democratic.
KOOZY: Grammie, it is.
GRAMMIE: Sounds very exciting. Where on Friday?
KOOZY: You'll come?
GRAMMIE: Sweetie, I wouldn't miss it.
KOOZY: Oh Grammie, thank you so much. As soon as I know where we're playing I'll let you know.
GRAMMIE: You don't know where yet?
KOOZY: Probably a mall, probably Aurora Mall. I don't know for sure yet because that's part of Fresh Virgins' credo—that we don't announce where or what time we're performing.
GRAMMIE: Because that would sort of detract from the spontaneity?
KOOZY: Grammie, yes!
GRAMMIE: And if people knew you were going to play they'd have to make a choice to see you or not.
KOOZY: Grammie, yes! We're eliminating choices.
GRAMMIE: Because life offers too many choices as it is?
KOOZY: Grammie, YOU should be a Fresh Virgin.
GRAMMIE: My day's come and gone, Sweetie.
    (Starts to wheel the tetherball pole away from the garden area)
KOOZY: No, really. I could talk to Case about it.
    (Helps Grammie with tetherball pole)
GRAMMIE: I'd really rather be a spectator, Sweetie.
KOOZY: Case is Head Virgin.
GRAMMIE: Case?
KOOZY: Yeah.

GRAMMIE: Is "Case" a family name?

KOOZY: No. Stage. Crank Case. And guess what he's studying at Career Education?

GRAMMIE: Something with automobiles?

KOOZY: Are you psychic or what? He's gonna be a Candy Striper.

GRAMMIE: Aren't they in the hospitals, Sweetie?

KOOZY: Candy apple paint. Car graphics. Scallops and flames and striping . . .

GRAMMIE: Does he do nails?

KOOZY: Fingernails?

GRAMMIE: You think he could do some little yellow happy faces on maybe a sky-blue background?

KOOZY: I could ask.

GRAMMIE: I've always wanted to be more daring with my nails.

KOOZY: So could you talk to Daddy? Please.

GRAMMIE: What would I say?

KOOZY: That I can't caddy. That I have to be on call for rehearsal any time of day. That I'm an adult.

GRAMMIE: All right, but since he knows as well as me you're only fifteen . . .

KOOZY: And five months . . .

GRAMMIE: Fifteen and five months.

KOOZY: Emotionally I'm an adult.

GRAMMIE: Emotionally I'm eleven.

KOOZY: Grammie, he'll listen if you tell him I should be a Fresh Virgin.

GRAMMIE: He can get his back up, Sweetie.

KOOZY: I know.

GRAMMIE: But he can be a dreamboat too. Like holding my hand in the doctor's office.

KOOZY: He's gonna say "no" I know it and I'll die.

GRAMMIE: Sweetie, since you're an adult emotionally, maybe it'd be better if you talk to him yourself.

KOOZY: No! Grammie, he gets so mad at me for the slightest thing.

GRAMMIE: That's because of me.

KOOZY: It isn't.

GRAMMIE: I'm being a burden.

(Tries out the tetherball, playing herself right hand against left hand)

KOOZY: You come every summer. He loves it.

GRAMMIE: I love it. I don't know about him.

KOOZY: He said I didn't have to go to Grandmother Craig's with Mom this summer if I make my own money caddying. But I couldn't

GRAMMIE (Ann Guilbert) and KOOZY (Melinda Deane) make room for a garden in the Gorman back yard.

know I'd get in Fresh Virgins could I? I couldn't know that on the second day of summer I'd get the absolute greatest career opportunity ever, could I?

GRAMMIE: Does Fresh Virgins pay?

KOOZY: Grammie, if art really-and-truly belongs to the people how can we charge for our gigs?

GRAMMIE: Good point, Sweetie.

KOOZY: Grammie, Fresh Virgins is the most important thing that's ever, EVER happened to me.

GRAMMIE: I wish I could help you, Sweetie. Financially.

KOOZY: Did you have to put yourself through college?

GRAMMIE: I found a way around that.

KOOZY: How?

GRAMMIE: I didn't go.
     (Starts working in the garden)

KOOZY: God, why didn't I think of that?

GRAMMIE: Koozy Marie Gorman, you'll get me in hot water up to my ears if you . . .

KOOZY: Grammie, it's just, I hate money when I don't have any.

(KRAUSBE calls from offstage. He's eighty, has a gravel voice, one leg that's plastic, gets around on crutches. He wears a greasy, grey short-brimmed welder's cap, red suspenders, grey workpants and workshirt. A police band radio is strapped to one crutch.)

KRAUSBE: *(Offstage)* HayTiger!

GRAMMIE: Sweety, Mister Krausbe's . . .

KRAUSBE: *(Offstage)* HayTiger!

GRAMMIE: *(Exchanges a look with Koozy)* Sweety, he couldn't mean me.

KOOZY: Grammie, sometimes he gives up if you don't pay any . . . Ask me about Case.

GRAMMIE: All right. How's Case, Sweetie?

KOOZY: I think . . . I'm not sure . . . It's possible, I'm falling in like . . . love with him.

GRAMMIE: That's exciting.

KOOZY: Not man-woman love though.

GRAMMIE: No?

KOOZY: Artistic love.

GRAMMIE: Well!

KOOZY: Not in love with his art, but in love one artist to another.

GRAMMIE: Artistic love.

KOOZY: Yes! And it's too-Herculean.

GRAMMIE: Uhhh-huh.

KOOZY: Because it's so BONDED.

KRAUSBE: *(Offstage)* HayTiger!

GRAMMIE: Sweetie, Mister Krausbe's not . . .

KOOZY: Grammie, what would you think about "Eight Easy Dinners From Cans?"

GRAMMIE: Well. That's a tough question.

KOOZY: As a piece. A Fresh Virgins' piece.

GRAMMIE: Well.

KRAUSBE: *(Enters)* HayTiger!

GRAMMIE: Hello, Mister Krausbe!

KRAUSBE: Gotta halfa minute, Missus?

KOOZY: Grammie, he'll talk FOREVER.

KRAUSBE: Burglary over on Tennyson, Missus.

GRAMMIE: Isn't Tennyson just two blocks . . .

KRAUSBE: Just come over the radio.

GRAMMIE: You've got yourself a police band radio.

KRAUSBE: Yes-sir. Radio Shack Realistic model.

GRAMMIE: Isn't that snazzy.

KRAUSBE: This Tennyson burglary just half-a-minute-or-so ago? Burglarized a fella's entire duck decoy collection.

GRAMMIE: Duck decoys are valuable, aren't they?

KRAUSBE: Yes-sir. Know how to call a duck, Missus?
GRAMMIE: Is it "Hey, duck?"
KRAUSBE: No-sir. But whatever you do? Don't blow.
GRAMMIE: No?
KRAUSBE: Grunt. Grunt and say the word.
GRAMMIE: The "quack" word?
KRAUSBE: No-sir. HayTiger, you know it?
KOOZY: *(Ignoring him, SHE plays a few notes on her keyboard.)*
KRAUSBE: Missus, three words call duck. *(Pause)* First one's
"Wick." *(Pause)* Second's "Tick-it."
GRAMMIE: Uh-huh . . .
KRAUSBE: And "Kak."
GRAMMIE: Not quack?
KRAUSBE: No-sir. Now them burglars? Could be cuttin' through
yards, headin' our way right this minute.
GRAMMIE: With their duck decoys?
KRAUSBE: Keep a eye peeled.
GRAMMIE: We most certainly will.
KRAUSBE: 'Course they could be escapin' inna motor cart.
GRAMMIE: You think?
KRAUSBE: Little wood cart. Lawn mower motor. Go like a bat
outta hell up 'n' down these alleys.
GRAMMIE: We'll certainly keep on the lookout.
KRAUSBE: We use-tuh race chugs.
GRAMMIE: Go carts?
KRAUSBE: Gravity cars.
     (Hands her a clipping)
GRAMMIE: The Soap Box Derby!
KRAUSBE: These days ya can buy a damn pre-fabberkated kit.
GRAMMIE: How interesting.
KRAUSBE: We use-tuh build our chugs outta linoleum. Yessir. Say,
you know my claim-tuh-fame, don't ya?
GRAMMIE: I don't think I do.
KRAUSBE: Nineteen forty-nine Great American Gravity Grand
Prix? *(Pause, wiggles his eyebrows)* I'm the guy what built the
Soap Box car that Hopalong Cassidy raced, and won, in the 1949
Great American Gravity Grand Prix Celebrity Race.
GRAMMIE: Congratulations.
KRAUSBE: Ya knew Hopalong whupped Jimmy Stewart's butt in
that race, didn't ya?
GRAMMIE: Well . . .
KRAUSBE: Yes-sir. *(Pause)* Where's Tom?
GRAMMIE: Squeezing in a few holes of golf.
KRAUSBE: Never miss his radio show.
GRAMMIE: Good for you.

GRAMMIE (Ann Guilbert) learns about gravity carts from next-door-neighbor KRAUSBE (Guy Raymond).

KRAUSBE: "Be a sport, listen to Tom Gorman's Sportsgab." *(Engages his crutches, stops)* Ask Tom, "when's he gonna gimme them tools a his?" *(Laughs)* Cuck-cuck-cuck . . .
        (Exits)
KOOZY: Grammie, how can you be so nice?
GRAMMIE: Wasn't that interesting about the duck calls?
KOOZY: No.
GRAMMIE: Tommy used to say something like "wick" whenever he wanted to tune me out.
KOOZY: He'd say "wick?"
GRAMMIE: He'd say . . . "Puttt."
KOOZY: Weird.
GRAMMIE: "Putt . . . Putt . . ." For hours . . . Well, Sweetie, would you like a lottery ticket?
KOOZY: Unscratched? *(Takes the ticket)* Grammie!! How can you not scratch immediately-if-not-sooner when you buy it?
GRAMMIE: You scratch them in the store?
KOOZY: Yesss!
GRAMMIE: Sweetie, no. No, no, no . . . Find the right aura, the right planetary alignment, the right feeling . . .

KOOZY: I always scratch the prize first.
GRAMIE: Me too!
      (THEY scratch.)
KOOZY: Hundred dollars!
GRAMMIE: Two dollars.
KOOZY: *(Scratches quickly, loses)*   Dog it, dog it, dog it . . .
GRAMIE: Sweetie, not so fast.
KOOZY: I can't help myself.
GRAMMIE: More you milk it . . . Double your pleasure . . .
KOOZY: I love baseball.
GRAMMIE: This game's baseball?
KOOZY: Yes . . . Grammie, you only need one run . . .
KOOZY & GRAMMIE: Winner!!!   *(Singing)*   Take me out to the ballgame . . . I don't care if we ever come back . . . For it's root, toot, toot for Koozy . . . Grammie . . . Gorman!
GRAMMIE: I'll get us two more tickets while you're out caddying.
KOOZY: Ohhh God! Grammie, will you please talk to him? Make him understand how important Fresh Virgins is?
GRAMMIE: I'll try, Sweetie.
KOOZY: Grammie, you are so wonderful.
GRAMMIE: I know. I'm a peach. Go caddy.
KOOZY: First, could you tell me what you think of "Eight Easy Dinners From Cans?"
GRAMMIE: All right.
KOOZY: Okay. Okay. So far? Right? This's just a two-character piece. You be the little boy who volunteers from the audience.
GRAMMIE: All righty.
KOOZY: So anyway after we wrap the little boy's head in Saran Wrap and do little punch-holes so we can stick two straws up his nostrils to breath, he says . . .
GRAMMIE: . . . "What's for dinner?"
KOOZY: Yesss! And I say . . .   *(Performing, robot-voice)*   "Eight Easy Dinners From Cans. Dinner Number One, Spam Hawaiian. First, remove the tops from a can of Spam and a can of Chopped Dole Pineapples. Mix well and serve. Dinner Number Two . . ."
GRAMMIE: Sweetie . . . Sweetie, something just popped into my head.
KOOZY: Okay.
GRAMMIE: Keep going and see how you like this.
KOOZY: Okay. *(Pause)* "Dinner Number Two. A Sixpack of The Famous Budweiser King of Beers."
GRAMMIE: *(Moving like a robot)*   "Wwwwwick!"
KOOZY: "Pop tops and serve."
GRAMMIE: "Tick-it!"
KOOZY: "Easy Dinner From Cans Number Three . . ."

GRAMMIE: "Kkkkkkak!"
KOOZY: "Solid white albacore Bumble Bee Tuna on a serrated sal-
tine . . ."
GRAMMIE: "Putt . . ."
KOOZY: "First, remove the top . . ."
GRAMMIE: "Wwwwwwwwick!"

(Lights bump to black. In the dark we hear dogs barking and howling, then the rollercoaster clacks downhill carrying scream- ing passengers.)

SCENE TWO

(Early that afternoon. TOM *enters the back yard and stomps with his golf clubs to the workbench alongside* KRAUSBE'S *fence. He dumps the clubs and heads into the garage. He emerges with a hacksaw.)*

GRAMMIE: *(Calling from house)* Can I fix you a sandwich?
  (Pause)
Tuna and crackers maybe?

  (Pause. TOM *begins tightening a golf club into a vise as* GRAM-MIE *enters.)*

How about a nice heaping portion of "Spam Hawaiian?" Special bonus, I'll even heat it.
  (TOM begins sawing the club into pieces with the hacksaw.)
How're you going to talk for four hours on radio on an empty stomach?

  (Enters house. TOM *dumps the pieces of the putter into the trash barrel.* GRAMMIE *returns with a six pack of Milwaukee's Best.)*

How about "Eight Easy Dinners From Cans Number Two?"
TOM: *(Carries the rest of his golfclubs toward the alley and dumps them into the trash bin, and returns)* So.
GRAMIE: Feel better?
TOM: *(Happily)* Much.
GRAMMIE: Sure I can't fix you something?
TOM: That's exactly the way I should've gone out of football, you know that.

GRAMMIE: With a hacksaw.

TOM: Flat out quitting.

GRAMMIE: Before you hit the goalposts five times in a row.

TOM: Mom, every goddamn one of those kicks could've bounced through.

GRAMMIE: No sense replaying it now.

TOM: *(Laughs)* Yesterday some guy calls the show and says, "I wanna talk to Mister Wide Right." It's been ten years and people still won't let me forget. *(Pause)* I'm still seventh on the all-time scoring list you know.

GRAMMIE: I thought you were fourth.

TOM: I was. But they play a sixteen-game schedule nowadays. Defenses are softer nowadays.

GRAMMIE: Tommy, I think you should talk to Koozy.

TOM: How come I never get a bounce?

GRAMMIE: Use a little psychology on her.

TOM: How come everything's psychology all of a sudden? Got a meeting with the station manager today. Now *he* wants to talk psychology.

GRAMMIE: Do you want to lose her, Tommy?

TOM: She's not going anywhere.

GRAMMIE: Like your father lost you?

TOM: He didn't lose me. He had a heart attack.

GRAMMIE: Before he could get you back.

TOM: He died, Mom. He lost everybody.

GRAMMIE: Don't you see the same cycle coming, Tommy?

TOM: No. Maybe you could use a little psychology on her.

GRAMMIE: How so?

TOM: Just . . . maybe . . . impress upon her . . . if you feel like it . . . the importance of caddying . . . of becoming responsible financially . . .

GRAMMIE: How about that she might be hurting your feelings?

TOM: Nah. You mean because she doesn't take much interest in sports? 'Course, talking on the phone to her friends is kind of a sport if you look at it a certain way . . . so . . .

GRAMMIE: Or that's she's tuned you out?

TOM: You know . . . I am . . . the most important person in her life. And does she care? Does she listen?

GRAMMIE: Do something together.

TOM: She doesn't wanta do things together anymore. Holy smokes, when she was ten, when she was playing soccer on the Rabbits? Remember? We were tight. If she'd stayed with soccer, who knows, maybe, possibly, she'd've become the first female placekicker in the National Football League. *(Pause)* When she took gymnastics from that Mrs. Hitler, we were tight.

GRAMMIE: Well, she's not ten anymore.

TOM: She is strange.

GRAMMIE: She is fifteen.

TOM: She doesn't respond.

GRAMMIE: There's a lot of you in her.

TOM: Me?

GRAMMIE: You should trust that.

TOM: Me? In her?

GRAMMIE: Caddying for instance.

TOM: Right. Caddying was good for me.

GRAMMIE: You hated it.

TOM: I loved caddying.

GRAMMIE: Your father'd drag you out of the house kicking and screaming, downshift our old Buick Skylark and push you out the door at the Country Club.

TOM: Mom, I know what she needs. She's the ace pitcher. Tempermental. Unpredictable. Raw. Very raw. But great potential. I'm her manager. I know how to pace her. Discipline her . . . Keep her focused . . . Mom, what're you doing? Mom, give me that . . .

(Tries to take the shovel away from GRAMMIE)

GRAMMIE: Tommy, let go.

TOM: Mom, what the hell're you doing wearing yourself out like this?

GRAMMIE: You want to tell me why in the name of Good-God you didn't turn my garden over this year?

TOM: Holy Smokes . . .

GRAMMIE: You thought I'd lost interest in growing things?

TOM: Mom, my ratings . . .

GRAMMIE: You thought I'd be in the ground before now?

TOM: . . . and Koozy . . . and my back's been acting up . . .

GRAMMIE: Is this your way of telling me I should give up?

TOM: Mom, give me the goddamn shovel. *(Takes it)*

(KRAUSBE enters unseen by them and takes a seat in his chair next to the fence in order to eavesdrop.)

GRAMMIE: I'm sorry if I'm a burden, Tommy.

TOM: Will you please let me do this?

GRAMMIE: I've got burial insurance.

TOM: Mom, you lost a few pounds. You don't need to be talking about funerals.

GRAMMIE: Yes I do.

TOM: You're doing great. Your blood's good. The chemo's working.

GRAMMIE: You know what bothers me about him? Doctor Frozen-Grin *(Pause)* He won't give me a time frame.

TOM: Because you're gonna live a long-long time. Look, your weight was down, we'll go to the dentist, you won't have any cavities, you'll

be hitting five hundred today. Ted Williams never hit five hundred.
Pete Rose. Five hundred's fantastic in anybody's league. *(Pause)*
Let me fix you a milkshake.
GRAMMIE: I want to talk about arrangements.
TOM: Put an egg in it? Hah? Sprinkle in a little wheat germ? Little
Emmett's Irish for flavor? Hah?
GRAMMIE: Tommy, I want everything taken care of, including my
obituary . . .
TOM: Geezus Friggin . . .
GRAMMIE: Which says my family was my greatest accomplishment.
And which I'd like you to, when the time comes, hand deliver to the
Rocky Mountain News and the *Denver Post* and make sure it gets
printed without some busybody inserting my age.
        (KRAUSBE'S *silently peering through the fence at them.)*
The mortuary I'll do today.
TOM: Mom, the sun's shining, birds're chirping, why today?
GRAMMIE: I want it done today.

        *(Trying to spade the garden, she can't break through the hard
        earth.)*

TOM: Mom, this . . . tumor's just a challenge. Together . . . we can
beat it. Just . . .
GRAMMIE: You don't think you should tell Koozy?
TOM: Why? You're in good shape.
GRAMMIE: Except for my hair falling out and my skin sagging right
off my face.
TOM: You look great. Look at Krausbe over there giving you the
oogle-eye. *(Pause)*   She's a kid. Why tell her when you're in such
good shape? When you're gonna beat it? What good's it gonna do
besides worry her?
GRAMMIE: I don't want to worry her.
TOM: Me neither.
GRAMMIE: Still, you should talk to her.
TOM: I talk. I talk till I'm blue.
        (Goes into the garage)
GRAMMIE: Maybe you should listen.
TOM: Where's the axe?
GRAMMIE: Would you try listening to her?
TOM: *(Emerges and moves toward the garden)*   Back up . . . Back
up . . . *(Raises the axe over his head and buries it in the ground
so deeply the head sticks)*   Shit!
GRAMMIE: That figures.
TOM: *(Trying to pull the axe free)*   I don't have time for this.
GRAMMIE: Fine. I'll cancel the dentist . . .

TOM: *(Overlapping)* Come on, you son-of-a-bitch!
GRAMMIE: . . . and do the garden and everything else myself.
TOM: *(Pulls it free)* Don't cancel. I got it. I got it.
GRAMMIE: *(Overlapping)* This is Mary Margaret Gorman and my son and I are having problems turning over the earth . . . so I will not make my appointment with Doctor Howard today. Thank you.
TOM: Look . . . Mom . . . I'm not wishing you gone . . . It's just . . . so much just doesn't get done anymore. All kinds of little things. And big things. Your garden . . .
GRAMMIE: I will do it myself. *(Now* SHE *buries the axe.)* Shit! *(Pause)* What about one of those jackhammers?
TOM: To turn over the garden?
GRAMMIE: Why the hell not?

(Lights bump to black. In the dark we hear KOOZY *warming up her keyboard.* SHE *tries a beat, then a few seconds of an instrumental, up-tempo version of "Take Me Out To The Ball Game."* SHE *chants the words along to the beat, but doesn't like the sound of it. Then* SHE *quickly segues into a new beat, and finds the right sound for "Hey Batter." We hear* KOOZY *say, "Yeah. Yeah!" Lights begin fading up.)*

SCENE THREE

(Late that night. KOOZY *enters from the back door with her keyboard and a tape recorder.* CASE *is asleep in a lawn chair atop the garage with Walkman radio headphones covering his ears.* KOOZY *sets up her tape recorder and keyboard atop the work table next to the fence in front of the garage.)*

KOOZY: *(Loud whisper)* Case . . . If you're asleep that's all right . . . I've figured it out . . . I'll write my Dad a piece . . . A sports piece . . . Then he'll understand . . . He'll tell me I was BORN to be a Fresh Virgin. And when we're famous, when Fresh Virgins is guest-hosting "Saturday Night Live," we'll dedicate the piece to my Dad . . . Would that be too-cool?

*(*KOOZY *goes into the garage and gets an infant crank-up swing, sets it up, sings and plays keyboard into a tape recorder.)*

Hey batter
Hey-hey batter

Hey batta-batta-batta
Heyyyyyyyy-yuh,
Hey,
Heyyyyyy-yuh . . .
     (SHE *sets the baby swing in motion, stands stock still, chants.*)
Go to first base.
Go to first base.
Hey badder, hey baddder, hey badder, hey!
Steal second base,
steal second base,
Hey! *(Pause)*
Hey-hey! *(Pause)*
Badder, badder, badder, badder, badder, badder, badder!
Third base!
Third base!
Home base!
Home base!
     (Building to a climax)
Hey,
hey,
hey,
hey,
hey,
hey,
hey,
SWING!!!

KRAUSBE: *(At the fence, hair mussed, wearing his night shirt)*
     HayTiger . . . That you?

KOOZY: *(Shuts off the tape and keyboard and stops the swing)*
     G'night, Mister Krausbe.

KRAUSBE: Just checkin . . .
     (Exits)

KOOZY: *(Plays and sings into tape recorder)* Steeeeeeee-rike
     one two three four,
     give us mo', give us mo'.
     Five six seven eight, who do we appreciate???
     Appreciate,
     appreciate,
     Who-oooh?
     Who-hoo-ooh! *(Pause)* Who-hoo-ooh!
     Who-hoo-ooh! *(Pause)* Who-hoo-ooh!

TOM: *(Enters)* Kooz.

KOOZY: Daddy! *(Shuts off her equipment)*

TOM: How 'bout a hug?

KOOZY: Uhhhhhh . . .

TOM: I NEED one.

KOOZY: Do I hafta?

TOM: 'Course you don't hafta.

KOOZY: Thanks, Daddy.

TOM: Brought you a present.

KOOZY: MADE you a present.

TOM: Nice.

KOOZY: It's not quite ready.

TOM: How 'bout a hug then instead?

KOOZY: Dadddyyyyy.

TOM: Okay. Okay. Want your present?

KOOZY: My birthday's in February.

TOM: *(Goes inside the back door)* This is just one of those Spur Of The Moments . . . Figured we oughtta do more . . . *(Returns with two cardboard boxes)* . . . father-daughter things . . . for that special rapport . . . sometimes happens between . . . you know . . . get back into some kind of . . . Anyway, anyway . . . Station's doing this promotion for National Artyfacts Week . . . Got a heckuva deal . . . Free . . . So . . . Close your eyes . . .

KOOZY: Daddy . . .

TOM: Come on, Kooz, you're gonna go crazy over this. Close 'em. Tight. No peeking. Hold out your hands. *(Puts one box in her hands)* Open 'em.

KOOZY: What is it?

TOM: What's it say?

KOOZY: White's Two Thousand.

TOM: Know what a White's Two Thousand is? White's??? Nothing but THE BEST METAL DETECTOR ON THE MARKET! Got one for you, one for me.

KOOZY: Why?

TOM: Why? Why??? Because you, and me, are gonna go . . . *(Makes a drumroll sound)* Treasure hunting! Evenings. Weekends. This is going to be our summer of DISCOVERY!

KOOZY: Daddy, no.

TOM: Metal detecting! THE family sport of the Nineties. Here, try on your headphones.

KOOZY: Daddy, no.

TOM: Kooz, this thing even tells you when it's a pop top or a nail so you don't go probing for nothing. Look. "Silver coin. Gold." Turn it on.

KOOZY: Daddy, no.

TOM: Who knows what's buried in our own back yard? *(Puts on the headphones, turns on the machine)* Who knows what long-forgotten treasure is lurking beneath the surface of our own back yard, eh buccaneer, just waiting for you and me to discover.

(TOM sweeps the detector back and forth in the sandbox. KOOZY watches.)

TOM: Hah! Lead! *(Kneels, digs)* Hang on! Hang on! Could just be an old pipe but you never . . . *(Pulls out a dirt encrusted piece)* A unicorn! Your unicorn! I gave you this on must've been your third, fourth birthday. I found your unicorn! Is this gonna be fantastic or what? You try.

KOOZY: Daddy, no.

TOM: Okay. Okay.

KOOZY: Daddy, are you mad? Are you mad at me?

TOM: No.

KOOZY: I don't want you to be mad at me.

TOM: It's late. We'll treasure hunt tomorrow. I'll be home early tomorrow. *(Sets down the machine)* How was your day?

KOOZY: Good.

TOM: My day was good too.
     (Sits at the table)

KOOZY: Good. *(Pause)* Daddy, did Grammie talk to you?

TOM: Minor setback at the station.

KOOZY: She said she was gonna.

TOM: Cut my show from four hours to two.

KOOZY: Ohhh . . .

TOM: Expanded "Love and Learn With Gloria Guardhausen" into my time slot.

KOOZY: I like her show.

TOM: Phoney as hell.

KOOZY: She is?

TOM: As a three-dollar bill.

KOOZY: She sounds incredibly caring.

TOM: Manipulative. Ultra-ambitious. Wears two tons of makeup. Just comes off sincere on radio.

KOOZY: Did Grammie tell you about . . .

TOM: *(Cuts her off)* You caddied today?

KOOZY: Will you please listen to me?

TOM: I always listen.

KOOZY: You never-ever do.

TOM: That's not true . . .

KOOZY: You just TELL ME what to do.

TOM: . . . not true at all.

KOOZY: When?

TOM: You're here instead of spending the summer with Mom and your Sisters in Grand Junction aren't you? Aren't you? Did I listen about that?

KOOZY: Yes, but . . .

TOM: So did you caddy or not?

KOOZY: I tried.

TOM: We made a deal.

KOOZY: I know.

TOM: "I'm mature."

KOOZY: I am.

TOM: "I'm the oldest. Let me stay home with you this summer instead of going to Grandma Craig's with Mom and The Girls, and I'll be responsible."

KOOZY: I will.

TOM: "Make money. Caddy . . .

KOOZY: *(Overlapping)* Daddy . . .

TOM: . . . My own money for clothes and albums . . .

KOOZY: Daddy . . .

TOM: . . . and college."

KOOZY: Daddy! *(Pause)*   There's two reasons. Okay? Why I can't caddy.

TOM: *(Game show host style)*   And the first reason is?

KOOZY: Caddying? Right? It's disgusting.

TOM: Caddying is an invaluable life experience.

KOOZY: Daddy, today. Right? I'm there. Right?

TOM: Right.

KOOZY: Denver Country Club.

TOM: Right.

KOOZY: Sitting in the caddyshack with like thirty-seven boys with buzz-top haircuts who think they're cooler than Tom Cruise or Emelio Estevez or Sean Penn. Right?

TOM: Thirty-seven boys and???

KOOZY: And Jeannette Hartshaw.

TOM: So it's not like you're the only girl.

KOOZY: Jeannette Hartshaw shaves. Her face. She wears ankle weights.

TOM: To increase her vertical leap.

KOOZY: Daddy, she sucks all day long on these Dynamic Muscle Builder Tablets with this rude-crude-and-socially-unattractive slurp-slurp noise.

TOM: Jeannette Hartshaw's father played pro football too you know.

KOOZY: I know. I know.

TOM: Jeannette Hartshaw's gonna make something of herself.

KOOZY: I know. A linebacker. And Daddy, first thing, the caddymaster slithers in and doesn't say a single-solitary word, and there's five-hundred-square-miles of grass out there bare minimum, but he spits this tobacco juice slop all over my shoe.

TOM: Fabulous!

KOOZY: Daddy, thanks a lot.

TOM: No. No. We had a caddymaster. Rick The Prick. He did exactly the same thing to me once. What's your guy's name?

KOOZY: Tad.

TOM: Tad the what?

KOOZY: Just plain Tad.

TOM: *(Overlapping)* Not Tad The Bad?

KOOZY: No.

TOM: RAD-ical Tad? Tad The Sad?

KOOZY: No. And Daddy, on the inside of his wrist he has a red tatoo of lips.

TOM: *(Pause)* Mouth lips?

KOOZY: Yesss. A tatoo of fat red mouth lips. And underneath? In blue cursive? It says "I Love Pussy."

TOM: Tad The Cad.

KOOZY: And he's always looking at me funny.

TOM: How funny?

KOOZY: Like he's seriously thinking about having twenty caddies pin me down so he can rip off my Fredricks of Hollywood panties.

TOM: I didn't know you . . .

KOOZY: *(Cutting him off)* I don't. But in his mind, Daddy. In his mind I wear superkinky underwear. And I know that's exactly what he's thinking because he's giving me exactly those kind of looks. And if I keep caddying one day he's going to order the boy caddies AND Jeannette Hartshaw to hold me down while he rapes me like twenty-six times in front of all the members of Denver Country Club and it's going to be on the ten o'clock news on Channel Four and you're going to be so ashamed of me you'll have to play the rest of your media-league softball games with a bag over your head. And Daddy, he's thinking of doing this in the VERY NEAR FUTURE!

TOM: *(Turns on the machine)* Nicest feature on this machine is you can go headphones or "sans" headphones. *(Sweeps the backyard, beep sounds)* Pop top. Don't get excited.

KOOZY: I sat there forever. He wouldn't send me out.

TOM: He send Jeanette Hartshaw out?

KOOZY: He's afraid of Jeanette Hartshaw.

TOM: Keep your mouth shut, pants zipped, nose to the grindstone, tomorrow he'll send you out.

KOOZY: Daddy, I'm not going back.

TOM: Caddying builds shoulder muscles, calf muscles and character. *(Sees* CASE *sleeping in the lawnchair atop the garage)* Who's this? Who the hell is this?

KOOZY: Daddy, shhhhh . . .

TOM: Shhhoosh? Some guy's sleeping on top of my garage.

KOOZY: Daddy, Case is part of the good news I was trying to tell you. Daddy, Case is the second reason . . .

TOM: How old is this guy?

KOOZY: I don't know. Twenty.

TOM: Twenty's too old. Much too old.

KOOZY: He's not a boyfriend.

TOM: What's he doing here?

KOOZY: His parents threw him out.

TOM: Kooz . . .

KOOZY: Daddy, his stepfather hit him with a beer bottle. In the head. For no reason. He got eight stitches. And his mother's so afraid of his stepfather she didn't even stick up for him. Daddy, eight stitches. Please, Daddy, one night. Please . . . *(Pause)* Oh thank you, Daddy. See, we're talking. We're actually talking. And the other thing I need to tell you about is this ad. See, there was this ad in "The Weekly" for Chick Performer Into Death Rock Who Can Write Lyrics. And I sent in this poem called "Pain" and . . . and . . . and . . . I got cast and we're called Fresh Virgins.

TOM: You cannot be in a band.

KOOZY: We're a political Performance Ensemble. I mean, we're so political you have to really BE a virgin to get cast.

TOM: Kooz, I wasn't born yesterday.

KOOZY: Daddy, pleeeeease . . .

TOM: Does it pay?

KOOZY: I even made you a piece.

TOM: Piece of what?

KOOZY: Performance piece. Especially for you. As a gift.

TOM: Okay . . .

KOOZY: So you'd understand Fresh Virgins is THE MOST IMPOR-TANT THING TO EVER HAPPEN IN MY ENTIRE LIFE!!!

TOM: I understand.

KOOZY: Then say "yes."

TOM: No.

KOOZY: Daddy, your piece is even about baseball!

TOM: *(Sarcastically)* Fabulous. Let's see it.

KOOZY: Forget it.

TOM: How would you like it if I took back your metal detector?

KOOZY: I wouldn't be caught dead with a metal detector.

TOM: Just put the head phones on, try it.

KOOZY: Daddy!!! *(Pause)* I'm giving you something so you'll give me something. Okay? Okay? This is for you. I wish this was "Saturday Night Live," but it isn't, but I still dedicate it to you. Okay?

(TOM nods. Turns on the tape recorder which plays "Hey, bat-ter" etc., and grabs one of the two pieces of the putter)

Hey batter . . . Swing!

*(Takes a vicious cut. KOOZY'S voice and music keep playing
out here.)*

Swing!

*(KOOZY takes another swing. She drops the half-putter, and
moves as if running the bases. Her movements are a combination
of modern dance, gymnastics and bunny hops. She sings along
to the tape recorded lyrics as she moves around TOM, who is
basically stunned by the oddness of it all.)*

Go to first base.
Go to first base.
Hey badder, hey badder, hey badder, hey!
Steal second base.
Steal second base.
Hey!
Hey-hey!
Badder, badder, badder, badder, badder, badder, badder!
Third base!
Third base!
Home base!
Home base!

*(Builds to the "swing" climax, swings, then drops to her knees
in front of TOM. Chants:)*

I'm out.
You're out.
Get out.
He's out.
She's out.
Get out . . .

*(Moves on her knees toward TOM half dancing, half pleading
as she sings along to the tape recording as it finishes with "Who-
hoo" etc.)*

TOM: *(Long pause)* That was . . . Without a doubt . . . I guess
there's a market for a routine like that. I . . . It was . . . Try that
for Tad The Cad tomorrow, he'll send you out first thing.

KOOZY: I knew you wouldn't "get it." Will you PLEASE just talk
to Grammie. PLEASE?

TOM: Why? No, why? Let's talk about this. Why?

KOOZY: She'll tell you why.

TOM: She's sleeping.

KOOZY: No she's not.

TOM: It's eleven thirty.

KOOZY: If she came home with you she can't be asleep yet.

TOM: She didn't come home with me.

KOOZY: Yes she did.

TOM: I haven't seen her since lunch.

KOOZY: She wasn't at your softball game?

TOM: Unh-uh.

KOOZY: I haven't seen her since I left to caddy this morning.

TOM: Check her room.

   (KOOZY exits into house.)

KRAUSBE: *(Enters and peers over the fence)* HayTom . . .

TOM: Mister Krausbe . . .

KRAUSBE: Auto-mo-beel theft on Colfax and Sheridan.

TOM: How 'bout that.

KRAUSBE: Suspect's a red-headed female, height approximately
 five foot, weight one hundred pounds.

TOM: Let me know how it comes out in the morning.

KRAUSBE: Pursuit in progress.

TOM: G'night then.

KOOZY: *(Calling inside the house)* Grammie!!!???

KRAUSBE: HayTom, what-chew got there?

TOM: Just a metal detector.

KRAUSBE: Don't you tell me "just." Heh-heh . . . Cuck-cuck . . .
 Snort-snort . . . That-uh good one?

TOM: The best. White's Two Thousand.

KRAUSBE: Always wanted one-uh them dee-tectors.

   (Exits into darkness of his yard)

KOOZY: *(Returning)* Daddy!

TOM: Gone?

KOOZY: Gone.

TOM: She's not gone.

KOOZY: Daddy!!!

TOM: Where the hell could she . . .

KOOZY: She could be hurt somewhere.

TOM: Let's not jump to . . .

KOOZY: In a shallow grave in a rocky field with just a torn-bloody
 strip of her blouse sticking up . . .

TOM: *(Overlapping)* Hey, hey . . . Let's not panic!

KOOZY: I'd better call Mom.

TOM: What's Mom gonna do about it?

KOOZY: I don't know. I'm worried.

TOM: So am I.

KOOZY: Should we tell Mister Krausbe?

TOM: What's he gonna do?

KOOZY: He's got the police radio and everything.

TOM: What color hair did she have?

KOOZY: When I left this morning?

TOM: Yeah.

KOOZY: You can't remember the color of your own mother's hair? No wonder she's not home.

TOM: She wears wigs.

KOOZY: Red.

TOM: She wouldn't steal a car.

KOOZY: Grammie?

TOM: Would she?

KOOZY: Did she say where she was going?

TOM: No. Yeah. The . . . uhhhh . . . Have you been on the phone tonight?

KOOZY: Just to Monica.

TOM: Shit! She probably tried to call, couldn't get through.

KRAUSBE: *(At the fence again)*   HayTiger, what-chew still doin' up this time-uh night?

TOM: So about that auto theft . . .

KOOZY: Grammie wouldn't steal a car.

KRAUSBE: TWO dee-tectors!?

TOM: Red-headed woman who stole the car?

KRAUSBE: If that don't frost my left ball!

TOM: Colfax and Sheridan?

KRAUSBE: If that ain't LUXURY!

TOM: Pursuit in progress??? Did they catch her?!!

KRAUSBE: Yes-sir. That red-headed female perpetrator? Turned out's a male juvenile.

TOM: Reason I ask, my mother's not home yet.

KRAUSBE: Where'd she go?

KOOZY: We don't know.

KRAUSBE: Oh.

TOM: If you hear anything on your . . .

KRAUSBE: She like to fight?

TOM: Whatta you mean?

KRAUSBE: Guess where a fight's broke out?

KOOZY: Grammie wouldn't fight.

KRAUSBE: Joe's Mambo Club over 34th Ave.

KOOZY: I'm gonna start calling hospitals.

     (Runs into the house)

TOM: She wouldn't be at Joe's Mambo Club.

KRAUSBE: One officer's already injured.

KOOZY: Emergency rooms . . .

     (Returns with the phonebook)

KRAUSBE: Riot squad's on the way . . .

TOM: I should've turned over her garden.

     (Lights bump to black.)

SCENE FOUR

(The next afternoon. VOICE OVER *of* TOM'S *radio talkshow is on the air. This scene plays out in the dark.)*

TOM: And we're back. This is Tom Gorman and you're listening to SportsGab on "KGST," the voice of the Rockies. And we're talking about the suicide squeeze. Is baseball's squeeze play the most dangerous and exciting play in all of sports or is it not? Does the squeeze encapsule life itself in its daring, complex nature, or does it not? But hey, holy smokes, I want to know what you think, and line four's winking at me. Hello, you're on SportsGab.

GRAMMIE: Tommy?

TOM: Mom?

GRAMMIE: We need to talk.

TOM: Fine. Whatta YOU think about the suicide squeeze?

GRAMMIE: I'm home.

TOM: Fabulous.

GRAMMIE: I've got a problem, Tommy.

TOM: Are you hurt?

GRAMMIE: No, I just feel so ashamed of myself for involving other people in my problem.

TOM: Mom, whatever it is we'll fix it. But right now we need your thoughts on the squeeze play. *(Pause)*   Mom?

GRAMMIE: Well. I didn't intend it as a squeeze play, but I suppose that's where we've ended up.

TOM: Mom, I don't know what you're talking about. But hey, line two's winking at me, and so's my engineer.

GRAMMIE: Tommy, Koozy's never going to forgive me.

TOM: Gotta go, Mom. And line two, you're on SportsGab.

(Lights begin coming up on the backyard.)

SCENE FIVE

(Early that evening. GRAMMIE *lies on a lawn chair with a paper grocery bag over her head—seeing and breathing through cut-out holes.* TOM *enters. Sees* GRAMMIE. TOM *drains his beer.)*

TOM: Look . . .

GRAMMIE: Don't apologize.

TOM: I had to keep the show moving . . .

GRAMMIE: You don't apologize, I won't.

TOM: Okay. *(Pause)* Mom . . . The garden . . .

GRAMMIE: I absolutely couldn't help what I've done.

TOM: End of the day, cultivated, fertilized. Plants'll jump outta that soil.

GRAMMIE: Will you forget the garden?

TOM: Right. *(Pause)* So why not call last night so we wouldn't worry?

GRAMMIE: Are you starting in?

TOM: I'm just asking.

GRAMMIE: The phone was busy.

TOM: Koozy was calling every hospital emergency room in the Yellow Pages.

GRAMMIE: I stayed at the Brown Palace Hotel. I splurged. Do I need your permission to live it up a little? *(Pause)* I brought you a towel.

TOM: *(Takes the towel)* What's going on?

GRAMMIE: I bought my box yesterday. Solid oak.

TOM: I thought we were done talking about arrangements.

GRAMMIE: We are, but this coffin's a little more expensive than my burial insurance covers, so I worked out sort of . . .
      (Pause)

TOM: Yeah?

GRAMMIE: Just a little swap. This for that.

TOM: Uh-huh . . .

GRAMMIE: But then a coffin is forever, so shouldn't I have what I really want?

TOM: Absolutely.

GRAMMIE: McMortenson even let me try it out first. Very comfortable. *(Pause)* I don't ever want to use it.

TOM: Mom, you're not gonna die. (SHE *and the bag give him a look.)* Okay. Everybody's gonna die. Someday. I'm gonna die. KOOZY'S gonna die.

GRAMMIE: I brought Koozy Brown Palace stationery and a shower cap.

TOM: She'll love it. So what'd you swap?

GRAMMIE: Remember when you and your father built that car?

TOM: No.

GRAMMIE: The Soap Box car?

TOM: Yes. Worst experience of my life. No matter what I did it was wrong.

GRAMMIE: We don't need to talk about this now.

TOM: No, let's.

GRAMMIE: Koozy's in the garage with a friend.

TOM: With no lights on? Who is she?

KRAUSBE: *(Returns)* HayTom . . .

TOM: Who is it? Monica?

KRAUSBE: HayTom . . .

GRAMMIE: A fellow artist.

KRAUSBE: HayTom, better keep yer girl away from them up on the corner.

TOM: She's got a boy in there?

KRAUSBE: They're smokin pot up on the corner.

TOM: *(Wants to knock, wants to rip open the door)* She's smarter than that . . .

KRAUSBE: Yes they are.

TOM: *(Peering through the cracks of the door)* Not that twenty-year-old?!!

KRAUSBE: HayTom . . . HayTom . . . Come 'ereTom.

> *(TOM gulps down his beer, tosses it over KRAUSBE'S fence. This presents an excruciating choice for KRAUSBE—the can or the conversation? He opts for conversation.)*

Give a sawbuck for that Jack Plane.

TOM: Mister Krausbe I'm trying to figure out . . .

KRAUSBE: *(Overlapping)* Give a double sawbuck.

TOM: Can't do it.

KRAUSBE: Wanna part with the lot of 'em, give a fair price.

TOM: Nah.

KRAUSBE: Give cash.

TOM: Nope.

KRAUSBE: Give a thousand dollars for the lot. Cash on the barrelhead.

TOM: They're not just tools.

KRAUSBE: No?

TOM: My Dad willed them to me.

KRAUSBE: I unnerstand.

TOM: Good.

> *(TOM gets on his knees and peers through the crack at the bottom of the garage door.)*

KRAUSBE: HayTom . . . I'd treat them tools like they's willed to me. Like they's given to me as a precious gift.

KOOZY: *(Opens the door, closes it fast)* Daddy. Grammie. He loves it!

TOM: Kooz, I hope you're smarter than to lock yourself up in a dark garage with a twenty-year-old man.

KOOZY: Daddy, remember the movie we made?

TOM: We made a lot of movies.

KOOZY: When I was like six? Remember? "Barbi Meets My Little Pony?" Case loves it. He thinks it might even be a piece. Grammie, you've GOT to see it. *(Grabs GRAMMIE to lead her into the garage)* And Grammie, I understand what you're saying with the bag.

TOM: Wait! What's she saying with the bag?

KOOZY: Daddy, don't you get it?

> *(Telephone rings. KOOZY races for the phone.)*

KOOZY: 'Lo . . . Yes she is may I tell her who's calling? *(To GRAMMIE)* John McMortenson from McMortenson's Mortuary?

GRAMMIE: *(Removes the bag from her head revealing a stunning blonde wig, answers)* Yes? Well yes, the body is brown. Red lettering would look very nice. No, no, not blood red, fire engine red. I'm glad you're excited about it. Yes . . . Goodbye . . . *(Hangs up, walks toward the house. TOM, KOOZY and KRAUSBE stare at her.)*

TOM: Mom? Mom?

GRAMMIE: What?

TOM: Mom, level with me. Are you planning to stencil some kinda message onto your body after you're dead? In fire engine red lettering?

> *(CASE enters from garage with the movie reel. He wears a bolo tie, bandaged head, black tux jacket, black jeans and bowling shoes, and coke-bottle black glasses. He looks like a mini-Elvis Costello, like Woody Allen's young, shorter cousin.)*

CASE: Tom, awesome film. Barbi and Junior Barbi driving their Corvette, lounging by the pool, and suddenly being attacked by Pirates of the Caribbean. My Little Pony flying out of the clouds to save them, and then riding into the sunset together. All told in two minutes. Tom, let's do some cutting and enter it in the Denver Film Festival.

TOM: Thanks, it's family property.

> *(Takes the film)*

CASE: Tom, it's got classic written all over it. Clear conflict between good and evil, plus two great looking dolls. Tom, with this film you could make a reputation.

TOM: I got a reputation—I'm the sports radio guy.

KOOZY: Daddy, you're embarrassing me.

TOM: Kooz, this movie's private.

KOOZY: Daddy, it's a thing. We can't own things. We only own our thoughts.

CASE: And as you probably know, Tom, we've all got a responsibility to share those.

(TOM *stares at* CASE, *thinks better of popping him, exits into the house.*)

GRAMMIE: Sweetie, on my lap here.

CASE: I am mad-mad-mad about your wig, Mature Lady.

GRAMMIE: Thank you.

KOOZY: Grammie, this is Case.

GRAMMIE: Thank you, Crank Case.

CASE: Woolworth's?

GRAMMIE: Yes. All Natural Hair, Mojave Desert Blond, from Woolworth's Wig Boutique.

KOOZY: Isn't she too-incredible. You look like Madonna or somebody, Grammie.

CASE: Marilyn Monroe.

GRAMMIE: Thank you, Crank Case. Sweetie, sit here.

TOM: *(Returns)* Yeah, Sweetie, sit there. *(Takes* CASE'S *arm off* KOOZY'S *shoulder)* Sweetie's not too big for her Grammie's lap.

GRAMMIE: I brought you a shower cap from the Brown Palace.

CASE: Too-cool!

TOM: Kooz, this is gonna be a "family" meeting.

KOOZY: Case is family.

TOM: No offense, you met him when? Yesterday?

KOOZY: Daddy, pleeeeeease don't do this to me.

KRAUSBE: HayTom, my offer's still good. One thousand simoleons.

TOM: Family meeting's in session now, Mister Krausbe.

KRAUSBE: Cash on the barrelhead.

GRAMMIE: *(To* KOOZY, *overlapping the above)* And I brought you some stationery, and a pillow and . . . *(Pulling things out of* HER *bag)* . . . and here's a nice authentic Brown Palace Hotel drinking glass, and a bible. Oh, and here's a complete set of silverware for one.

TOM: What's the punchline, Mom?

GRAMMIE: Well.

TOM: What're you buttering her up for?

GRAMMIE: I'm not buttering anyone.

TOM: What's the deal with McMortenson?

KOOZY: Daddy, leave her alone.

GRAMMIE: Sweetie, it's okay . . . My burial insurance only gets me a plastic coffin. Looks like a great big piece of tupperware.

KOOZY: Grammie, a coffin?

TOM: Kooz. Kooz, she's fine.

KOOZY: Grammie, are you sick?

TOM: Kooz. She just wants to get her affairs in order. She's sixty-four. People get their affairs in order at sixty-four. Now what the hell happened at the funeral home?

GRAMMIE: *(Sits on the edge of the sandbox)*   Well. To get the box I really wanted, the oak one, McMortenson wanted two thousand more dollars.

TOM: So you traded something for the oak coffin? What? The house?

GRAMMIE: Advertising.

CASE: Too-cool. Bartering is like the only true measure of exchange.

TOM: What kind of advertising?

GRAMMIE: Soap Box Derby cars have advertising on them.

KRAUSBE: HayTom!

TOM: *(To GRAMMIE, ignoring KRAUSBE)*   Uh-huh?

GRAMMIE: Businesses sponsor the cost of building the cars and in return get their logo painted on the side of the car.

KRAUSBE: HayTom! You know my claim-tuh-fame don't ya?

TOM: Case do me a favor?

CASE: You name it, Tom.   *(Slaps TOM on the shoulder)*

TOM: Bag of Diet Shasta Cherry Cola cans in the garage there? Sitting atop the lawnmower? Grab 'em and pitch 'em at Krausbe. Keep him occupied a few minutes. Thank you.   *(To KOOZY)*   Good kid.   *(To GRAMMIE)*   So, Mom, straighten me out. Where the hell'd you get a soap box derby car?

GRAMMIE: Sweetie, could you help me out?

KOOZY: God, Grammie. Anything.

GRAMMIE: Build me a Soap Box Derby Car.

KOOZY: I don't know diddly about cars.

KRAUSBE: HayTiger!

TOM: You traded advertising on a Soap Box Derby car for an oak coffin?

GRAMMIE: Sweetie, your father's got a garage-full of tools.

TOM: And the car doesn't exist?

KOOZY: I don't know diddly about tools.

KRAUSBE: HayTiger!

TOM: Mom, you know what we're talking?

GRAMMIE: Sweetie, I wouldn't ask if it wasn't something I really wanted.

TOM: Mom, don't tune me out. Does McMortenson know there's no car?

GRAMMIE: No.

TOM: Mom! What the hell?

KRAUSBE: HayTom, don't you tell me you don't know my claim tuh fame.

GRAMMIE: Haven't you ever wanted anything, Tommy?

TOM: Yeah, but Geezus Friggin Christmas! Mom, we're talking crime.

GRAMMIE: But if Koozy builds the car . . .

TOM: She's got to caddy.

KOOZY: I am not gonna caddy!

TOM: Then I'm putting you on a bus to your mother in Grand Junction.

KRAUSBE: HayTom!

CASE: *(Returns from dumping the cans into* KRAUSBE'S *yard)* Sorry, Tom. He won't bite.

KRAUSBE: HayTom!

TOM: What the hell were you thinking, Mom?

KOOZY: Grammie, ME build a Soap Box Derby car?

GRAMMIE: There is a lot of prize money involved, and since your father's so gung-ho about making money . . .

KOOZY: Grammie, it's too-geeky! I'd have to wear a bag over my head my entire high school career. Wouldn't I, Case?

CASE: Not necessarily.

TOM: Mom, I haven't got the extra two thousand dollars. Okay? But what we can do . . .

KRAUSBE: HayTom, make you a deal.

TOM: Just a sec. Mom, isn't there anything you like somewhere between the oak coffin and the tupperware?

KRAUSBE: HayTom, come 'ere. Come 'ere, Tom. *(TOM reluctantly goes to him.)* HayTom, I build the chug. And you pay me by givin me your tools.

TOM: Mister Krausbe, we're gonna settle this internally.

KRAUSBE: You ain't never gonna use them tools.

CASE: Tom, no problem. I'll build the car.

TOM: Look, she's my mother. I'll handle this.

CASE: Kooz, the car could be a piece.

KOOZY: Really?

CASE: We could race it down the escalator at Aurora Mall.

KOOZY: Really?

CASE: Think of the statement that'll make.

KOOZY: And we could make a video of us building it.

CASE: Yes! You're sitting in this white blank space, and the car begins to evolve around you, and you'll dress in like skin tight black leather pants . . .

KOOZY: Yeah!

CASE: . . . And a little black leather vest that cross-laces across the chest but doesn't quite close so there's like an inch and a half of bare milky-white skin so we can just see the rising mound of . . .

TOM: *(Overlapping)* Hey . . . Hey . . . Koozy's got other things going. Either she caddies or she's on the bus.

KOOZY: Daddy, Grammie's in trouble.

TOM: And I'll get her out of it.

KRAUSBE: HayTom, I'll getter out of it.

GRAMMIE: Tommy, wouldn't this be an interesting project for the two of you?

KOOZY: And what's wrong with me making money my own way?

TOM: You're not building any car.

GRAMMIE: *(Overlapping)*   Tommy . . .

KOOZY: Why not?

TOM: I just told . . .

KOOZY: *(Cuts him off)*   Because it's not your idea? Because it's not what you want me to do?

TOM: You made a commitment.

GRAMMIE: *(Overlapping)*   Tommy . . .

KOOZY: To make money.

TOM: There's no money in building a car.

GRAMMIE: *(Pulls out the clipping)*   Tommy, you wouldn't believe the scholarships and prize money.

   (Phone rings, TOM answers.)

TOM: SportsGab! Sorry. Gorman's residence. Yeah . . . Listen, about the deal you cut with my mother for the coffin . . . Yeah I'm the dad . . . Well yeah, we do have a special father/daughter rapport. Really? Only three weeks till race day. How 'bout that. The car? Well. Holy Smokes. The car. Well, why don't I let my daughter tell you about HER car . . .

   (Hands phone to KOOZY. Lights bump to black.)

END OF ACT ONE

ACT TWO

SCENE ONE

(A week later. Late afternoon. The garage doors are open. Tools are scattered around and two saw horses are set up with several one-by-eights atop them. A gaudily-constructed wooden car shell lies on the ground. Nothing's poking up in the garden yet. We hear the sound of Gloria Guardhausen's radio show.)

GLORIA'S VOICE: This is "Love and Learn" and I'm Gloria and our lines are open and we have Joe on the line. Hi, Joe!

JOE'S VOICE: Hi, Gloria. I sure do like your show. I'm a first-time caller.

(KOOZY, wearing a wide leather tool belt, turns on a power saw. The saw roars, KOOZY struggles to keep her balance and to prevent the saw from lurching out of her grip. SHE manages to turn the saw off.)

KOOZY: Shit!

(KOOZY sits, tries to compose herself. GLORIA's show comes in loud and clear again.)

GLORIA'S VOICE: Give yourself a big hug for that, Joe. Mmmmmmmm . . . Isn't that Yummy. Mmmmm-mmmm . . . What's REALLY on your mind today, Joe?

JOE'S VOICE: I think it's great you're not just hosting "Love And Learn," but the station's made you co-host of "SportsGab" too, Gloria.

GLORIA'S VOICE: I think it's GREAT too, Joe. It's always been a FANTASY to co-host Sportsgab. And I think it's DELICIOUS when our fantasies come true, don't you, Joe?

JOE: Yeah!

GLORIA: Confide in me, Joe. What else is on your mind today?

JOE'S VOICE: I was wondering where you and your stepson got the idea to build a soap box derby car.

GLORIA'S VOICE: Joe, I got the INSPIRATION to begin this EXCITING, COLLABORATIVE journey with my stepson Jason when a "Sportsgab" caller told me how much fun he'd had building a gravity car for Jimmy Stewart . . .

KRAUSBE: *(Overlapping, peering over the fence at KOOZY)* Hopalong Cassidy, goddammitt!

GLORIA'S VOICE: . . . I said to myself. I said to my INNER
  VOICE, Joe. I said, YES!
KRAUSBE: *(Overlapping)* 'Scuze my French, Tiger.
JOE'S VOICE: I built a car.
GLORIA'S VOICE: Did you?
JOE'S VOICE: When I was a boy. In Shoshone, Wyoming.
GLORIA'S VOICE: And was it REALLY a positive experience?
JOE'S VOICE: It was, what's that word you use . . . It was . . .
GLORIA'S VOICE: Bonding?
JOE'S VOICE: Yeah, bonding.
GLORIA'S VOICE: Isn't bonding YUMMY, Joe?
JOE'S VOICE: Yeah. I never knew my Dad. Never really . . .
  Ummmm . . . What's the word?
GLORIA: LOVED, Joe?
JOE: Never really loved my Dad, until we built that car together.
GLORIA'S VOICE: I'm so WARMED to hear that, Joe, because, as
  you know, I rate feelings as YUM or YUCK. And the feelings
  EMANATING from the ADVENTURE that Jason and I have EM-
  BARKED upon are Yum . . . Yum . . . Yum . . . Yum . . . Yum
  . . . Five Yums, Joe. So I don't have to tell YOU how MEANING-
  FUL building our car is in terms of INTERPERSONAL DEVELOP-
  MENT . . . I'm sure that you and your Dad . . .
KRAUSBE: HayTiger, turn that goddamn racket off!
  (KOOZY clicks off the radio.)
She really frosts my left ball. Jimmy Stewart! SportsGab! Weaslin'
her way onto Tom's show. Why she don't know the difference be-
tween a base and a ball goddamnit!

  *(KOOZY tosses an empty aluminum can into KRAUSBE'S
  yard.)*

KRAUSBE: HayTiger, where's Boyfriend?
KOOZY: I don't need any help. Okay?
KRAUSBE: Yes-sir. *(Pause)* Two weeks ta race day.
KOOZY: I know that. Okay?
KRAUSBE: Yes-sir.
KOOZY: I'm doing fine. Okay?
KRAUSBE: Yes-sir. *(Pause)* Give ya a hint?
KOOZY: No thanks.
KRAUSBE: Gonna need wheels ta roll down the hill.
KOOZY: Case is getting the wheels. Okay? Okay? He's just . . .
  Okay? He's bringing them.
KRAUSBE: HayTiger, come 'ere. Come 'ere. Tiger. Looky here.
  (Shows her the wagon on his side of the fence) Little bastard up
the street name a TimBo? Little bastard wakes me up every mornin'

ridin' them damn Big Wheels up'n'down the sidewalk? TimBo tries
to tell ya them wheels are his? Cup yer hands together like this'n
box his ears like you was playin' the cymbals.

KOOZY: I don't want stolen property.

KRAUSBE: I give 'em the wagon inna first place, I can confiscate
it back.

KOOZY: I don't need any help!
   (Goes back to the car shell)

KRAUSBE: Boyfriend take a hike, did he?

KOOZY: Mister Krausbe, I'm really frustrated.

KRAUSBE: How you think I feel watchin ya?

KOOZY: I need to do this myself.

KRAUSBE: Don't you tell me "myself."

KOOZY: I do!

KRAUSBE: Don't you tell me you didn't jump into this rain barrel
with yer head greased.

KOOZY: Rain barrel?

KRAUSBE: 'Fore you ever started, you knew you needed somebody
knows what they're doin.

KOOZY: Case knows what he's doing.

KRAUSBE: Cuck-cuck-cuck . . .

KOOZY: He does!

KRAUSBE: Snort, snort, snort . . .

   *(KOOZY tries to cut out a pattern with a hand saw, but gets
   nowhere.)*

KOOZY: This is so ignorant!
   (Throws the saw)

KRAUSBE: Ya need a jigsaw.

KOOZY: Leave me alone.   *(Covers HER face)*

KRAUSBE: HayTiger . . . Awwww, HayTiger . . . I'm on yer side
. . . HayTiger, wanna punch me upside my ugly old bean? Make ya
feel better . . . Wanna kick me in my good leg? Kick me in my bum
leg? Release some a them fruss-rations . . . *(Pause)* HayTiger
. . . Hand me a crescent . . .

KOOZY: What's a crescent?

KRAUSBE: It ain't a French donut. Cuck-cuck-cuck. Crescent's a
wrench, Tiger. Got a little doo-hickey you fiddle with ta open'n'close
the size a yer gap.

KOOZY: *(Digs in the huge toolbox sitting next to the fence.)*   This?
   (Holds up a plumber's wrench)

KRAUSBE: That's a goddamn pipe wrench.

KOOZY: How about?   *(Holds up another)*

KRAUSBE: That's a goddamn box wrench!

KOOZY: How'm I supposed to know what a GODDAMN crescent wrench looks like! *(Finds it)* Okay?!

KRAUSBE: That's it. That's it, Tiger. *(Takes the crescent from her)* Now we're cookin with gas! *(Trying to remove the wheels from the wagon)* Now, when Tom comes home, you tell 'im I'm yer partner. Tell 'im ya traded tools for expert-tease. Damn. Little bastard TimBo boobytrapped me with bubblegum. You know TimBo?

KOOZY: I used to babysit him.

KRAUSBE: His momma denies it, but I'd bet my crutches TimBo's a die-rect descendent of Mass Murderer Charles Manson. Got that same smirk. *(Unscrewing a nut)* Now we're cookin with gas.

        (TOM *enters, beer in hand.*)

HayTom . . .

TOM: Mister Krausbe.

KRAUSBE: HayTom, Tiger's took me on as her partner.

KOOZY: No I haven't.

KRAUSBE: But I give my word I won't move yer tools into my garage till after the chug's finished.

        (TOM *tosses his empty beer into* KRAUSBE'S *yard.*)

ThanksTom.

        (HE *exits.*)

TOM: Kooz. Kooz.

KOOZY: What?!!!

TOM: Tune in with me on this. *(Pause)* My Very Eager Mother Just Served Us Nine Pickles. *(Pause)* Okay?

KOOZY: Okay what?

TOM: Are we in tune? My Very Eager Mother Just Served Us Nine Pickles?

KOOZY: Daddy, I've got a major problem.

TOM: Kooz, that's the planets in order of distance from the sun. I'm driving home. I'm thinking how tight we used to be. Kooz, Mercury, Venus, Earth, Mars, Jupiter, Saturn, Uranus, Neptune, Pluto. WE STUDIED THE PLANETS TOGETHER. Kooz, we can build this.

KOOZY: Daddy, no.

TOM: Then tell your grandmother you can't do it.

KOOZY: I can do it.

TOM: Without me? Realistically?

KOOZY: When Case's thumb is better . . .

TOM: Broke his thumb AGAIN?

KOOZY: Not "again."

TOM: Same thumb he hit with the hammer last week? *(*KOOZY *shoots him a look)* Kooz, I know you want my help.

KOOZY: Daddy, how many times do I hafta . . .

TOM: But you're just too stubborn to ask.

KOOZY: No!

TOM: Kooz, all you got's a shell here.

KOOZY: It's the body.

TOM: You start with the floorboard.

KOOZY: That's so boring.

TOM: It's the foundation. You need more than looks. You got a base you're creative on top of it. Otherwise all you got's style. You're not flimsy. Don't make your car flimsy.

KOOZY: I'm not trying to make it flimsy.

TOM: Kooz, I want in.

KOOZY: Daddy, it just looks like I'm not making any progress.

TOM: Gloria's got a team of structural engineers building her car.

KOOZY: Daddy, you are so transparent.

TOM: Test running it in a wind tunnel.

KOOZY: All you want is to show up Gloria.

TOM: What's wrong with that?

KOOZY: It's totally selfish.

TOM: Kooz, I'm going under at the station. Kooz, we're talking basketball today. Hoops. We're talking how many minutes Larry Bird can play before he needs a blow. I say he can go eighteen hard minutes before he needs a blow. Right? And Gloria . . . Gloria launches into how oral sex has the ultimate potential to achieve world peace.

KOOZY: Daddy, if you're leading into a talk between us about oral sex, I just wanta tell you I'm feeling very fragile right now.

TOM: No, Kooz. And guess what the kicker is? This is SportsGab. My SportsGab. She says "oral sex" and the phone lines light up like a goddamn Christmas tree. What the hell is happening, Kooz?

KOOZY: Daddy, I know you're upset about work but . . .

TOM: And she steals our Soap Box Derby idea and makes like she invented it. Like she's got the perfect parent-child relationship. Kooz, tell me why I wouldn't want to kick her snotty, stuck-up, psychological . . .

KOOZY: *(Overlapping)* Daddy, I am in PAIN.

TOM: Kooz, I am in PAIN too!

KRAUSBE: *(Returns)* HayTom, where's Missus?

TOM: Mister Krausbe, please. Not now.

KRAUSBE: She givin' off any odor yet?

TOM: She's lying down.

KOOZY: Grammie?

KRAUSBE: You sure she ain't givin off any odor?

KOOZY: She's got the flu.

KRAUSBE: I clipped a article for her. Tells how ta think the badness outta yer body. Yes-sir. Soon's I get these goddamn wheels off . . .

(Starts removing the second set)

KOOZY: Daddy, could you try and get in tune with me for one second?

TOM: I'm in tune. *(Pause)* I am.

KOOZY: Daddy, at our first-and-only gig last week? At the junkyard? When you were too busy playing softball?

TOM: Kooz, softball is not recreation it is essential job politics.

KOOZY: Daddy, a Doberman started howling during "HeyBatter" and wouldn't stop. Like it was my fault.

TOM: It's okay.

KOOZY: And now Case hates me.

TOM: I understand.

KOOZY: I haven't seen him in a whole week.

TOM: It'll be all right.

KOOZY: Daddy, I'm so hurt.

TOM: I know. Kooz . . . *(Moves behind KOOZY, but can't quite allow himself to touch her)* I'm . . . You know, I'm inside . . . the moment for you . . . I'm . . . here for you . . . I want to . . . *(Moves toward the car shell)* EMBARK . . . MEANING-FUL . . . Foundation . . . I know tools . . . So what do you say? I want to win, Kooz. I want to win at something. Okay??? So we don't lose each other.

   (Dogs bark loudly. CASE enters from alley, stops. His thumb and head are bandaged. He and KOOZY stare at each other. She moves tentatively toward him.)

KOOZY: Hi.

CASE: Sorry.

KOOZY: That's okay.

CASE: My mom and my step-father split up.

KOOZY: Oh.

CASE: I've been helping her move.

KOOZY: Oh.

CASE: And I was depressed.

KOOZY: I was too.

CASE: About the gig?

KOOZY: Yeah.

CASE: I hate Dobermans.

KOOZY: Dobermans are so ignorant.

CASE: Axles. *(Holds them up)*

KOOZY: Thanks.

CASE: Video. *(Holds up the camera)*

KOOZY: Too-cool.

CASE: I really feel like we could create something.

KOOZY: The car. A piece.

CASE: Yeah. And . . .

KOOZY: Me too.
CASE: And . . . Create something with you.
KOOZY: I'd like to create something with you too.

   (TOM *picks up the handsaw, bends it between his knees, begins "playing" it softly.*)

KOOZY: He really badly wants to help.
CASE: Sure.
KOOZY: He knows about tools.
CASE: We have a definite need for that.
KOOZY: Daddy, what are you doing?
CASE: Playing the saw.
CASE: Too-cool, Tom.
TOM: Saw's got teeth, it oughta be able to sing the blues.
CASE: Massive concept!
TOM: A saw doesn't cut. *(Saws a board)* Saw gnaws. Hear it? Teeth are taking tiny bites.
KRAUSBE: There you go! *(Dumps the second set of wheels over the fence)* HayTom, I'll fetch that article for the Missus.
   (Exits)
TOM: So.
CASE: So.
KOOZY: So.
CASE: Krausbe gave us this wood.
KOOZY: Mahogany.
TOM: Heartwood. Excellent. Your Grandpa used to say "heartwood's got a soul."
CASE: Yeah?
TOM: You got bark. You got sapwood. You got heartwood. *(To CASE)* No offense, you're sapwood. *(To KOOZY)* Grammie's heartwood. Heartwood looks dead . . .
KOOZY: Daddy!
TOM: No. Looks dead but it's not. Stillbreathes, still absorbs. Still . . . You cut down a tree, take heartwood and make a desk. Chair. Whatever. Tree's soul doesn't die, just takes on a new shape, new form.
CASE: Too-cool!
KOOZY: Yeah.
CASE: Could you say that again after I get the camera rolling, Tom?
TOM: Tell you something else to keep in mind before we jump in here. Jason? Gloria's Jason? Collects Nazi memorabilia. *(Pause)* So whatta you say? Let's build something that'll blow Jason and Gloria Guardhausen right outta the water!
   (Measuring and marking the wood)

CASE: Tom, I've got doubts about coming from that POV.

KOOZY: Yeah.

TOM: Doubts about beating the woman who's destroying my livelihood?

CASE: Competition's why the world's all messed up, Tom.

TOM: Yeah?

KOOZY: Daddy, that's true.

CASE: Instead of competing, we need to focus on becoming the very best individual we can be with the gifts the Supreme Being has given us, Tom.

TOM: Let's cut the bullshit and play to win. Okay?

CASE: I'm not knocking playing to win, Tom.

TOM: Oh no?

CASE: Know why I said "yes" to this project, Tom?

TOM: Is it a three letter word, starts with S, ends with X?

KOOZY: Daddyyyy!

CASE: To make a statement about mankind rediscovering the ability to travel without dumping noxious fumes into the atmosphere. Right, Kooz?

KOOZY: I was thinking . . . Never mind . . .

CASE: No, what?

KOOZY: It's too embarrassing.

TOM: You're doing it to win money.

CASE: She's doing it to make a political statement.

KOOZY: Ummmmm . . .

TOM: To win a college scholarship.

CASE: A statement about rediscovering the collaborative relationship between the wheel and gravity.

KOOZY: I was thinking that we would be, you know, creating something really beautiful together on an artistic/emotional level.

CASE: That's a major part of it too.

KOOZY: Really?

CASE: Really.

    (Kisses KOOZY *lightly on the lips)*

TOM: *(To himself)* I was thinking the same thing.

CASE: I am juiced about creating with you because you know WHAT IS WHAT.

    (THEY *move to kiss again, but* TOM *interrupts.)*

TOM: We get rolling, save the saw dust. Mix it with a little glue. Patch holes.

KOOZY: Daddy, do you want a hug?

TOM: No thanks.

KOOZY: Daddy, I want to give you one.

TOM: No, I'm fine.

KOOZY: Daddy, please let me. Daddy, what you said about the fact
our car's gonna have a soul was so beautiful.

TOM: Thank you.

KOOZY: Are you sure you don't want a hug?

TOM: I want a chalkline. We start with the floorboard.

CASE: I was thinking we'd start with a shot of the brown cloud
during morning rush hour.

KOOZY: And the background score's this awful wheezing and cough-
ing and gasping do you think?

TOM: *(Measuring)* Get me a goddamn chalkline. Two weeks we
got? Two weeks ain't near enough time to build this thing unless we
get humping now.

CASE: This's supposed to be a democratic process, Tom.

TOM: Yeah, well . . . *(Takes the chalkline from KOOZY)* Hold
that end on the mark. *(KOOZY does)* Pull it away from the wood
gently in the center. Snap it.

KOOZY: Blueline!

TOM: Now we cut on this line. Watch me. Some things you just need
to watch, then do what you see. *(Sawing)* Gotta remember wood's
stubborn. You don't force the saw. Guide it. Guide it. Force wood,
it splinters.

KRAUSBE: HayTiger come 'ere. HayTiger . . . *(KOOZY goes to
him.)* Give this ta Missus.

KOOZY: *(Looks at the clip and calls to KRAUSBE as he disappears)* She doesn't have cancer.

TOM: *(Stops sawing)* That's for me.

KOOZY: He says it's for Grammie.

TOM: For . . . For a friend of mine.

KOOZY: She doesn't have cancer. *(Pause)* Does she? *(Pause)*
Does she? *(Pause)* Daddy, does she?

TOM: Kooz, everybody who gets cancer doesn't die.

KOOZY: Why didn't you tell me? Why didn't you?

TOM: I didn't want . . .

KOOZY: What?!!

TOM: Didn't want to . . .

KOOZY: What?!!! Treat me like a half-way intelligent human being?!!

TOM: Worry you.

KOOZY: Like a person?

TOM: Kooz, my intentions were . . .

KOOZY: Worry me?

TOM: Yeah.

KOOZY: Worry me?!

TOM: Yes.

KOOZY: I had a right to know.

TOM: I did what I thought was best.

KOOZY: You don't have the faintest idea what's best for me.

TOM: Who the hell you think you're . . .

KOOZY: Embarrassing me in front of a friend is good for me?

TOM: How did I embarrass . . .

KOOZY: Forcing me to caddy. Hiding Grammie being sick from me like I'm a baby is good for me?

TOM: You're too busy singing with The Dobermans to care what happens around here anyway?

KOOZY: I can't believe you said that.

TOM: Truth hurt?

KOOZY: You are such a jerk.

TOM: Watch your mouth.

KOOZY: You are such an ass.

TOM: You are not too old to . . .

KOOZY: Making fun of the fact I'm a performer is good for me?

TOM: Will you get off my goddamn back?

KOOZY: You want me to get off your goddamn back?

TOM: I want you to start taking my advice . . .

KOOZY: *(Overlapping)* Do you?

TOM: . . . for a change because you are in drastic . . .

KOOZY: . . . Do you??

TOM: . . . need of it.

KOOZY: Do you?!!!

TOM: Do I what?

KOOZY: Want me to get off your goddamn back?

TOM: Yes!

KOOZY: Then get off my goddamn back. Permanently.

(KOOZY stomps into the house. TOM stares, picks up a hammer, smashes the floorboard he's just cut as the lights bump to black.)

SCENE TWO

(Late that night. In the dark, we hear Monica's answering machine—Julie Browne's "I Like 'Em Big And Stupid" plays. Then Monica's voice comes on the line.)

MONICA'S VOICE: Hi, this is Monica. And even if you're not big and stupid, I still want to hear from you. So like leave a message at the tone or beep or whatever. Okay? Here it comes . . . *(Beep sounds.)*

KOOZY'S VOICE: Monica, I love your new message, but where are you? I need to talk to you about my grandmother. Monica, I can't talk to her about it. God. And my father . . . God Monica, it's too complex. Monica, call me. I'm sleeping outside tonight, as far away from my father as possible. So call me tonight no matter what time. Monica, it's URGENT!

(Dream music plays. Weird moonlight comes up on KOOZY sleeping in the lawn chair in the backyard. The rough shape of the soap box car emerges, sitting atop two saw horses. Softly, a pirates' chant and the sound of waves are heard.)

SCENE THREE

(The same. KOOZY dreams. The garage becomes a ship. The Pirate ship sails the sea. The skull-and-crossbones is hoisted high. The Pirates' singing grows louder. Pirate Number One (CASE) comes on deck dressed in pirate/football costume, followed by GRAMMIE—her body bound by thick rope and her mouth gagged. Pirate Number One puts the plank in place as Pirate Number Three (KRAUSBE) enters below with a hook for a hand and a parrot perched on his single crutch.)

THREE PIRATES: *(Singing)*   Deep, deep, down to the deep
   Deep, deep, down to the deep
   Gonna toss this woman way down to the deep . . .
   Toss her way down to the deep.
   Gonna toss this woman way down to the deep
   Down to the deep,
   She's gonna sleep,
   Sleep, sleep, she's gonna sleep
   In the deep, deep, deep
   In the deep, deep, deep
   In the deep, deep, deep . . .
TOM'S VOICE: *(Oddly distorted, and commenting as the singing fades)*   This is Tom Gorman on KSEX and we're bringing you live coverage of the INTERNATIONAL PLANK WALKING CHAMPIONSHIPS!
   (Stadium ambience)
   The Three Pirates have thrown anchor and are making final preparations . . . The plank is almost in place . . . And their victim today is one Mary Margaret Gormando. Gormando! Who is bound and

gagged and not going anywhere but down, down, down to the deep
in just a few moments! SportsFans, let's pick up the action . . .
PIRATE NUMBER ONE: The plank we're gonna be using, Tom, is
the finest heartwood mahogany available in the world today.
PIRATE NUMBER THREE: HayTom, I use-ta build my planks
outta linoleum.
KOOZY: Oh my God! No! Grammie!

>   *(Jumps from the lawnchair into the soap box car shell and
>   paddles out to sea toward the ship)*

PIRATE NUMBER THREE: HayTom, after we eighty-six the old
bimbo, our next victim's a little bastard name a TimBo. You know
TimBo, Tom.
PIRATE NUMBER ONE: You know TimBoTom, TimBo?
KOOZY: Grammie!
TOM'S VOICE: Righto, Pirates! And tell me, will you be trying to
break your World Record today?
PIRATE NUMBER ONE: We're only competing with ourselves, eh
captain???

>   *(A snatch of Johnny Carson theme music plays as Pirate
>   Number Two (TOM) wobbles onstage dressed in a pirate captain's
>   costume and carrying a golf club.)*

PIRATE NUMBER TWO: Aye-aye, maties. We don't force, we don't
force, we don't force the victim to walk the plank. We guide the
victim.
ALL PIRATES: Har, har har!
PIRATE NUMBER THREE: HayTom, I'm the guy what built the
plank Jimmy Stewart walked in "Miracle on Thirty-Fourth Street."
TOM'S VOICE: Is that a fact?
ALL THREE PIRATES: Yesssssssssssss-sir!
KOOZY: *(In* HER *dinghy)* Not so fast, buccaneers! That's my
Grammie and she's comin with me.
THREE PIRATES: Noooooooooo-sir!
KOOZY: Hand her over or I'll. . .I'll. . . *(Jumps from the dinghy
and looks for a weapon, finds a metal detector)*
TOM'S VOICE: The action is underway, ladies and gentlemen, and
not only is Pirate Koozy's team undermanned, but she's got no dag-
ger.

>   *(KOOZY zaps Pirate Number Two with the detector as if it were
>   a laser gun, then zaps Pirate Number One.)*

PIRATE NUMBER ONE: Say, swashbuckler, take your shirt off and give us a peek at your pecks.

PIRATE NUMBER THREE: Now we're cookin with gas!

KOOZY: Could I give you a kiss instead?

PIRATE NUMBER TWO: No kissing. I said no kissing!

　　　(KOOZY and PIRATE NUMBER ONE kiss, separate.)

KOOZY: Thanks. I needed that.

PIRATE NUMBER ONE: What's your name?

KOOZY: My name? They call me The Swashbuckler.

PIRATE NUMBER THREE: You ain't TimBo is ya?

KOOZY: No.

PIRATE NUMBER THREE: *(Exiting in search of TimBo)* Where's that little bastard TimBo?

PIRATE NUMBER ONE: Gimme another kiss, Swashbuckler.

KOOZY: Sorry, only one kiss to a customer.

PIRATE NUMBER ONE: But I love you. And I'd rather die than live without another kiss.

KOOZY: I love you too, but my father says only one kiss to a customer.

PIRATE NUMBER ONE: You're just saying that because I'm not big and stupid.

KOOZY: No! Don't!

PIRATE NUMBER ONE: Timberrrrrr!

　　　(PIRATE NUMBER ONE jumps overboard. Loud scream, splash, and crash of aluminum cans)

TOM'S VOICE: *(Always oddly distorted and coming from the heavens)* Steeeeeeeeerike One!

PIRATE NUMBER TWO: I'll take my kiss now, Swashbuckler.

KOOZY: Kiss YOU? Are you serious?

PIRATE NUMBER TWO: *(Pursuing her)* Pucker up, buttercup.

KOOZY: You are disgusting!

PIRATE NUMBER TWO: You're not too big to pucker up, buttercup.

KOOZY: You've got an overactive imagination if you think I'm ever gonna kiss you.

　　　(Lights change.)

PIRATE NUMBER TWO: Fine! Then don't!

KOOZY: Fine! I won't!

PIRATE NUMBER TWO: Then you're grounded for the rest of the summer.

KOOZY: You wouldn't.

PIRATE NUMBER TWO: For the next three summers.

KOOZY: You can't. I am an adult.

(Lights back to eerie pirates at sea.)

PIRATE NUMBER TWO: You're a child.

KOOZY: I've been watching R-rated movies since I was seven.

PIRATE NUMBER TWO: *(Singing, Lounge Lizard style)* Tell me you love me, love me, love me.

KOOZY: Never.

PIRATE NUMBER TWO: *(Singing)* Tell me you need me, need me, need me more than any other man.

KOOZY: I'd rather die.

PIRATE NUMBER TWO: Please tell me you love me.

KOOZY: No. *(Hands him a tiny pink Care Bear suitcase)* And get off of my goddamn boat. Permanently.

PIRATE NUMBER TWO: But I can't swim.

KOOZY: Then take the bus to Grand Junction. *(Bus engine revs, horn sounds. He exits despondently.)*

BUS DISPATCHER'S VOICE: *(Overlapping)* Last chance for Albuquerque . . . Kookamunga . . . and Grand Junction . . .

KOOZY: *(Overlapping)* Now. Go. And don't ever try to control me again. You hear me? I'm out of control. I'm out of control. You hear me?

TOM'S VOICE: Righto, Swashbuckler, I hear ya loud 'n'clear. But before you save the day, let's pause for station identification.

(Standing in her dinghy, KOOZY is caught in a bizarre white light. Pirate ship disappears.)

GLORIA'S VOICE: *(Sinisterly distorted)* This is Gloria! And you're live on "Love and Learn." Who's ready to confide? Who's ready to confide?

KOOZY: Hi, Gloria, this is Koozy.

GLORIA'S VOICE: Cousy?

KOOZY: Yes.

GLORIA'S VOICE: Isn't that a basketball name? Cousy.

KOOZY: Yes. Oh Gloria, you are so sensitive and perceptive.

GLORIA: I know that!

KOOZY: My father named me after Bob Cousy of the Boston Celtics. He wanted a boy and when he didn't get one he punished me with my name.

GLORIA'S VOICE: I sense some HOSTILITY in your voice, Cousy.

KOOZY: Gloria, if I was a boy he'd take me duck hunting and teach me how to change the oil and say things like "put a little hair around it . . ." *(Pirate laughs echo.)* But instead he just humiliates me in front of my friends.

GLORIA'S VOICE: *(Totally bored)* Tell me more, Bob Cousy. Confide in me, Bob Cousy.

KOOZY: Gloria? Gloria? I'm unique. I'm mature. I'm really-and-truly
uniquely mature.

(Police siren wails. Lights flash. KRAUSBE, *dressed in convict
stripes, charges into the scene.)*

CONVICT: HayTiger, just come over my Realistic Radio Shack, the
police're headed this way.
(Police siren wails loudly, dies out.)
CONVICT: HayTiger, police're here to lock us up.
(Blue-and-red lights flash, siren swells.)
KOOZY: What've we done?
CONVICT: I just wrung TimBo's neck, and you kissed a boy ta
death.
KOOZY: But I only did it to save Grammie.
POLICEMAN'S MEGAPHONE VOICE: Koozy Gorman! This is
Police Commissioner Tad The Cad. Come out with your hands up
and we won't shoot.
CONVICT: HayTiger, what're pennies made from?
KOOZY: What?!
CONVICT: What're pennies made from?
KOOZY: *(Shouting)* Dirty copper!
CONVICT: Cuck-snort, cuck-snort . . .

(The Police fire a burst of gunfire. CONVICT *runs off toward
the loud gunfire.)*

You'll never take me alive, Copper! Toppa da woild, Ma!
*(*GRAMMIE *hops toward* KOOZY.*)*
GRAMMIE: Save me, Sweetie. Save me, Sweetie.
KOOZY: Grammie!
(Unties her as the gunfire grows louder)
GRAMMIE: Sweetie, you did it. Sweetie, you saved me.
KOOZY: Grammie. Quick. Into my dinghy before the police . . .

(They climb into KOOZY'S *dinghy as bullets ping and ricochet
around them.)*

KOOZY: We're safe. Grammie, we're safe. Grammie, you don't have
to walk the plank. I saved you.
GRAMMIE: Stop da music! *(Silence)* Sweetie, did you know this
boat is leaking?
KOOZY: Oh my God!
GRAMMIE: Sweetie, no problem. I'll just hot wire a car.

(Exits as the bullets sound again, only now they have the intensity of a war zone. KOOZY chases after her but collapses on the lawn lounger.)

KOOZY: Grammie, don't steal a car. Grammie! Grammie, it's just a little leak. Grammie, I'll patch the leak. Grammie, I built this boat. Grammie it's fixed. The boat's not leaking anymore. Grammie, I swear it's like better than ever. Grammie . . . Grammie . . .

(Dream music and Pirates' chant slowly fade out with the lights.)

SCENE FOUR

(The next morning. GRAMMIE waters the garden with a watering can—a few green stalks have pushed upwards. She's even thinner now. KRAUSBE'S police scanner sqawks but he's not in sight. KOOZY comes quietly through the back door and begins taking photos of GRAMMIE. GRAMMIE stops watering, sees KOOZY.)

GRAMIE: Started this garden too damn late. *(KOOZY clicks off another photo.)* I smell rain. *(KOOZY moves for a different angle.)* Make your bed for you. *(Begins folding up the blanket. KOOZY clicks another photo.)* What in the name of good-God are you doing?

KOOZY: I don't have any good photos of you.

GRAMMIE: That's because there's no such thing.

KOOZY: You look cute . . . *(Clicking away)*

GRAMMIE: I look like a rag. *(Turns her back to KOOZY)* With the exception of my Purple Passion Woolworth's Wig Boutique hair.

KOOZY: Turn around.

GRAMMIE: What has gotten into you, Sweetie.

KOOZY: Grammie, let me capture you.

GRAMMIE: *(Sits at the table)* You know, don't you?

KOOZY: Grammie, could you give me a little smile maybe?

GRAMMIE: What should I smile about?

KOOZY: I don't know.

GRAMMIE: I don't know either. *(Clicks a photo)* You know or not?

KOOZY: Know what?

GRAMMIE: Why I've been dragging myself around?

KOOZY: Flu.

GRAMMIE: Why my stomach pooches out a little more each day?

KOOZY: Desserts?

GRAMMIE: Want me to say it out loud? *(Pause)* Sweetie . . . Brace yourself . . . I'm pregnant.

KOOZY: Grammie . . . *(Laughs)* Mister Krausbe clipped this for you.

GRAMMIE: *(Takes the article)* "How to Beat The Odds." Did you read it?

KOOZY: Yeah.

GRAMMIE: Is it about playing blackjack in Las Vegas?
     (KOOZY shakes her head.)

GRAMIE: I figured. *(Pause)* Come here. *(KOOZY sits on her lap and she hugs her.)*

KOOZY: Grammie, I'm so scared.

GRAMMIE: Me too.

KOOZY: Why didn't he tell me?

GRAMMIE: Do me a favor, Sweetie. Forgive him. You're hurting him as much as . . .

KOOZY: *(Stands)* I haven't done anything to him.

GRAMMIE: Then do me the favor and forgive him.

KOOZY: Here. *(Hands GRAMMIE an envelope)* My savings. From birthdays and babysitting. Eight hundred and twenty-seven dollars.

GRAMMIE: For my coffin?

KOOZY: Case thinks he can sell his compressor and spray gun for the rest and then I'll eventually pay him back.

GRAMMIE: Sweetie, just build the car.

KOOZY: I can't.

GRAMMIE: Sweetie, every project has its ups and downs.

KOOZY: I know you really want the oak coffin so I'm getting it for you.

GRAMMIE: Sweetie, I want something even more than the box.

KOOZY: You said . . .

GRAMMIE: *(Overlapping)* I want you and your daddy doing The Piece.

KOOZY: But I can't do it. I can't work with him.

GRAMMIE: So what do I do? Assume one day you and your father'll talk to each other again? After I'm dead?

KOOZY: You're not gonna . . .

GRAMMIE: *(Overlapping)* I'm gonna beat the odds?

KOOZY: Yes.

GRAMMIE: How?

KOOZY: You're supposed to mentally picture yourself healthy. And if you want it bad enough the picture comes true. And you're supposed to get mad too.

GRAMMIE: Then let's fight.

KOOZY: Grammie, I couldn't fight with you.

GRAMMIE: Sure you could.

KOOZY: Over what?

GRAMMIE: The car.

KOOZY: Grammie, I'll get the rest of the money by tomorrow or the next day.

GRAMMIE: I WANT THE CAR.

KOOZY: Grammie, I tried.

GRAMMIE: Try again.

KOOZY: Grammie . . .

GRAMMIE: He thinks his father never gave him anything but a bad time.

KOOZY: That's all he ever gives me.

GRAMMIE: Your grandpa did give him something though.

KOOZY: Tools . . .

GRAMMIE: Not just tools.

KOOZY: . . . and one day I inherit them and give them to my kids, not that I'm ever gonna have any.

GRAMMIE: Don't you be flip with me! The gift isn't the tools. It's how to use the damn tools.

KOOZY: I'm sorry.

GRAMMIE: And Tommy doesn't even know that's what his father really gave him and that's what he's got to give you.

KOOZY: Don't be mad at me.

GRAMMIE: Damnit, I'm not mad at you! I just want you to understand that there's nothing wrong with either you or your father accepting a damn gift, damnit. Damnit. Sweetie, you have got to help me stop cussing.

KOOZY: Okay.

GRAMMIE: Okay. *(Pause)* I want everything square with you and me, and you and your daddy. I've got to pick my fights carefully nowadays and when I do I want to make darn sure I win.

KOOZY: I'm sorry.

GRAMMIE: For what?!!

KOOZY: For not being able to give you what you want.

GRAMMIE: All I want is you and Tommy to love each other and to build me a small wooden car, WHICH DOESN'T EVEN HAVE AN ENGINE! Is that a lot to ask for?

KOOZY: Yeah.

GRAMMIE: You think I'm being selfish?

KOOZY: Sort of.

GRAMMIE: Good. I wanta be selfish as hell, damnit. Because I am not going out of this life without leaving something behind even if it is no more than a damn soap box derby car.

KOOZY: Grammie, you're not going anywhere.

GRAMMIE: Well, Sweetie, I am.

KOOZY: Grammie, no.

GRAMMIE: This afternoon.

KOOZY: Grammie, you're gonna give up . . . this afternoon?

GRAMMIE: Hell no. I'm going in St. Anthony's to have a chemo drip inserted next to my liver.

KOOZY: God, Grammie, not the hospital.

GRAMMIE: Why not?

KOOZY: Because . . . I don't know.

GRAMMIE: Because you're scared I won't come out?

KOOZY: Yeah. *(Pause)* I never even told you I love you.

GRAMMIE: Sweetie, let your fingers do the talking. *(Gives KOOZY a hammer)* And when I come out of St. Anthony's I want to see some progress.

KOOZY: This is so unfair.

GRAMMIE: Well Sweetie, life's like that. *(Gives back the envelope with KOOZY'S savings in it)*

KOOZY: Grammie, please just take the money.

GRAMMIE: Beat the damn odds, Sweetie. *(Pause)* Okay?

KOOZY: *(Pause)* Okay.

GRAMMIE: You got film in that camera?

KOOZY: Yes.

GRAMMIE: Good. *(Poses)* Come on. *(Gives KOOZY a model-ly smile)* Shoot me . . .

(KOOZY aims, clicks, lights bump to black.)

SCENE FIVE

(Early that evening. GLORIA'S radio show comes over the radio. Lights come up on TOM piling tools into open toolboxes. KRAUSBE watches intently.)

GLORIA'S VOICE: . . . got a week and a half to test drive on the official hill and FINE TUNE before the big day . . . And by FINE TUNE I mean both the car and our relationship so that no matter what our differences as Jason EMBARKS on his solo flight across the GREAT EXPANSE OF ADULTHOOD, we will always be friends, we will always have something MEANINGFUL that we can RECALL to remind ourselves that we care, that we love, that we have the EMOTIONAL CAPACITY to share a moment. So,

Jason, if you're listening, give yourself a big hug. Mmmmmmmmmmm-
yum! Now let's go back to our phone lines. And we have Wendy.
Confide in me, Wendy.
 (TOM disappears into the garage for more tools.)
KOOZY'S VOICE: Gloria, I want to EMBARK and EVOLVE with
this person but we have trouble . . . you know . . .
GLORIA'S VOICE: COLLABORATING?
KOOZY'S VOICE: Yes.
 (TOM returns.)
GLORIA: Wendy, I have an INTUITIVE FEELING about you.
Are you married?
KOOZY'S VOICE: No.
GLORIA: Divorced?
KOOZY'S VOICE: No.
GLORIA: Involved with more than this one person?
KOOZY'S VOICE: Yes.
GLORIA: I sensed that, Wendy. Tell me more.
 (TOM clicks off the radio.)
KRAUSBE: Thanks Tom. *(Pause)* HayTom, you throwin' in them
dee-tectors fer good measure?
TOM: For an extra two hundred apiece yeah.
KRAUSBE: Cuck-cuck-cuck . . . Keep 'em. Ya might need ta go
treasure huntin full time, ya don't get that goddamn Gloria in line
down the station.
TOM: You got my cash?
KRAUSBE: That the last of 'em?
TOM: That's all you paid for.
KRAUSBE: Bring 'em around here while I fetch yer money.

 *(KRAUSBE disappears. TOM exits for KRAUSBE'S yard with
the boxes of tools. KOOZY comes through the back door and picks
up a metal detector. She turns it on, sweeps it across the lawn.
It beeps. She hones in on the spot, drops to her knees and probes
with her fingers. She finds a coin, works the dirt off. TOM returns.)*

TOM: Getting your hands dirty. Better go take your fifth shower of
the day.
KOOZY: I'm not gonna fight with you.
TOM: That'd be a first.
KOOZY: I am trying really hard to connect with you, Daddy.
TOM: Probe with a screwdriver, keep your hands clean.
KOOZY: Found a penny.
TOM: Your lucky day.
KOOZY: Nineteen-eighty-six.
TOM: Want me to pitch this shell?

KOOZY: Daddy, I wrote a song for you.

TOM: Maybe later. I want to get this stuff cleaned up.

    (Throws a board in the trash)

KOOZY: The song is like the answer to whether I want you to pitch the car or not.

TOM: Kooz, why don't we try talking to each other first, maybe progress to songs say when you're in your twenties.

KOOZY: I can't believe somebody writes a song and you . . .

TOM: Can I pitch this in the trash bin?

KOOZY: Can you PLEASE listen to my song first?

TOM: Sing.

KOOZY: Why do you have to tell me to sing?

TOM: Because I haven't got all night.

KOOZY: My song is a gift. Why can't you just accept a gift?

TOM: *(Pause)* Okay . . .

KOOZY: Okay. *(Pause)* It's kinda Country 'cause I know Country's your . . . Okay, you haven't got all goddamn night.

    (A Cappella)

Hey, Daddy, you're my old man . . .

gonna tell ya just where I stand

'cause I been feelin like a piece of solid wood

and I been splintered

I been splintered

yeah my heartwood's been splintered good . . .

and maybe your heart's been splintered too

maybe you've been splintered too

but I'm ready for a new beginning

yeah I'm ready to play to win

Hey, Daddy, let's play to win

Hey, Daddy, let's play to win . . .

TOM: Nice.

KOOZY: Thanks.

TOM: Heartwood.

KOOZY: Splinters.

TOM: Splinters . . . Kooz, I'm sorry I'm not . . .

KOOZY: I'm sorry for being so rude yesterday.

TOM: . . . I'm not giving you what you want.

KOOZY: I'm sorry I'm not what you want.

TOM: My Dad never even came to a ballgame.

KOOZY: Never saw you play?

TOM: He thought sports were stupid.

KOOZY: Really?!!

TOM: Maybe next time you do a . . . a . . . you know . . .

KOOZY: Piece.

TOM: Maybe I could come.

KOOZY: You wouldn't hafta.

TOM: Things get straightened out at the station. Gloria. She's having this torrid affair with the station manager.

KOOZY: You're kidding.

TOM: Bob. Gave me the metal detectors. I'll introduce you at the company picnic next month. Mom and The Girls'll be home by then.

KOOZY: I guess I haven't been here for you about work.

TOM: Hey, I haven't been here for you about . . . what?

KOOZY: Everything.

TOM: Everything??

KOOZY: It's okay.

TOM: It's not okay.

KOOZY: Thanks for the metal detector.

TOM: Sure. *(Pause)* Do you want to go out and . . .

KOOZY: Case is coming over.

TOM: Sure. Case. Why not.

KOOZY: Daddy, please don't hate him.

TOM: I don't hate him.

KOOZY: He's really sweet to me.

TOM: Kooz, he ever . . . Or any guy, ever hurts you . . . Tell me. I'll break his legs for you.

KOOZY: Oh thanks.

TOM: Kooz . . . You know what I mean . . .

KOOZY: Daddy, I don't.

TOM: I . . . I want to get back what we used to . . . Kooz, we need to . . . FINE TUNE our relationship.

KOOZY: I agree.

TOM: Kooz, I . . .

KOOZY: Daddy, what?

TOM: I don't know how.

KOOZY: Me neither.

TOM: Yeah . . . So . . . You want to cancel Case? Go metal detecting or take me to a rock concert or . . . or . . .

KOOZY: Daddy, why don't we just try to build the car together.

TOM: The car.

KOOZY: Without fighting.

TOM: I took care of the car.

KOOZY: You built one without me?

TOM: I uhhhh . . . Mister Krausbe . . .

KOOZY: Daddy, what?!

TOM: Mister Krausbe's got the tools.

KOOZY: My tools?!

TOM: Kooz, they're not your tools.

KOOZY: They're supposed to be. One day.

TOM: Yeah. Well.

KOOZY: Daddy, did you trade Mister Krausbe the tools in exchange
for him building the car?

TOM: No.

KOOZY: Daddy, what?! What?!!

TOM: I sort of sold him some of the tools.

KOOZY: You sold my tools?

TOM: Kooz . . .

KOOZY: *(Overlapping)* Daddy, I can't believe you'd do this to me.
And to Grammie.

TOM: I did it for Grammie.

KOOZY: Daddy, she wants the car.

TOM: She wants the oak coffin. Now I've got enough money to pay
for it.

KOOZY: Grammie wants us to build the car together. She wants us
to prove we love each other. She doesn't want to die without her
family being tight.

TOM: You don't care diddly about the car.

KOOZY: I do.

TOM: You don't care diddly about tools.

KOOZY: Daddy, I do. Daddy, we studied the PLANETS together.
We can build a little wooden car that doesn't even have an engine!

TOM: Kooz, these cars are complicated.

KOOZY: Buy the tools back.

TOM: Gloria's team of engineers took two weeks to . . .

KOOZY: Daddy, let's throw some cans. Get him over here. *(Grabs
a bag of cans, starts throwing)* Mister Krausbe! Daddy, he is AL-
WAYS here and now he's gone. Mister Krausbe! *(Climbs atop the
workbench to look into KRAUSBE'S yard)* Come here! He's going
cuck-cuck-cuck. *(Starts to hurl a can, stops just as KRAUSBE
comes into view)*

KRAUSBE: *(Enters)* HayTiger, what-chew doin?

TOM: Mister Krausbe we uhhh . . . need to talk for a second.

KRAUSBE: Yes-sir.

TOM: About the tools.

KOOZY: My tools.

KRAUSBE: Yer tools?

KOOZY: Yeah. One day.

TOM: Can we buy them back?

KRAUSBE: What kinda swindle're you two pullin?

TOM: You said if I changed my mind . . .

KRAUSBE: That's before I had another offer.

KOOZY: Please Mister Krausbe.

KRAUSBE: Fella's gonna trade one a them three-wheeler, battery-
charged Get-Abouts fer the tools.

TOM: I give you the money back you can buy the Get-About.

KRAUSBE: No-sir.

KOOZY: Sure you could.

KRAUSBE: No-sir.

KOOZY: Why not?

KRAUSBE: Take all of the fun outta it, I just pay for it.

KOOZY: Oh my God!!!

TOM: Look, we're gonna have to work round the clock to get this thing finished in time so . . . What the hell do you want?

KRAUSBE: *(Seductively wiggles his eyebrows)* HayTom, you know what I want.

KOOZY: What Mister Krausbe?

KRAUSBE: I got a picture a me EMBARKIN . . .

KOOZY: Embarkin?

KRAUSBE: On a CO-LABOR-ATION.

TOM: Building the car?

KRAUSBE: HayTiger, you got doubts, you ask Hopalong Cassidy.

KOOZY: What if you help build, but you can't come over the fence?

TOM: A consultant.

KOOZY: Adviser.

KOOZY (Melinda Deane) and her father, TOM (Jim Baker), negotiate buying back their tools from next-door-neighbor KRAUSBE (Guy Raymond).

KRAUSBE: And what else?

TOM: What else do you want?

KRAUSBE: HayTiger, you know what I'm after?

KOOZY: The metal detector?

KRAUSBE: Can ya part with it, Tiger?

KOOZY: Daddy?

KRAUSBE: I'll take care of it like it's WILLED ta me.

TOM: He can have mine.

KOOZY: No, he can have mine.   *(Gives* KRAUSBE *the detector)*

TOM: We'll share this one.

KRAUSBE: Thanks, Tom. Ya can pick up yer tools anytime.
   (Exits)

TOM: Can we do this?

KOOZY: Yes.

TOM: Without killing each other?

KOOZY: Daddy, yes.

TOM: Okay. Start planing the rough edges of the body and I'll get
   going on the floorboard again.   *(KOOZY stares at him.)*   What?
   (Pause)   Oh. Okay. Kooz, what do you think we ought to do first?

KOOZY: I'm glad you asked me that question, Daddy. I think I should
   start planing and you should get going on the floorboard.

TOM: Great idea.   *(KOOZY planes.)*

KOOZY: Like this?

TOM: Yeah. That's it. That's it. Feel the wood?

KOOZY: Yes.

TOM: Feel how close to the wood you are?   *(Helping her plane)*

KOOZY: Yes.

TOM: Shape it.

KOOZY: Don't force.

TOM: Right. Don't force.   *(He steps away from* KOOZY *and watches
   her plane by herself.)*   You can make a plane sing if you get in the
   right rhythm.

KOOZY: Really?

TOM: You're doing it right now. Hear it? The plane shaping the wood?

   (Lights fade down on them as KOOZY'S *plane sings.* TOM *and*
   GLORIA'S *radio show fades up simultaneously.)*

SCENE SIX

   (Darkness. We hear Tom on radio.)

TOM'S VOICE: This's Tom Gorman . . .

GLORIA'S VOICE: Along with Gloria Guardhausen . . .

TOM'S VOICE: And before we wrap up I just want to wish you and Jason the best of luck in the race tomorrow, Gloria.

GLORIA'S VOICE: And I hope you and your daughter break your legs, Tom.

TOM'S VOICE: Thanks, Gloria.

GLORIA'S VOICE: Finished your car?

TOM'S VOICE: We think so.

GLORIA'S VOICE: You think so?

TOM'S VOICE: Yeah, we think so. We haven't actually given it a test run yet but we're gonna do that this evening so I'll let you know when I see you in the pits tomorrow.

GLORIA'S VOICE: "In the pits!" Tom, you and your sports expressions are so yummy.

TOM'S VOICE: Yeah . . .

GLORIA'S VOICE: Well, that wraps up "Sports'n'Stuff" for today. Stay tuned for "Love and Learn" with MOI . . .

(Moonlight fades up on the backyard. Late night. TOM, KOOZY and GRAMMIE are looking at the finished car, which has both "McMortenson's Mortuary" and "Koozy's Piece" emblazoned across its mahogany finish.)

GRAMMIE: Now you're sure this brake works?

KOOZY: It does, Grammie.

TOM: Mom, put your helmet on.

GRAMMIE: If it's not dangerous, why do I need a helmet?

KOOZY: *(Helping GRAMMIE with the helmet)* Case and Mister Krausbe are watching for traffic.

GRAMMIE: The wheels are on tight?

TOM: Wheels are on tight.

KOOZY: Ready?

GRAMMIE: *(Climbing into the car)* Sweetie, how can anybody be ready for something like this.

TOM: Krausbe thinks TimBo oughtta take the first run.

GRAMMIE: That's comforting.

KOOZY: Grammie, you don't have to if you don't want to.

GRAMMIE: Sweetie, don't worry about me. *(Looks back at TOM)* Well. *(Gives TOM the thumbs-up sign, then to KOOZY)* Give me the green light.

KOOZY: *(Calling downhill)* All clear?

CASE: *(Offstage)* All clear!

KRAUSBE: *(Offstage)* Yes-sir!

KOOZY: Bon voyage, Grammie.

GRAMMIE: Bon voyage, Sweetie.

(KOOZY gives the car a shove. GRAMMIE rolls downhill.)

GRAMMIE: Yeahhhhhhhhh!!!
ALL: Yeahhhhh!!!

*(TOM and KOOZY watch GRAMMIE disappear down the hill.
THEY turn toward each other. KOOZY runs into TOM'S arms
and hugs him. TOM tentatively hugs KOOZY, then pulls her
tightly to himself in a full embrace. A rollercoaster clacks rapidly
downhill as we hear the joyous screams from the amusement park
in the distance. And the lights fade slowly to black.)*

END OF PLAY

Frank X. Hogan, author of *Koozy's Piece*
Koozy's Piece, selected for production from PrimaFacie III, is the
fourth of Denver playwright Frank Hogan's plays to premiere at
the DCTC. A member of the Playwrights Unit, editor of the DCTC's
1985 and 1986 anthologies of new plays, and a recent Rockefeller
Playwrights-in-Residence Grant recipient, Frank's other plays include *Ringers* (The Source 1984-85), *Pleasuring Ground* (The Source
1986-87), *Denver Messiah* (The Lab 1981-82), *New Kid on the Block*,
Wet Paint and *Little Flames*. His play *One Leaf Falls* was the
winner of the 1986 Marvin Taylor Playwriting Award and opened
at the Sierra Repertory Theatre in Sonora, California.

Veterans Day
Donald Freed

Veterans Day was first performed as a staged reading in *US West's PrimaFacie III*—A Presentation of New American Plays at the Denver Center Theatre Company in March of 1987.

*VETERANS DAY
by Donald Freed

Directed by Laird Williamson

THE CAST—PRIMAFACIE III

Leslie R. Holloway .... Archie Smith
John MacCormick Butts .... James J. Lawless
Walter Kercelik .... Byron Jennings

*originally titled VETS

The Denver Center Theatre Company, Donovan Marley, Artistic Director, presented the World Premiere of *Veterans Day* in the Source Theatre, as part of the DCTC's 1986-87 season, with the following artists:

Directed by Laird Williamson
Scenic and Costume Design by Andrew V. Yelusich
Lighting Design by Daniel L. Murray
Sound Design by Thomas James Falgien
Stage Manager, Paul Jefferson

THE CAST

Leslie R. Holloway, born 1900; "shell shocked" at the
Battle of the Marne, 1918 .... Archie Smith
John MacCormick Butts, 65 years old;
a veteran of World War II .... James J. Lawless
Walter Kercelik, Colonel U.S. Army, 45 years old, the most
highly decorated soldier of the Vietnam war .. James Kiberd

TIME: Veterans Day, the present. The action is continuous from 4:00 p.m.
(The DCTC production was performed without an intermission.)

PLACE: A small day room in a large Veterans Administration Hospital. A military band practices outside.

Veterans Day

(*Veterans Day, the present. The action is continuous from 4 p.m., on Veterans Day, November 11th.*)

(*A small day-room in a large Veterans Administration (V.A.) Hospital. The room is outfitted with old furniture, a vending machine, a water cooler, magazine racks, old books, a piano, a T.V., P.A. speaker, a bulletin board. A waxing machine, a broom, etc. are in one corner. Screens blur some of the bright sunlight. The "fourth wall" is windows looking out on the V.A. grounds below. Old photos and portraits of generals are hung on the walls. There is also a larger-than-life-size highly colored recruitment poster: it pictures Colonel Walter Kercelik beckoning as a modern Uncle Sam. The legend reads "Uncle Sam Wants You!"*)

(LESLIE R. HOLLOWAY *sits motionless in a wheel chair, in a corner, behind a piece of furniture. HE is wrapped in a blanket almost up to his ears. We do not yet notice him. In the distance,*

*a military band is practicing. Then, an announcement over the
P.A. system, as the lights come up.)*

P.A. ANNOUNCEMENT: All volunteer ushers report to Patton
Auditorium for rehearsals at 13:30 hours . . . repeat: All . . .

*(Silence, again, then distant band music. Outside the double
doors we hear the voice of* JOHN M. BUTTS *calling to an orderly,
but we do not see him.)*

BUTTS: *(Off)*   Hey, Dick, hey *paisan*—I'm holding that camper for
you—Huh?
ORDERLY: *(Off)*   You gonna lend me the money?
BUTTS: *(Off)*   You got it. Hey, Dick, does that buy me protection
from you-know-who? *La Coster Nostro*, or whatever the hell it is.
    (Loud laughter, then very close to the door.)
ORDERLY: *(Off)*   . . . bastard, you—hey, hold it down, Holloway's
already in there waitin' for you bastards.
    (BUTTS sticks his head inside the door, still talking.)
BUTTS: Huh? O.K.—Where is he? Are you—oh, yeah, O.K., I see
him. *(Whispering, off)*   I'll see you, *paisan*.

*(Inside the room, BUTTS stands staring over at the figure of
HOLLOWAY in his wheelchair. BUTTS is expensively dressed
in the California style, flashy rings and a watch decorate his
hands. HIS hair is dyed. After a moment HE steps over to the
inert figure in the wheel chair and peers down at HOLLOWAY.)*

BUTTS: How you doin', old timer?—You awake?—Who the hell put
you in the g'damn corner like that—huh?

*(BUTTS wheels HOLLOWAY out into the room. The old man
gives no sign of life. BUTTS sniffs at some odor, then checks his
watch and looks out the window and hums along with the band.)*

"Keep the home fires burning . . ." I bet you remember that one,
don't ya, uh . . .?

*(HE goes over to check the old man's dog tag. The old man
stares out, unmoving.)*

. . . Leslie.—You remember that one— ". . . and the caissons go
rolling along . . ." Huh?—Or was that after your war?

*(The medley ends. In the silence BUTTS roams around the
room, checks the corridor, returns and sits at the piano after*

*studying the Kercelik recruitment poster with wonder. HE tries
the T.V.—it doesn't work; the panel comes off in his hand.)*

Crap . . . I bet I know your favorite.

*(BUTTS plays and sings "Over There." HIS back is to the doors
and HE does not see WALTER KERCELIK enter. KERCELIK
is in full uniform, covered with medals. HE carries a case and
walks with a slight limp. KERCELIK stands ramrod straight
watching and listening, then sings along softly. BUTTS finishes
and swivels around, seeing KERCELIK. Pause.)*

Colonel Kercelik. I recognize your picture. I mean, uh. . . Kercelik?
(HE mispronounces the name (Ker-chē-lik) both times.)
KERCELIK: Yeah. Kercelik.
BUTTS: That's it. Kercelik . . . Geez, you're everywhere! *(Indi-
cating the poster)* C'mon in . . . This young man, here, is, uh,
Leslie R. Holloway, private, uh . . . *(Pulls out a program)*
American Expeditionary Force, uh, "Big Red" Division, uh,
"wounded in the battle of the Marne, July the 21st, 1918."
(Pause) Tore up a Heiney machine gun nest, single-handed.
(Studies program) Uh, they're gonna introduce him right after
me—after I get my special award—Let's see . . . yeah, you're first,
then me, then young private Holloway, here. Then we eat—no, then
the guy from Washington—Espinoza—says a few words, *then* we
eat, then I'm taking some of the brass over to Scotch 'n' Sirloin for
a couple of belts, then who knows?—You're my guest, if you can
make it.
KERCELIK: Thanks.
BUTTS: Name's Jack Butts.
    (THEY shake hands. BUTTS sings an advertising slogan.)
"Oh, John MacCormick Butts has all the cars and trucks . . ."
    (BUTTS goes to piano and sings in full voice.)
Huh? You watch the late movie?—I do my own ads.
    (Repeats refrain)
"Low down payments to Vets!"

    *(BUTTS plays an introduction, then begins his sales pitch try-
ing to stand on his head.)*

I got three guys, help me stand on my head on T.V. . . . "Hi, folks,
this is Ol' Mac Butts, standing on his head to make you an offer.
(Sings) "You can't turn down, You won't turn down, You'll never
turn down." I'll make you the same offer I've been offering any
American veteran since 1952, when we first opened. So come down

to the Sierra Grande exit on the Garden Grove Freeway, day or
night, seven days a week. And you Vets get down here on the double
and help me destroy this incredible inventory. Inventory!—That's
the enemy, Vets—and together we can conquer that enemy, annnd—
  (HE plays and sings to the tune of "Over There.")
"Cars and trucks
Cars and trucks
Cars and trucks
O, the vets are comin!
The vets are comin!
The freeway's hummin' to Jack Butts' . . ."
  (BUTTS laughs and shakes hands again with KERCELIK.)
BUTTS: Well, it don't rhyme but it sells cars, know what I mean?
  And I got three more lots under a different name—"Kilroy's Cars
  and Trucks"—outside a' Long Beach—Yeah, well, hell, it's a living,
  and a lot more, and the best deal in the country for Vets. How 'bout
  you, Colonel, you ready for a trade-in?
KERCELIK: I don't live here.
BUTTS: Makes no difference—"Any Vet, Any Time, Anywhere,"
  that's my slogan. I got the greatest thing goin' since the GI Bill.
  Well, crap, I figure that any hometown boy that ever put his ass on
  the line for Uncle Sam's got a break comin'. I know it sounds corny
  but, well, jeez, you know what I mean. Yassuh! . . . Where you
  stationed, Colonel?
KERCELIK: West Point.
BUTTS: The Point! You, uh—
KERCELIK: I teach there.
BUTTS: You do? What do you, uh—
KERCELIK: Military History.
BUTTS: Uh-huh. Well, that's terrific. Great . . . excuse me a minute
  I just wanna—

  *(BUTTS checks his watch, then exits into the corridor. Alone,
  KERCELIK goes over and stares into the face of the old man in
  the wheelchair. KERCELIK sings a verse softly, along with the
  band music in the distance.)*

KERCELIK: "America, America, God mend thy every flaw, Confirm
  thy soul in self-control, thy liberty in law."
BUTTS: *(Re-enters talking)* Of course, they're runnin' an hour late
  already. I got my Thanksgiving rush, but, no, "Report at 16 hundred
  hours." I coulda told 'em, anything that's got to do with Washington's
  gonna be all fouled up. Ah, well shoot, that's the Army—hurry up
  and wait. *(Nodding to HOLLOWAY)* Anyway, he don't care, do
  ya, young feller? Christ, he's been around these VA joints for, what?

Seventy some odd years. Jesus. Poor bastard. Sixty-five, seventy years, since, uh—well, I just hope he knows his picture'll be on T.V. and all. *(Pause)* Your family gonna' be here to see you get another one?

KERCELIK: No.

BUTTS: *(Reading program)* "Walter Kercelik, Colonel, United States Army . . . the most highly decorated service man of the Vietnam action."—Some "action," huh?—You were on the cover of *Time* magazine, weren't ya?—Sure. Let's face it, old Leslie here and me are just window ressin' for you today. You're the guy on the enlistment posters. I'm only here 'cause I give 'em a hundred thousand bucks a year for special USO entertainment, and I spent two goldarn months here with malaria after I got shipped out of the Philippines . . . And old Leslie, here, figures to crap out any minute—someone said they got a guy from the Spanish-American war back east somewhere, Christ that'd make him—what?—a hundred and somethin'—so they figure they'll pin one more on old Leslie. It'll look good on T.V.—one of us from each war. Of course, Korea, but then, that was a . . . yeah, it'll look good, in the papers, you know, when budget time comes around—yeah. *(Reads program)* "The Battle Hymn of the Republic and a medley of marching songs . . Marine Honor Guard . . . Closing prayer, the Reverend James Lawson . . ." *(Pause)* Your family comin'? No, that's right. My secretary'll be here, and my kid—if he remembers. No, he's on the floor today for the Thanksgiving rush. *(Laughs)* The fuckin' Japs—we dropped the A-bomb on 'em, and now they're back in Long Beach and Garden Grove beatin' the you-know-what out of us all over again. *(Laughs)*

KERCELIK: What?

BUTTS: Cars! I've got three franchises with the biggest inventory of American cars in eight states, and the fuckin' Japs are outsellin' us two to one. It's *crazy!*

KERCELIK: Yeah.

(KERCELIK opens his other case and takes out his full-dress regalia, including: red sash, more medal ribbons, a dress hat, Sam Browne belt, etc. HE begins to dress. BUTTS helps him, wrapping him in the sash, etc.)

It's time.

BUTTS: Oh, boy . . . Here, let me give yuh a hand . . . Here we go—God, you're gonna look great . . . All the trimmins.

(KERCELIK stands on a chair, as BUTTS wraps him in the red sash.)

BUTTS: *(Sings)* "My country 'tis of thee . . ." Gives me a lump in
the throat—this is America. America! And right or wrong, we're
right! Am I right? . . . You know what I can't stand? When they
start clappin' before they finish the "Star Spangled Banner," before
the game. . . Wait—O.K.—there you go! Where's a mirror? Perfect!
Wait, let me get that dust on the shoes. O.K. Now you look like the
poster. Hey, I wanna get your autograph—for my son.
  (Hands over program and pen to KERCELIK to sign)
You're a hero, Colonel, I salute you. You are the last of a kind
. . . *(Then reads)* "Kilroy was here—good luck."—Thanks, Col-
onel, thanks a million.
KERCELIK: Thank you, Mr. Butts. I'm ready now.
  (KERCELIK takes out a small tin container from his case.)
BUTTS: What's that? *(Takes it and reads)* "Imperium Britan-
nicum . . . Christmas 1914"—What is it?
KERCELIK: They put a piece of Christmas cake and tobacco in it,
and sent it to the boys at the front . . . Keep it.
BUTTS: Me?—Jeez, thanks.
  (BUTTS goes to the recruitment poster of KERCELIK.)
God, that looks good! Like a . . . whew!
  (Puts on an American Legion fatigue cap and salutes)
There you go. I could never wear clothes—till a few years ago, here,
I started to get tailor-made. My kid, though—hey, would I like him
to meet you, see what a real man's made of.
  (BUTTS plays softly at the piano. KERCELIK hums.)
"Pack up your troubles . . ." Remember that one? . . . "In your
old kit bag and smile, smile, smile . . ." Can he hear, do you think?
. . . I wonder where his home town was.
KERCELIK: He's from Illinois.
BUTTS: Is that right?
KERCELIK: Downstate. Cairo.
BUTTS: Is that a fact? *(Looks at program)* Where do you see that?
KERCELIK: No, I've just done my homework. That was fishing and
hunting country, in those days.
BUTTS: Oh—Sure. I went big game hunting in Wyoming, here, about
a year ago this Thanksgiving. Took my boy.
KERCELIK: . . . They all knew him. His dad had a little bottomland
farm. There were three boys . . . His mother was from the old
country.
BUTTS: Alfalfa, and all?
KERCELIK: Roger.
BUTTS: Pigs.
KERCELIK: Roger.
BUTTS: Alfalfa—that's hard work. The windrower.
KERCELIK: Click—click—click.

(BUTTS *chuckles.*)
    Alfalfa, hay, corn, pigs, two cows, milk—the old dog, Mike.
BUTTS: Hey, you gotta whichamacallit, a photographic memory!
    (Stares at HOLLOWAY*)*   Do you think he can hear us at all?—Well
    . . . So he was a country boy, huh?
KERCELIK: He was.
BUTTS: A home boy.
KERCELIK: True.
BUTTS: Southern Illinois.
KERCELIK: You been there?
BUTTS: I, myself, personally?
KERCELIK: Uh-huh.
BUTTS: Yeah, I been down there . . . Kinda corny . . .
KERCELIK: Affirmative.

    (HE *plucks a few notes on the piano, of the traditional hymn,*
    "Up in My Father's House.")

    "Oh, it's joy, joy, joy up in my Father's House . . ."
    (BUTTS *is affected, singing along.*)
BUTTS: God, that's an old one, Colonel.
KERCELIK: That it is, Sergeant.
    (BUTTS *reacts.*)
BUTTS: Sergeant? . . . You guessed right—forty g'damn years
    ago.   *(Long pause)*   So he was a country boy, huh?

KERCELIK (James Kiberd) and BUTTS (James J. Lawless) sing softly at
the piano, while HOLLOWAY (Archie Smith) remains motionless in his wheel-
chair.

KERCELIK: Roger.
BUTTS: A hay-shaker.   *(At the piano, slow and soft. KERCELIK
joins in.)*   "How you gonna keep 'em down on the farm, after they've
seen Paree . . ."

> *(Silence. All three men staring out—their thoughts far away.
> Then BUTTS rises and checks the corridor, returns and crosses
> to the windows. HE belches.)*

Excuuuuuuuuuse me.

> *(BUTTS stares out the window, checks his watch, consults his
> program, sprays with a breath product, hums an old war song,
> marches about to the music.)*

Hup-hup-hup-hup . . .!   *(Etc.)*   "There's a silver lining . . ." Says
you're gonna lay a wreath—Last year there was a couple of Vietnam
vets on a hunger strike over there. They had to drag 'em out before
we could march over to give the salute.   *(Stares out window)*   Fuckin' Jane Fondas hang out in that garden and they—
KERCELIK: Where?
BUTTS: Down there. They're supposed to plant vegetables and stuff
to—I helped raise money, for 'em, with the Christmas show—yeah, .
but they're growin' stuff to give to a Catholic charity that's feedin'
the bums down in the bay area.
KERCELIK: They do?
BUTTS: Yeah, right over there. See those guards in the tan shirts—
None of that madness today.   *(HE sings and dances "I'll Get By.")*
. . . Spencer Tracy . . .

> *(KERCELIK sits and opens his briefcase in order to look at
> several documents. BUTTS wanders to the piano and picks out
> a few bars of patriotic gore. Then he goes to the soft drink machine.)*

Wanna Coke?
KERCELIK: Thanks.
BUTTS: I need some food. That banquet's gonna make me puke. I
know it— Gas . . . My stomach's never been the same since the
Pacific. Very delicate . . . C'mon!
> *(Machine eats BUTTS' coins but does not function.)*
I shoulda got some disability but they said it was all in my head,
but I know my stomach and it was never the same after the war.
So when these kids from Vietnam talk about this "Agent Orange" I
give 'em the benefit of the doubt, know what I mean?
> *(KERCELIK smiles and nods.)*

I mean some of 'em . . . a lot of 'em are NG, bums, protestors, long hair— *(Laughs)* from the back you can't tell if they're male or shemale— *(HE pounds the machine.)* C'mon—Dr. Garabedian, over here, he won't let 'em even say the words.

KERCELIK: What words?

BUTTS: "Agent Orange"—You believe in it, or you think it's all, uh, mental?

KERCELIK: I believe it's "mental"—

BUTTS: You do? So do I.

KERCELIK: And physical.

BUTTS: Yeah, me too—But you didn't, uh, you weren't, uh . . .

KERCELIK: Exposed to it?

    (KERCELIK plugs in and uses an electric razor.)

BUTTS: Yeah.

KERCELIK: I was.

BUTTS: You were?

KERCELIK: Roger.

BUTTS: No kidding. You don't look it. I mean, you look like . . . a poster.

KERCELIK: It's all inside—It works on your inside.

BUTTS: On the inside? *(Feels his own gut)*

KERCELIK: Roger—Inside, I'm about, ah, two-hundred-years old. *(HE smiles.)*

BUTTS: Well, you look like the All-American boy to me. *(Laughs)* Now, you're puttin' me on, Colonel. That's a good one. Two hundred years old—that'd make you older than Pop, here.

    (BOTH laugh.)

Don't think they can't drive you nuts over here, in these hospitals, because they *can!* *(Shakes machine)*

KERCELIK: They can?

BUTTS: Alright, count to ten, now. I'm gonna give you one more chance. *(Anger rising)* Do you know how much money I've raised to fix up these stinking recreation rooms? Forget it. *(Walks away, then pounding the machine)* Do you know how many tax deductible items I've gotten donated to this joint? Fuck it! *(Walks away, then kicking the machine.)* They don't care—they don't care whether these poor bastards here *live or die!* Nothing works here! *(Screaming)* Phonies! Fucking phonies—nothing works here and nobody cares!

KERCELIK: Easy! Who don't care?

BUTTS: The VA, Washington, the government—they *don't care!* *(Exhausted)* That's why us guys, the "Private Sector," has to do everything—*Everything.* That's why I'm out raising dough for these poor bastards here, twelve months a year. Never take a vacation. Wrecked my marriage—"Why don't you go and live there at the

Hospital," she said—Tried to get my kid involved . . . Phonies.
Period. Buncha phonies.
KERCELIK: Who?
BUTTS: All of 'em.

*(A sweeping gesture, including an old dusty picture of General
Pershing.)*

KERCELIK: You're right. *(Pause)* Who's that walking over
there?—Is that Jane Fonda?
BUTTS: *(Jumps to the window)* Where?!—Huh?
KERCELIK: Over there . . . No. No, it's one of the nurses. My
mistake.
BUTTS: Huh?—Crap.
        (Pause. BUTTS goes to the piano.)
"Someday I'm gonna moider da bugler . . ."
KERCELIK: *(Cutting under)* "Someday I'm going to murder him
dead . . ." ·
BUTTS: *(Looks, then cheerfully)* "And then I'll get that other
pup . . ."
KERCELIK: "The one that wakes the bugler up . . ."
BUTTS: "And like Pop, here, *(Referring to HOLLOWAY)* We'll
spend the rest of our life in bed!"
        (Pause. BUTTS stares at HOLLOWAY.)
Hey, old man wake up. "It's a long way to Tipperary, it's a long
way to go . . ." *(Pause)* Last year, what's-his-name, from Gre-
nada, laid the wreath . . . you divorced?
KERCELIK: Mmm?
BUTTS: No, didn't they make a T.V. movie out of you bein' a POW,
or was that—you were on "60 Minutes," too, weren't ya—that Mike
Wallace, that slimey son-of-a-bitch, those New York pricks lost the
war for us—am I right? I mean you oughta know—while you guys
were rotting in a concentration camp.
KERCELIK: Viet Nam?
BUTTS: Huh?—That whole Kennedy crowd of queers and hippies.
I had two dealerships from '66 on and we had the MIA/POW office
in the—after '71, I gave 'em space, the wives, we musta passed out
a million bracelets "POW/MIA"—And of course, the VFW and the
Legion, and we had "Vets for Viet Nam," so we were behind you
all the way. My kid had a college deferment, but he had a POW/MIA
table right out in front of the ROTC building at Long Beach State,
so—but I wish now that he'd gone in because it might've made a
man out of him—

*(BUTTS is interrupted by an announcement over the P.A. sys-
tem:)*

P.A. ANNOUNCEMENT: Attention, all administrative staff, attention, all administrative staff: report to Patton Auditorium imediately.
Attention, all security staff, report to the auditorium immediately—
immediately.

*(Sound of running from the corridor. There is a bang on the
double door and the sound of the ORDERLY'S VOICE shouting.)*

ORDERLY'S VOICE: Hey, Mac, he's comin', he's comin'!
BUTTS: Now what?—Keerist!

*(BUTTS runs out. The band starts up, again, with "Hail to the
Chief." KERCELIK limps to the window to watch. Sounds of
police sirens and helicopters flood the room. Sirens and sounds
build, the P.A. blares.)*

*(KERCELIK stares out. HE takes out binoculars from case.
HIS lips begin to twist and move. HIS curses are drowned out by
the noise. BUTTS runs back in, shouting.)*

He's comin', the President's comin'! Holy Cow! He's comin' to give
us the medals. It's Katy-bar-the-door! The Secret Service is all over
the g'damn hospital to—
KERCELIK: What? What did you say?
BUTTS: The President! The fuckin' President—to give us the medals!
He'll be here in an hour, I gotta call my boy!

*(BUTTS rushes out. Slowly the noise subsides, leaving only the
sound of the band in the distance. KERCELIK steps into the
corridor, then returns to stare at the motionless old man, HOLLO-
WAY. KERCELIK speaks quietly in HOLLOWAY'S ear.)*

ORDERLY'S VOICE: Security report to the Wilshire entrance—security report to the . . .
KERCELIK: Private Holloway?—Sir? Can you hear me? . . .

*(KERCELIK slips out a small gun from his briefcase, puts it
in the old man's hand, and tucks it under HOLLOWAY'S blanket,
just as BUTTS re-enters.)*

BUTTS: This place's gone nuts! Get the old man ready. The place's
crawlin' with Secret Service and LAPD—It's you, brother.
KERCELIK: What?
BUTTS: *You!* They're all saying the President wants his first official
picture after the election with *you.* You're money in the bank. You

know, if you wanted to, you could probably run for Governor or even—what's the matter, is the old man awake?
KERCELIK: No.
BUTTS: Hey, wake up, Private!

KERCELIK (James Kiberd) waits for BUTTS to return after planting gun on HOLLOWAY (Archie Smith).

(At the piano, BUTTS sings and plays Irving Berlin's, "You Gotta Get Up In The Morning" . . . Pause.)

KERCELIK: Leave him alone.
BUTTS: Aw, hey, this is the biggest day of his life, for God's sake.

(Sirens and helicopters in, again, then quiet except for the band in the distance. Then:)

KERCELIK: Biggest day—of our lives.
BUTTS: Sure!

(Sound of running in the corridor, then silence. The band is silent.)

KERCELIK: Security.

BUTTS: And how! Christ, if he ain't safe at the VA, he ain't safe anywhere. Am I right?

KERCELIK: You're right—

BUTTS: G'damn right—

KERCELIK: He ain't safe anywhere.

BUTTS: Huh?

KERCELIK: The Commander-in-Chief—he's not safe anywhere. Especially here.

(Pause)

BUTTS: He's not?

KERCELIK: Hell, no.

BUTTS: No?—How come?

KERCELIK: Think about it.

BUTTS: Huh?

KERCELIK: You have a hospital full of men.

BUTTS: Yeah.

KERCELIK: Each one—torn up by war.

BUTTS: Yeah.

KERCELIK: By the Commander-in-Chief. . . So any one of them's liable to carve him up.

BUTTS: Who?

KERCELIK: The Commander-in-Chief.

BUTTS: Wait a minute. Who's the Commander-in-Chief?

KERCELIK: The President?

BUTTS: The President!?

KERCELIK: Right.

(Band starts, again, in the distance. BUTTS *tries to change the subject.)*

BUTTS: The freeway'll be gridlocked now with the motorcade and my kid'll be trying' to jump the railing . . . *(Laughs)* You're not serious are ya, about . . . Naw, they got the psychos here so doped up they can't even find the head to take a crap. I mean, this is the safest place on earth for him. You ever seen the whole place? The ones that ain't doped up are drunk—I mean we got hot dogs around here that'll say anything—One guy, they call him "Nigger Nate," swears that his platoon—*(Laughs)*—uh, they, uh, that they ate human flesh in Korea! *(Wipes his eyes and nose, and sighs deeply)* Christ, I bring the comics and showgirls out here every year for Christmas and the poor bastards can't even clap their hands right. I mean we had Bob Hope here a couple years ago, and one guy fell asleep and fell out of his wheelchair—it was pathetic. Boy, was Hope ever sore. *(Pause)*

KERCELIK: They might get *him*, too.

BUTTS: Who, Bob Hope? *(Laughs)*

KERCELIK: Why not?

BUTTS: Colonel, you're a comedian yourself. You're what they call a poker-face comedian—*(Laughs and checks his watch)*—Listen to that band—gives you a thrill, don't it? *(HE hums along.)*

KERCELIK: "Military music is to music what military justice is to justice."
        (Pause)

BUTTS: You're terrific. You gonna tell jokes when you make your speech? They'll love it. *(Laughs)* I'll never forget Milney Bay, in New Guinea, I was in charge of all the USO talent. We had Hope and Crosby, all of 'em, and the chorus girls. Oh boy! Ten thousand dog faces—screaming with laughter, and tryin' to reach up and touch some of that pin-up pussy, boy-oh-boy! *(HE hums along with the band.)* And the parties at the Officer's Club afterwards! Of course, I had to chaperone the talent—and just between you and me, Colonel, we went through all that fine pussy like a dose of salts. I mean these were *movie stars*—that was *"eatin' pussy"*—and the brass and the big stars, they drank and they drank, and *they ate that starlet pussy all night*! And I was just a kid—my eyes were poppin' outta my head.

   (BUTTS roars with laughter, throws himself at the piano and launches into the chorus of "Praise the Lord and Pass the Ammunition." "Praise the Lord and pass the starlet pussy—All aboard, it's so nice and juicy." KERCELIK cuts in.)

KERCELIK: New Guinea?

BUTTS: Goodenough Island is where I started, then Woodlark and Morsby, all around there, Abau Island—but we worked the USO shows out of Brisbane and Sydney. It was big-time, I'm talking Broadway producers, Hollywood big shots, stars—and I ran the nuts and bolts, Generals called *me* to get good seats for their friends and get fixed up with the starlets—I'm gonna tell you something: I've made a couple of million dollars since then, but in terms of *fun*—nothing but I mean nothin' even comes close to the war.

   (BUTTS sings and pounds out a few bars of "Don't Sit Under the Apple Tree." Then silence.)

KERCELIK: When did you get your wound?

BUTTS: Huh?

KERCELIK: Your wound.

BUTTS: Oh—Well, musta been around Luzon . . . Dengue, uh, you know, malaria . . . Fuckin' Luzon—lyin' there crazy with Dengue, listenin' to that cunt Tokyo Rose . . . Yeah, so, anyway, I was out of the USO, in Luzon, and we were movin' out of Okinawa for staging and then we were goin' in, invading Japan, and then they dropped the A-bomb. And that was it: I'm alive today because of the bomb When I got back here the fever started up again so I checked in here a while, got to know the brass, looked up some of my old USO buddies from Hollywood . . .

KERCELIK: But you missed it, didn't you?

BUTTS: What?

KERCELIK: The war.

BUTTS: Well . . . You know how it is. "Uncle Sam Wants You!" And you're scared to death, but then . . . Well, you're just a kid and it's like there's no tomorrow. I mean, you're all in it together, and the money flows and the liquor flows and you don't think about tomorrow . . . But I mean, that's when you're on leave or R. and R.—When you're back in the line it's hell. Then it's hell.

KERCELIK: War is hell?

BUTTS: You know, like they say.

KERCELIK: I know—But I've seen ordinary men, like you, when they were fighting for their lives, blind with blood, going under direct fire to save their buddies—calling their names, sobbing—

BUTTS: *(Overlapping)* It's hell.

KERCELIK: Sobbing—with love.

BUTTS: Love?

KERCELIK: Affirmative. Because they had never before and never would again feel anything like that comradeship . . .

BUTTS: Oh . . . Well, yeah—sure. They were, uh—

KERCELIK: Happy.

BUTTS: Well . . .

KERCELIK: They were happy—Because before that, and after that, they were nothing.

BUTTS: Yeah . . . Drinking up their pensions, walkin' the streets, screaming in their sleep—nothing . . . you know, it's funny—my old man—he was in the first war—told me that they'd've shot their own officers if they—when the Yanks and Heinies, at Christmas time, came up out of their trenches and sang songs together . . . one time, at Christmas time . . . they'd have shot their own officers . . . but I figured that was the old man's liquor talkin'.

KERCELIK: No. That was the mutinies.

BUTTS: Oh . . . Yeah, maybe . . . The what?

KERCELIK: The mutinies.

BUTTS: Hey, pretty soon, now. Let's see, where's my speech?

(Finds HIS *speech)*   Here we are: "Mr. Espinoza, Colonel Kercelik, Dr. Garabedian, Congressman Levy . . ." Crap. It's not gonna be any good. Now if I could stand on my head and do it.   *(HE tries.)* "Mr. President, Colonel Kercelik, uh, Dr. Frankenstein—"
    *(*BOTH *men laugh.)*
Blah, blah, blah—What're you gonna say?
KERCELIK: Something about the Unknown Soldier. *(Takes a plastic encased paper from his briefcase)* "Dear Ma . . . the cannon exploded . . . the trees caught on fire, it was a sheet of flame . . . and then the mules caught fire . . ."
BUTTS: No, jeez, don't read that. We gotta keep it upbeat. I mean, no disrespect but it's like the President said on T.V., "America's Back on Top Again"—something like that. So tell one of your jokes, lighten it up. Know why I voted for him? Because he started out as a salesman, like me. Like you—I mean, this poster is big time—you're sellin' America!
    *(*KERCELIK *takes out another paper.)*
KERCELIK: "Dear Pop and Laurie . . . Last night we sat around the camp fire and sang songs until . . ." *(Pause)*
BUTTS: Yeah, well, that's a little better . . . *(Picks at piano)* "Tenting tonight, tenting tonight . . ."
    *(*KERCELIK *joins in, softly.)*
KERCELIK: "Many are the boys who are dying tonight, Dying on the old campground . . ." I've got more.
BUTTS: No, no, that'll be perfect.
    (The sound of helicopter draws BUTTS to the window.)
Official! I bet they're gonna put marksmen on the roofs. Won't be long now.
    *(*KERCELIK *joins him at the window.)*
KERCELIK: Yeah . . . But that's not going to do him any good.
BUTTS: Well, you know, ever since Dallas—the Secret Service fouled up the—
    *(*THEY *overlap the following.)*
KERCELIK: The Secret Service was hungover and half drunk in Dallas—
BUTTS: —Yeah, that's what I—
KERCELIK: —But that wouldn't of saved him, because—
BUTTS: Who Kennedy?—
KERCELIK: —Because he was a dead man, and they—
BUTTS: Well, I never believed all that garbage about—
KERCELIK: —They would have got him in Miami or New Orleans or they—
BUTTS: —I always said that, what's-his-name, I swore was a—
KERCELIK: *—They could have got him in L.A.!*

(BUTTS is stopped by the bitter intensity of KERCELIK'S tone. BUTTS turns from the window to stare at KERCELIK. Silence)

BUTTS: . . . What 'ya mean?

P.A. ANNOUNCEMENT: Captain Dean, please report to Administration. Captain Dean, please report to Administration.

KERCELIK: The guys on the roof can't help him. *(Pause)* He's going to get it from three feet away. *(Pause)* From the head table. *(Pause, band music in the distance)* Private Holloway. *(Pause)*

BUTTS: The old man?

(KERCELIK nods, then walks over to HOLLOWAY, pulls open the old man's blanket to reveal the gun that he, KERCELIK, has planted in the old man's hand. BUTTS comes over to stare at the gun, than at HOLLOWAY, and, finally, at KERCELIK.)

BUTTS: You're kidding.

KERCELIK: What?

BUTTS: You gotta' be kidding.

KERCELIK: Why?

BUTTS: Hold it, Colonel, I mean like you don't kid about bombs when you're standing in line waitin' to get on a plane. *(Pause)* You can't kid about, uh, terrorism or, uh . . . not these days, you don't.

KERCELIK: You think Private Holloway is kidding?

BUTTS: C'mon, Colonel, the old man's out of it, he's a vegetable, he hasn't opened his eyes in ten years, they feed him through a straw— You gotta be kidding, I know you're not drunk—are ya?

KERCELIK: No.

BUTTS: I know you're not . . . C'mon, Colonel, we better go and see if they want us to—

KERCELIK: I'm not drunk. And Private Holloway, he's not drunk— And he's not crazy.

BUTTS: I don't believe this. Maybe I'm crazy. *Somebody's* crazy!

KERCELIK: Roger that. The Commander-in-Chief . . .

BUTTS: The President?

KERCELIK: The Commander-in-Chief.

BUTTS: What about him?

KERCELIK: Private Holloway states that the Commander is a homicidal maniac, and Private Holloway's going to shoot him down, like a mad dog—that's what he just told me.

(BUTTS stares, then starts to walk toward the door. KERCELIK moves quickly to block his way. The band music stops. Pause)

BUTTS: It's not loaded—The gun.

KERCELIK: Of course it's loaded.

BUTTS: Naw, one of the psychos musta planted it on him for a gag.
—How did you know he had it?—I get it—you thought was loaded.
(Laughs) Here, I'll prove it to you. Poor old bastard.
     (BUTTS *starts towards the wheelchair.)*

KERCELIK: Watch out or he'll shoot *you.*

BUTTS: Naw, it's a gag, he's in a coma, for Christ's sake—

KERCELIK: No. He's not—He's faking. He's been faking for fifty
years. Waiting for his chance.

BUTTS: Nooo!

KERCELIK: It's true. He told me.

BUTTS: He told you?

KERCELIK: Roger.

BUTTS: He *told* you?

KERCELIK: That's right. He told me all about it.

BUTTS: I don't believe it. What?

KERCELIK: He told me . . .

BUTTS: When?

KERCELIK: While you were running back and forth chasing that
parade out there.
     (Pause)

BUTTS: O.K.—What'd he say, then?

KERCELIK: Well . . . Let's move over here.

BUTTS: What for?

KERCELIK: He's resting now.

BUTTS: He looks exactly the same to me.

KERCELIK: No. All the talking's worn him out.

BUTTS: Well, Christ, I was only gone for about a minute.

KERCELIK: Keep it down. Come over here if you want me to tell
you what he said. I think it's important for you to hear this.

     *(A suspicious BUTTS studies KERCELIK and HOLLOWAY,
     then slowly joins KERCELIK, away from the old man. KER-
     CELIK talks in a low intensive tone so as not to wake HOLLO-
     WAY.)*

KERCELIK: You've never spent any time here, have you?—I mean
on the permanent wards.

BUTTS: What?

KERCELIK: Keep your voice down—You come here at Christmas,
right?

BUTTS: Right. Why?—I spent a month here when I—

KERCELIK: I know, but that's it. I'm talking about the custodial
wards.

BUTTS: What about it?

KERCELIK: Unless you know the ward life, here, you can't understand where Private Holloway's coming from.

BUTTS: Well, what about it?

KERCELIK: O.K. The first thing's the food. They ran an experimen-
tal program here for some of these long-term "shell-shock" cases—
this was thirty, forty years ago—I know this for a fact, and they
loaded 'em up with Librium and Valium. Now when you mix Valium
and Librium you're turning a man into a time bomb.

*(Sound of sirens and helicopters again. BUTTS moves away
towards the window. KERCELIK crosses to the doors and locks
them. BUTTS reacts.)*

BUTTS: Hey, we better go and find out what's going on.

KERCELIK: No. I think we better decide what to do about Private
Holloway, first.

BUTTS: Huh?

KERCELIK: Do we turn him in, report him, warn the Secret Service?—Or do we cover for him? Except we have problems with each
of those choices, don't we? . . . Anyway, let me finish telling you
what he said.

*(KERCELIK stands blocking the locked double-doors. The
noise fades slightly. Confused, BUTTS pretends to be looking out
the window.)*

BUTTS: Yeah, yeah, go ahead, I'm listenin'—there's a bunch of T.V.
trucks down there. They're gonna tear up the garden—O.K.—hurry
up, will ya?

KERCELIK: Yeah. Well, you understand that they keep 'em all on
Lithium and Thorazine?

BUTTS: Yeah, so?

KERCELIK: Well, that slows everything down.

BUTTS: Yeah.

KERCELIK: Way down—So ten years—when you're on that kind
of medication—is like a month to you or me. *(Pause)* You know—
like in the *Bible*.

BUTTS: What's that?

KERCELIK: The *Bible*. Remember? "And Abraham lived eight
hundred years." *(Pause)*

BUTTS: Oh, you mean, uh—

KERCELIK: Methusalah lived, mm, "nine hundred years"—you remember that?

BUTTS: I'm a Methodist.

KERCELIK: Yeah, well . . .

BUTTS: Well, I know all about it—the first war—my old man was
  with the Marine Brigade at Belleau Wood. Used to get plastered
  and act out the whole g'damn battle. Always called it the "Big War,"
  or the "Great War."

KERCELIK: What'd he tell you?

BUTTS: Said it was nauseating—stale mustard gas hangin'
  everywhere, and they were covered with lice—the old man used to
  dance around when he got loaded, laughin' and scratchin' . . .
  (Dances) They had a helluva time, he said.

KERCELIK: Not so loud—I know, it was on June 23rd—Belleau
  Wood.

BUTTS: It was? My old man?

KERCELIK: Yeah. They went in after dark, your father and the
  Third Battalion—What else did he tell you?

BUTTS: Nothin' much. Just, you know, uh, it was—

KERCELIK: A slaughter . . . There was a cold rain, that morning
  . . . The Germans started pouring high explosive and toxic shells
  on top of them and the Marines got disoriented, caught in the middle
  between the French snipers and the German cannon. The noise—the
  screams and the concussion of the guns: you know, when the blood
  drains out of you, you lose control—and the Doughboys crawled back
  through their own blood and waste.
  (Pause)

BUTTS: Jesus. I never heard any of that.

KERCELIK: That was Belleau Wood—Your father.

BUTTS: Jesus. You sure know your history, don't you?

KERCELIK: He was very lucky, your father.

BUTTS: Yeah, I guess so. He got to come home and drink himself
  to death in one of these joints. *(Pause)* So, anyway, what about
  the old guy, here?

KERCELIK: The point—if I get it—is that Private Holloway's
  operating on the fact that he's only been here about six months—To
  him—the war's still going on and any day now he's going to "buy
  the farm."
  (Pause)

BUTTS: You mean he, uh—

KERCELIK: He's going to get killed any day now—like all his buddies—So he figures his only chance is to join one of the mutinies.

BUTTS: Mutinies?

KERCELIK: Sure. You know about that, don't you?

BUTTS: The mutinies? When? In the Navy?

KERCELIK: No. The Army.

BUTTS: The Army?

KERCELIK: Right. It started with the French and English—on the

Western Front. After Flanders and Verdun, after they lost all their boys. Sixty thousand a day until they ran out of boys—420,000, alone, in the battle of the Somme—That's when the French began to kill their officers . . . This is what was going on when your father and Private Holloway and the Doughboys landed in 1917. They saw it all: units, detachments, battalions buried alive in their trenches by the German shells—So, it was a terrible shock to the old man.

BUTTS: Which old man?

KERCELIK: All of them.

(Pause)

BUTTS: He told you all this stuff?

KERCELIK: And it's all true.

BUTTS: All while I was out in the hall?

(KERCELIK nods.)

It's crazy.

KERCELIK: *(With great quiet staccato)*   No. It's *true* . . . You see, at first, he said, they paid no attention. The Doughboys were gung-ho—they wanted to kill Germans. That's all they wanted, all they thought about—And they did. They did. The French were stalled, wouldn't fight, but the Americans just threw themselves on the Germans. Went right straight ahead, wiping out one machine gun nest after another, and when they ran out of ammunition, finishing 'em off with bayonets and pick-axes hand to hand. Unbelievable! And Private Holloway was in the middle of it with his whole company—M Company, 9th Infantry—You get the picture?

(Pause)

BUTTS: When was all this?

KERCELIK: Hm? I think he said it was November, 1917. Yeah. Three o'clock in the morning—snow on the ground—you could see your breath—all hell broke loose. He said a German assault company stormed down on them, blasting with Bangalore torpedoes. It was all over in three minutes—pistols, bayonets, knives. Three of his buddies died at his feet: Corporal James B. Gresham, Private Thomas F. Enright, and Private Merle D. Hay.—But they held, the Doughboys held.

BUTTS: *(Softly)*   They did?

(KERCELIK nods.)

Jesus!

KERCELIK: Yeah. The "Big Red One" held. And there were more slaughters, worse than that. Much worse.

(Pause)

BUTTS: The big red one?

KERCELIK: The 1st Division—they wore a big red number "one" on their shoulder patches.

(HE rubs BUTTS' shoulder.)

BUTTS: Oh . . . My pop was attached to the 3rd Army. I don't even
know what division.

KERCELIK: "Black Horse."

BUTTS: Huh?

KERCELIK: Your pop fought with the old 84th—they called it the
"Black Horse."
　　(Pause)

BUTTS: Yeah . . . Seems like I remember somethin' like that . . .
You know, he told me once that all the crap on Veterans Day,
Armistice Day, Poppy Day, you know sellin' poppies like they used
to, and, uh, droppin' bags a water out of the window of the Muhlbach
Hotel in K.C., uh, whenever they had the old Legion conventions,
goosin' the girls with the electric canes and the "joy buzzers," the
shockers . . . the old man told me that all they ever cared about,
really, was each other and all the hell they'd been through. Oh, sure,
the flag and all, but . . . I can still smell his breath . . .

KERCELIK: They cared about each other. They understood. No one
else.

BUTTS: That was it. Period. That's what my poor ol' crazy drunk
of a pop said . . . *(Very sadly)* Today it's different. Oh, yeah—
that's why I joined AA.

KERCELIK: Why?

BUTTS: I was always scared I might get to be like my old man.
(Shudders and uses breath spray)   Anyway, fuck it.

KERCELIK: So the "Big Red One" was relieved and they fell back
around Base 8 Hospital at Savenay, and that's where Private Holloway learned the song. Boys without jaws, with no bodies at all—
monsters—singing the song.

BUTTS: What song?

　　*(KERCELIK sings softly to the tune of "In the Good Old Sum-
　　mertime.")*

KERCELIK: "In the base at Savenay,
Where the sick and wounded lay,
Running up their temperatures,
More and more each day . . ."
　　(HE smiles. Pause.)
So that's our problem. Private Holloway is still back on the base at
Savenay in the field hospital—in his mind.
　　(Pause)

BUTTS: You're on the level, aren't ya?—Or are ya?—You got me
goin' now—You know what they say about salesmen—well, you
coulda been one helluva salesman—no wonder they got you on that
poster! Because you're Uncle Sam's number one salesman . . .

Yeah. *(Laughs)* You tell a great war story, Colonel. *(Crosses towards the door)*

KERCELIK: At ease, Mr. Butts. I promised Private Holloway that none of us would leave here until we took a vote on what to do about the "problem."

BUTTS: Promised—Vote?

KERCELIK: Shhh. I gave him my word.

BUTTS: O.K., now, Colonel—I mean—we know some of the great horseshit artists in this world are in the U.S. Army. And in my racket—shit, I *am* the greatest horseshit artist since Mad Man Muntz—remember him?—But I mean this stuff you're feedin' me makes the grass grow green. *(Laughs)*

(KERCELIK unlocks the doors.)

KERCELIK: It's up to you.

(BUTTS crosses slowly.)

But you have to know that Private Holloway intends to shoot him in the face at point blank range—Look, here's the Commander-in-Chief. *(Placing the recruitment poster)* Here's you—me—and Private Holloway, here. *(Moving wheelchair)*

(BUTTS stops.)

And the Secret Service—the S.S.—is going to open up. And you'll be standing there right next to the Private, right *in* the line of fire. In the crossfire.

(KERCELIK steps away from the doors. BUTTS is utterly baffled.)

BUTTS: Now, look, Colonel—whatever this is—I am not involved. Period.

KERCELIK: Well, I'm sorry, Mr. Butts, but both of us are going to be standing there, right in the line of fire—Private Holloway says that he is not taking any casualities today—and neither will the Security Services. A *hail* of bullets. Period.

(Pause)

BUTTS: Wait a minute. O.K., O.K., then, let's take the g'damn gun away from him, while he's asleep, before he gets us all killed.

(Band music up. BUTTS starts to walk slowly toward the wheelchair . . . BUTTS is advancing on the old man. KERCELIK'S voice is a hoarse whisper.)

KERCELIK: Hold it.—That won't work.

(Helicopter rockets in, freezing the action.)

BUTTS: *(Shouting over the din)* Why not?*

(Silence)

---

*(If desired, break the first act at this point.)

KERCELIK: They'll find the gun on you, when they search us—before the ceremony.

BUTTS: Huh?

KERCELIK: They're going to search everybody before they let the Commander-in-Chief in here   *(Pause)*   Don't wake him up, now, he might start shooting. Come over here and we'll figure something out.—Come on.

(Slowly, BUTTS *joins* KERCELIK. *Sounds of helicopters and sirens)*

BUTTS: This is getting out of hand, here.

KERCELIK: I know—Where do you stand?

BUTTS: What'ya mean? We got to take the gun away from him.

KERCELIK: Look, let me lay it out for you! If you get the gun away from Private Holloway—I say "if" because he's got the reflexes of a twenty-year-old man, don't let that act he's putting on fool you— "if," then they are going to hassle us about whose gun it is, until hell won't have it—They're going to say it's yours. I mean, they are not going to believe us—that the gun belongs to Private Holloway— are they?

BUTTS: *(Pause)*   No . . . But they know me here! I know all the shots—all the big shots. I've raised more than a million dollars—

KERCELIK: *(Overlapping)*   That cuts no ice with the DIA. I know these people, you don't.

BUTTS: Who?—No, but're ya tryin' to tell me that these guys—I don't care how gung-ho they are—are gonna try to give *you* a hard time?—I mean, God, look at you, you're Uncle Sam's pride and joy. They know you. After today, the President's gonna make you a General, for Christ's sake!

KERCELIK: Hold it down—You see, Mr. Butts, it doesn't work that way. Wait a second—O.K., I'm going to tell you how it works. You've known G2 and CID people?

BUTTS: Sure, yeah, of course—buncha pricks, but they're not gonna—

KERCELIK: *(Overlapping)*   Wait—We're talking about way beyond the old G2 or CID or CIC or any of the old military intelligence groups. We're not even talking about the Secret Service—they are just here for show, they've been out of it since Dallas.

BUTTS: What are we talkin' about then?

KERCELIK: The DIA and NSA.

BUTTS: The CIA?

KERCELIK: The DIA, Defense Intelligence Agency. The National Security Agency.

   (Pause)

BUTTS: Well, so what?—They know who we are.

KERCELIK: That's the catch.

BUTTS: What?

KERCELIK: Well—you see, they don't go by these. *(Indicating his medals)* Or by your television commercials, or even by your Christmas shows you put on here.

BUTTS: They don't?

KERCELIK: No, they don't.

BUTTS: Well, then, what in the fuck do they go by?

KERCELIK: There you go! Now you're starting to read me loud and clear.

BUTTS: I am?

KERCELIK: Roger.

BUTTS: What'ya mean?—The, uh, the DI, uh—

KERCELIK: DIA.

BUTTS: They got something on, uh—

KERCELIK: On me. Roger.

BUTTS: On you?

KERCELIK: That's a Roger—And on you.
    (Pause)

BUTTS: Me? What the fuck are you talkin' about?

KERCELIK: Keep it down, now.

BUTTS: Me? Me?

KERCELIK: You're airborne now, Butts.—You and me.
    (Pause)

BUTTS: I pay my taxes. I got one of the top accountants! We were in the service together—Manny Rosenthal. He's the best—sharp little guy from New York, but he's careful, oh yeah! They've got nothin' on me. Period.

KERCELIK: We're not talking about right now, Butts.

BUTTS: We're not?

KERCELIK: No.

BUTTS: Oh . . . well, then, what are we talking about?

KERCELIK: The records—The records, the files, the dossiers, the micro-film.

BUTTS: My records?
    (KERCELIK smiles.)
Bull-shit, I don't have any records.

KERCELIK: That's a negative. Everybody has a record, you know that.

BUTTS: Wait a second, I got an honorable discharge. I got letters of commendation from Bob Hope and all the shots—I got the "USO Man of the Year" award—so fuck them in their fucking ass. Excuse my French, but if this DIA tries to fuck with me—watch out!
    (Pause. Band Music)

KERCELIK: You're not reading me.

BUTTS: I'm a veteran, goddamnit, I'm an Elk. I'm VFW and Legion.
I'm Rotary. I'm a Moose, I'm a Lion, Shit! I'm an Oddfellow!—You
tell 'em to check me out with Captain Smoot, Long Beach PD, LBPD
You can bet on it—I'm in with the brass, I give 'em vet's prices on
their new cars. I'm in with 'em, I'm *wired*.

KERCELIK: Come here—I'll tell you what's "wired." This hospital's
wired, so keep it down to a roar. You don't think that the Commander-
in-Chief decided to come here today on the spur of the moment do
you?

> *(HE points towards the ceiling and lowers his voice. BUTTS is
> shaken. KERCELIK checks several locations for "bugs.")*

The DIA has this entire country "wired." They've got your ass wired
. . . These are the "animals," these are not CIA yuppies, these are
not CIA drunks, or FBI Mormon straight arrows—these are not
Captain Smoot and the boys in blue of the LBPD This is the DIA.
No married men allowed in. These are the anti-terrorist elite, not
a bunch of rough trade Rambos from Muscle Beach. These guys take
no prisoners, they kill everybody and let God sort 'em out—I'm sorry
to brace you like this Mr. Butts, but I'm letting you in on what's
happening, on a strictly "need to know" basis—This is National Security now. These people spell "America" with a "K." *(Pause)*
And you fit the "profile."

BUTTS: I do?—What "profile?"

KERCELIK: The DIA profile.

> *(From the corridor, a wave of security radio static and sounds
> of running, doors slamming, etc. Then, the doors open half-way
> and an AGENT sticks his head and shoulders into the room. The
> AGENT wears dark glasses, his gun is drawn. BUTTS, who has
> worked his way near to the door, jumps back. The AGENT stares,
> then sees KERCELIK and salutes.)*

AGENT: . . . Colonel.
> *(Exits)*

BUTTS: Jesus . . . Who are these guys?—Who controls 'em?

KERCELIK: I'm sorry, but you're not cleared for that. They were
formed after Dallas—and their orders are to take out anybody—I'm
saying anybody—and I mean Admirals, Generals, Cabinet members—the director of the Central Intelligence Agency—anybody—
whoever potentially threatens the Commander-in-Chief—I'm sorry
to have to do this to you.

P.A. ANNOUNCEMENT: All caterers and volunteers please report
to the main reception area. Repeat: . . .

(KERCELIK opens his briefcase and hands a slim manilla folder to BUTTS. BUTTS reads and turns pale. KERCELIK takes back the folder and returns it to the briefcase. Police sirens)

BUTTS: Huh? . . . *(Whispering)* What is this?

KERCELIK: Part of your papers.

BUTTS: My discharge papers?—Part of my record. This?

KERCELIK: That's a Roger.

BUTTS: Where'd you get it?

KERCELIK: CGSC.

BUTTS: What's that?

KERCELIK: The computer bank at the Command and General Staff College. I'm a consultant there.

BUTTS: You are? And they gave you this?

KERCELIK: No. But I have clearance so I ran a printout on everybody on the program, here, with me. You and Private Holloway, and the others.

   (Long pause)

So you see why I say if they find a gun on you or even if you try to turn it in—if you can get the drop on Private Holloway, which I do not believe you can—it's not just going to be, "Thank you, Mr. Butts, and here's another USO Service Award" . . .

BUTTS: I gotta take a leak . . . I can't believe this. Can I see it again?

KERCELIK: I don't think it's a good idea. You saw it—Why don't you urinate over there in that trophy.

BUTTS: Huh?

KERCELIK: So you won't have to leave here until we figure out some kind of, ah, "order-of-battle"—The gun, Mr. Butts. Remember?

   (BUTTS stares, then goes U.S. and tries to urinate in a large hollow trophy. Then he goes to the window.)

BUTTS: Ah, the hell with it . . . They got agents all over the garden, down there.

KERCELIK: Sure.

BUTTS: Is that the, the DIA?

KERCELIK: No. You won't see them.

BUTTS: What'ya mean?

KERCELIK: They work "deep cover." They'll be infiltrated all through the hospital. Anybody could be one.

   (BUTTS turns from the window to stare at KERCELIK.)

BUTTS: Anybody?

   (KERCELIK nods.)

You? Could you be one?

KERCELIK: *(Smiles)* Don't go Section Eight on us now, Mr. Butts.

BUTTS: No, but I mean, you said ya had, uh, "clearance," and you could be checking on all of us, because I mean, I'm all for it—because, today, with terrorists and all, *I believe in total security.* And, believe me, I got nothin' to hide, *nothin'*—and I wanta explain that, uh, report to you, because I say, "Hang 'em at the airport!"—I'll take a urinalysis right now. *(Pointing at the trophy)* —This report—I wanna tell you just how phoney it is.

KERCELIK: Take it easy, it's not necessary.

BUTTS: Oh, it is—it is—You see, we were in Tokyo gettin' ready to make our Christmas tour of the islands, and we—

KERCELIK: I don't want to hear it, Mr. Butts, it's not—

BUTTS: *(Overlapping)* Well, you're gonna hear it, by God—I don't care if you are an undercover DIA man—because they promised me—those fuckin' MPs in Tokyo promised me that if I covered his ass that they'd—I'm talking about . . .

(BUTTS whispers the name of a famous comedian in KER-CELIK'S ear: 15 seconds.)

KERCELIK: Easy, Butts, that's not our problem now—

BUTTS: Listen to me! He was drunk. We all were. And he told me to bring the sailor and, uh, the starlet up to his room. So I did, and I swear to you on my mother's grave that's all I did.
    (Pause)

KERCELIK: I believe you.

BUTTS: And that morning, the next morning, the MPs told me that if I, you know, if I . . . because the starlet, the girl . . . I mean who are they gonna believe? Me, or a big name like Georgie Jessel?—This could *ruin* me, for God's sake!
    (BUTTS is on the verge of tears.)

KERCELIK: I know, I know.

BUTTS: I mean, for God's sake, it was war . . . It was all booze and black market and cigarettes for somebody's sister—war.

KERCELIK: Yeah, I know.

BUTTS: War!

(BUTTS staggers upstage and vomits. KERCELIK leaps to help him.)

KERCELIK: OK., OK., mister. Take it easy. Sit down, here. Drink some water.
    (KERCELIK pours BUTTS a cup of water, and wipes his brow.)

BUTTS: *(Whispers)* War . . .

KERCELIK: The old man knew all about it.

BUTTS: The old man? *(Indicating HOLLOWAY)*

KERCELIK: No, your father.

BUTTS: *(Picking at the piano keys)* . . . Just another drunk . . .
Windbetreben, something like that, he'd yell that out and laugh like
a son-of-a-bitch. *Windbetreben*—they'd call out to the Germans . . .
He used to say that there was a blind girl in the War Department
. . . that drew all the numbers out of a fishbowl—crap like that . . .
And he'd sing the old crap . . .

> *(BUTTS plays and sings with mixed feelings.)*
>
> "Oh, the General got the Croix de Guerre,
> Parley-voo
> Oh, the General got the Croix de Guerre,
> Parley-voo
>
> *(KERCELIK joins in.)*
>
> Yes, the General got the Croix de Guerre,
> but the sonofabitch wasn't even there;
> Hinky-dinky, parley-voo."

KERCELIK: *(Pause)* Yeah—He knew the score.

BUTTS: Yeah, I guess so.

KERCELIK: Right . . . Now, we've got to move on, here. The MPs
were covering their behinds so they turned you in, but the brass
covered it up to save *their* skins. SOP.

BUTTS: Yeah.

KERCELIK: So that's that. Period—Now let's move on. What do
we do about Private Holloway and his gun?

BUTTS: Huh?—Oh yeah . . . well, you'll have to, uh, tell 'em, or,
uh—

KERCELIK: *(Overlapping)* Can't do that. No way.

BUTTS: Why not?

KERCELIK: I told you—There's paper on me, too.

BUTTS: I don't get it. You got "clearance," don't ya? They're gonna
make you a General—you're gettin' your picture with the President—
I mean, you got *clearance!*

KERCELIK: Affirmative, I got it.

BUTTS: Well, that's O.K. then, isn't it?

> *(KERCELIK opens the briefcase and hands BUTTS another
> folder. BUTTS studies it.)*

"Lieutenant Walter Charles Kercelik is hereby awarded the Congres-
sional Medal of Honor"—That's what it says. Right here. The
C.M.H.!

KERCELIK: That's right.

BUTTS: Well, I mean, that's the highest medal they can give *anyone*.
Isn't it?

KERCELIK: That's right.

BUTTS: Sure it is. So all you have to do—
KERCELIK: No, you're not reading me.
BUTTS: Well, then tell me, will ya? What's the catch?
KERCELIK: I will, if you will hold it down. Here's the "catch"—A
  C.M.H. citation is a . . . knife that cuts both ways.—Relax, I'm
  going to lay it out for you by the book.
P.A. ANNOUNCEMENT: Doctor Richard and Captain Brusima,
  please contact Administration.
KERCELIK: This, ah, citation gives you the official line.

> (KERCELIK *reads an occasional word or phrase from the ci-*
> *tation as he speaks with leashed agitation.)*

The village was south of the Hoi An River. Ninety eight percent
"unpacified," Brigade said, but I figured it was closer to 100%. Anyway. . . *(Reading)* "The 173rd . . ." that was my shock troops—
"Cordon and Search mission on the night and morning of . . ." You
see, what the VC did was bury their *material* and documents under
the mud in the pigsties, or tunnel it in under the buffalo manure
right in the stall with the animals, where our people never went
near enough to "search" much less "destroy." But I told Brigade
that I'd personally go in with the 173rd on a night operation. Well,
I guess they figured that *Time* magazine's favorite Green Beanie'd
get his ass blown up, so they let me go in—And then, we dug up
the VC documents and blew away . . . *(Reading)* "220 enemy
cadre, while taking prisoner 25 agents of the . . ." and, naturally,
Brigade claimed the credit. MAC-V held a special press conference,
they flew me into Saigon for a "photo opportunity" at the Embassy,
and because they said that . . . *(Reads)* "He personally risked
his life under heavy enemy fire to rescue his own men, Lieutenant
Kercelik . . ." And I'd been wounded, too, in the leg—so it all came
together in the dispatches and the CMH was in the bag.
> (HE *takes off the medal and looks at it, then tosses it to* BUTTS.)
BUTTS: Man-O Man. Great!
KERCELIK: Oh, yeah—Except, that's not the way it went down,
  and Brigade knew it, MAC-V knew it, and the Pentagon—and right
  now, *they* know it—the DIA.
> (*Pause.* KERCELIK *controls his breathing.*)
BUTTS: Knows what?
KERCELIK: That I'll kill an American as quick as I will a Com-
  munist—if it comes down to it. And if I will—anybody will—if it
  comes down to it.
BUTTS: Down to it?
KERCELIK: That's a Roger—What happened was this.—I was up
  to my knees in pig-shit making sure the Delta Company people were

going down in it to "search" for VC documents—lists of names of
agents—so we could "interrogate" and torture and "neutralize" some
real 100% VC people, for once, instead of the usual crowd of old men
and women and children . . when I heard . . . mmm . . .

*(KERCELIK rubs his temples and takes a sip of water and a
deep breath, then resumes as HE looks out the window. Band
Music starts up again. Slanting light catches KERCELIK'S face
as HE stands behind HOLLOWAY'S chair.)*

BUTTS: Jesus Christ—You're sweatin' blood.
KERCELIK: Mm. We'd caught them flat-footed, for once, because
they believed that we never would come in after dark, because MAC-
V, and Westmoreland kept saying—"The Night Belongs to the Viet-
Cong—Belongs to the Viet-Cong"—like one of your damned car com-
mercials—So, we were all over them before they could get it together
and it was a blood-bath, and we only took three wounded and eleven
killed.—And I killed five of those myself.
  (Pause)
BUTTS: You mean, uh, you killed five of the, uh, the uh, the Viet—
KERCELIK: No.—I shot four of my own men . . . And I strangled
the fifth. So that's five.
  (Pause)
BUTTS: Why, what happened?
KERCELIK: Well—I was there, in the pigsty, when I heard Acousti,
my Top Sergeant, screaming at somebody in English, if you want
to call it that.

*(KERCELIK'S voice is soft and distant. Tears run down HOL-
LOWAY'S cheeks.)*

"You scum-bag, cock-sucking, mother-fucking animals . . ." In Eng-
lish, so I knew he was screaming at our people . . . So, I ran over
there—Acousti had been my Top in I Corps, I trusted him with my
life—and Acousti was faced off with five of our Delta Company,
screaming—and he was crying . . . because those men from Delta
had been—he'd caught them cutting up a VC baby—a baby—
BUTTS: I don't wanna hear it—
KERCELIK: *(Inaudibly)* . . . And eating it.
BUTTS: And what?
KERCELIK: *Eating* it . . . They said it was a pig . . .
BUTTS: Was it? . . .
KERCELIK: So, then I shot them, four of 'em—And my Top just
stood there frozen, crying—Tough wop street kid, bawling so loud

you could hear him over the sound of the mopping up—and the
general racket of the screaming women. He couldn't stop.
    (Pause. HOLLOWAY *"sleeps" again.)*
So, of course, I made a deal with Brigade—and it never happened.—
Except it did, and the DIA has the "paper" on it.
BUTTS: They do?
KERCELIK: That's a Roger. And if they have to "neutralize" me,
   or you, that "paper" will be out on the wire services—before our
   bodies're cold—to tell the American public how you and I, or both
   of us, "had a long history of mental illness, according to high Pentagon
   sources."
    *(*BUTTS *moves closer to* KERCELIK.)*
BUTTS: But, listen, Colonel, I mean you couldn't help it—it was
   war, for God's sake.
KERCELIK: *(Laughing)*   Airborne, Mr. Butts. It was war. And in
   war, everybody goes crazy or they die—right?
BUTTS: That's right.
KERCELIK: Except that I didn't and I couldn't—that was my prob-
   lem. The Generals, MAC-V, they did: Westmoreland, Abrams, Ros-
   son, DePuy, Richardson, Ewell, Ramsey—all of them—they did.
BUTTS: What?
KERCELIK: Go crazy—Because to them Vietnam was a "Brown
   Disneyland"—they believed that—and "six flags over nothing."—
   They believed that. The WPPA.
BUTTS: Who's that?
KERCELIK: The "West Point Protective Association."
BUTTS: Oh.
    (Pause)
KERCELIK: You get the big picture now? A couple "heroes" like
   us are just two more "suspects" when it comes to the records. And
   nothing you or I will ever do can change that. Because those facts
   are freeze dried.
BUTTS: I'm sick to my stomach. You telling me a man can't start
   over anymore—in America?
KERCELIK: Not anymore . . . So—we're back at ground zero with
   Private Holloway. And here's how I read it. A) We report him—ex-
   cept, then, they, the DIA targets us—so we don't report him. B)
   We kill him and—
BUTTS: *(Overlapping)*   Wait, now, wait a—
KERCELIK: *(Overlapping)*   Keep it down! We kill him because
   then it's SOP all over again, from the top, down.
BUTTS: Wait, I can't let you—
KERCELIK: Yes, you can. We kill him. We're heroes again. We
   both get CMH's. We saved the life of the Commander-in-Chief, the
   leader of the Free World—Think about it.

(BUTTS *recovers. In extreme agitation* HE *paces and mumbles to himself, while* KERCELIK *hums along with the band music.*)

BUTTS: You're serious. You're *not* serious.

KERCELIK: Think about it. They make me a General. And you get elected to Congress on the Commander's coat tails, or maybe they even make you Secretary of Veterans Affairs.

(Pause)

BUTTS: *(Softly)* My God . . . the poor bastard: I mean he's half dead, already . . . But, but, I mean, uh, how would you do it?

KERCELIK: Well, the two of us—together—could slip up on him, while he's, ah, resting, and then just shoot him "in the struggle."

BUTTS: *(Half whispering)* In the struggle?—Oh, yeah, yeah, "in the struggle."

KERCELIK: Yeah. Well, it's one choice.

BUTTS: Yeah, well, anything's possible these days. It's like they say, "the lesser of two evils," because, you know, if you had to choose between the old man and the President—I mean what choice is there?

(Pause)

KERCELIK: Is it a "go," then?

BUTTS: Huh?

KERCELIK: Is that it—is that your decision?

BUTTS: No! It's not *my*, it's not *my*—it's not *me! You* said—what about *you?*

KERCELIK: You said that if we had "to choose" between Private Holloway and the Commander-in-Chief, that there *was* no choice.

BUTTS: Alright, yes, I *said* it, but that don't mean that we—

KERCELIK: *(Overlapping)* But is it true?

BUTTS: Is what true?

KERCELIK: The only choice: Kill him—we're patriots; don't—we're patsies?

BUTTS: Colonel, I'm not a well man.

KERCELIK: Choices, Mr. Butts—To make the optimum choice you have to have the optimum intelligence, you know that.—Now, I haven't told you everything that Private Holloway told me. And you need to hear it all—so that you can tell it later.

BUTTS: Tell it later?

KERCELIK: Roger—As I understand it, his position is that we should help him kill the Commander-in-Chief because . . .

(BUTTS *shuffles.*)

—hold it, keep quiet now, just shut up for once and listen . . . O.K., we should kill the Commander and not him, the Private, because he, the Private, and all of his men are real flesh and blood human beings—or they were—and the Commander doesn't actually exist, at all—He's a phoney. *(Gestures)* A picture on the wall.

BUTTS: If he said *that*, we *should* shoot him, like a mad dog that you—

KERCELIK: *(Overlapping)*   According to him, the Commander is just a figurehead, you know, a symbol, a photo-opportunity, an office, a title—*a haircut*. He's alive, the 5 piece suit in the Man-Tan makeup, carrying the "First Dog," saluting the doorman, waving and pointing off camera to all the ghosts that line the tarmac—he's alive, alright— he eats all that chicken at all those banquets, and evacuates it every other day, and he fucks his wife once a year, so he's alive, as far as that goes. But he doesn't count—until today.
   (Touching the poster of himself)

BUTTS: Meaning?

KERCELIK: Meaning he doesn't count the way Private Holloway or you or I "count"—in the "Body Count."

BUTTS: "Body Count?"

KERCELIK: When *we* die in a war, they count us—so they can tell who won. *We count*. The Commander, he *doesn't* count—He counts *us*, after we're dead, so they'll know who won.

   (BUTTS *shakes his head in growing confusion.* KERCELIK *takes* BUTTS *to the window.*)

All those acres of crosses out there, as far as you can see, *everyone* of them counts. Especially the ones without names—Kilroy, G.I. Joe, the Unknown Soldier. The years mean nothing to them, he says. And then there's the Doughboys: the Big Red One, all the Race Horse Brigades, the Wild West, the Ivy Leafs, Iron Jaws, Rainbow Ohio, All American—there's the Black Horse and your old man, and all the rest—millions and millions on his side. All present and accounted for, they say.

BUTTS: They? Who else is in on this?

KERCELIK: Christian Hornbeck and Arthur Reed.

BUTTS: Who're they?

KERCELIK: Corporal Hornbeck—107 years old, he saw action in Manilla, enlisted when he was thirteen . . . and Private First Class Arthur Reed is 123.

BUTTS: No!

KERCELIK: Affirmative. His mother cooked for Union Troops in the Civil War. Private Reed shot his first rebel when he was nine, and was a PFC at eleven.   *(Pause)*   Those're the only names he'd give me. There's more, but he calls all the rest "The Kilroy Company."

BUTTS: Those guys aren't here, I'll tell you that.

KERCELIK: He says they are. Over in the—is it the Wadsworth Facility?

BUTTS: Yuh.

KERCELIK: He says there's whole wards of men warehoused over there, all of 'em well over a hundred years old.

BUTTS: I been over there at Christmas.

KERCELIK: In *every* ward.

BUTTS: . . . No . . .

KERCELIK: Well, he has no reason to lie about it . . . The point is . . . these men hold that the Commander—whether it's Lincoln or McKinley or Wilson or Roosevelt or whoever—has sucked the blood out of every white cross out there, out of every Yankee or Rebel or Rough Rider or Doughboy or G.I. That these so-called Commanders are just zombies living off that young flesh. So that if you shoot them, these zombies come right back to what we call life under another name, just in time for the next war. And then they need a whole new Army of grunts and dogfaces and Kilroys to feed on, so that McKinley or Wilson or Smith, or Kercelik, or whatever they call the new Commander can count bodies, so that the nation can know it won or lost, so that it can know that it *exists*—win *or* lose . . .

    (BUTTS is staring in fear at KERCELIK.)

So what they say—Holloway and Hornbeck and Reed, and the others—what they say, and they *are* the majority by a count of millions to one, is that the *only* choice we have is between Kilroy and the Commander.

    (BUTTS starts to back away.)

Do we kill Kilroy or the Commander?—That's our marching music out there.

    (KERCELIK puts the CMH on BUTTS. The failing light glints on the medals.)

BUTTS: What are you doing? Are you completely insane?

KERCELIK: No.

BUTTS: Well, I think you are.

KERCELIK: No. Not anymore. *(Pause)*

BUTTS: Then you're a goddam phoney—you're one of those, uh, secret agents, aren't you, trying to test me?

KERCELIK: I am.

BUTTS: I knew it! *Thank God!* . . . I knew you were workin' for the President! *Thank Christ!*

KERCELIK: I was—but now, I'm Private Holloway's man.

    (HE straightens up HOLLOWAY'S blankets.)

BUTTS: Who are you? How did you know the President was comin'? You knew he was comin'! You're protecting him, aren't ya?—Look, I'm on your side!

KERCELIK: Why don't you stand at ease for a minute?

BUTTS: It's almost time. We gotta go out there, in—

KERCELIK: *(Overlapping)*   I'm watching the time. Stay here, Sergeant!

BUTTS: You don't give me orders, Colonel, I don't care who you're supposed to be!

  (KERCELIK "stands" on his head. BUTTS stops.)

KERCELIK: Hey, Butts, I'm standing on my head . . . John Mac-Cormick "Jack" Butts—Now hear this: Private Holloway told me to tell you something.

  (KERCELIK'S voice becomes ancient. HE "crawls" through war towards BUTTS.)

(As HOLLOWAY)   "Dear Ma . . . It was terrible, what happened to the poor mules . . ."   *(Sings)*
"Oh, the General got the Croix de Guerre,
Parley-voo
Yes, the General got the Croix de Guerre,
But the sonofabitch wasn't even there;
Hinky-dinky, parley-voo."

BUTTS: Why are you doing this to me?

  (KERCELIK stands upright.)

KERCELIK: Belleau Woods burned like a torch in the night. The mules exploded in flames.

BUTTS: The mules?

KERCELIK: The burning mules. The letter. Your old man's letter.

  (HE puts letter in BUTT'S pocket.)

BUTTS: Why me?

KERCELIK: Because you assassinated that Coke machine. And you called them by their rightful name—"phonies." Because—underneath that sales pitch is a *man!*

BUTTS: *(Whispers)*   But why pick on me?

KERCELIK: You or me—one of us has to help him—And you're here. And you're everybody . . . and after I'm gone, you'll tell the story.

BUTTS: But why today?

KERCELIK: He sees there's another war coming. The "Great War."

BUTTS: Is it?

  (KERCELIK nods.)

KERCELIK: So that's why it's got to be today.

  (Sirens)

We are going to have some "military music"—and "military justice," here, in about seven and a half minutes. This is his last chance . . . This is not Lee Harvey Oswald. This is Leslie Robert Holloway—and he-is-not-alone.

BUTTS: I'm sick. I'm no kid, you know.

KERCELIK: Yes, you are . . . And you have got to tell it, later.

    (HE buckles on his sabre. BUTTS screams.)

BUTTS: I'm not going to tell it later! You're lying. You've been lying since you walked in here. Goddamnit, *who are you?*

KERCELIK: Kilroy . . . *"Homo Americanus*—Late in the Age of Atoms—Now extinct."

BUTTS: What?

    (KERCELIK puts on dress Gold Braid.)

KERCELIK: I said, "I'm a dead man."

BUTTS: Tell me the truth.

KERCELIK: A two hundred-year-old dead man.

    (Then, P.A. ANNOUNCEMENT:*)*

P.A.: All personnel to the Parade Ground and the Auditorium.

    (BUTTS goes up to the poster of KERCELIK *and touches it. The light is fading.)*

BUTTS: I don't get it. A man like you. It don't add up.

    (KERCELIK joins BUTTS at the poster. HE touches it as HE talks. THEIR tone is intimate.)

KERCELIK: Yes, it does . . . We have to go down: the Commander-in-Chief; Uncle Sam; and *me.*

BUTTS: Please don't say that, son.

KERCELIK: And you have to stay here—and take care of Kilroy, and tell our story.

    (BUTTS comes very close to KERCELIK. HE begins to weep.)

BUTTS: What is it? Is it the Agent Orange? I could understand that . . . Listen, Please, don't do it, Colonel . . . Please, for God's sake, he's our leader, he's the only President we got. We can't take any more, this country'll go nuts, if you do this—I mean, what'll happen to *us? (Raging)* It's not fair: We came home in '46 and *Life* magazine showed pictures of cars shaped like raindrops, sittin' in the driveway of our new "ranch style" house, bought for "nothin' down" on the G.I. Bill—and in the doorway, waitin'—was our wife and kid— *(HE starts to shake.)* and they loved us . . . And the cars—they were shaped like tear drops . . . So, alright, fuck the brass and the big shots, you're right, but what about us, the little guy—*you gotta remember the poor fucking American people!*

KERCELIK: I remember them! *(Looking out at the crosses)* I can still see their faces . . . Whitney and Kraft and Clark and Pappas . . .

(As KERCELIK *calls out the litany,* BUTTS, *in desperation, tries to communicate with* HOLLOWAY.*)*

KERCELIK: Rasmussen, Pierce, Whatley, Vernon, Broome, Heidt,
                 Washington, MacConnell, Forquet, Weil, Massey,
AND   Eliot, Mauro,DiSoma, Guinne, Lieberman, Dobbs,
                 Dowling, Dobrinski—*Butts! Kercelik!*

BUTTS: Listen, Can you hear me?—Try to hear me. Do you
                 understand what's happening?—Mr. Holloway, Pri-
TOGETHER   vate Holloway? Do you know him? Sir? do you know
                 Colonel Kercelik? Is any of this true? Is it? He's gonna
                 do something terrible—he's gonna, hey, wake up!
                 Wake up you stinkin' old phoney! *(Shaking him vio-
                 lently)*

(HOLLOWAY—*in* BUTTS' *arms—opens his mouth in a scream or howl of profound and pent up anguish and grief and loss so prolonged and unremitting as to fill up the theatre and the world. Then he sinks back down into his wheelchair.* BUTTS *is half dead with terror.)*

BUTTS: *(Softly)* Oh, my God . . .
KERCELIK: What's the matter?
BUTTS: I shit my pants.
KERCELIK: I know. War. *(Putting on white dress gloves)*
BUTTS: Please!
KERCELIK: What?—I won't tell anyone. You'll just smell like
everyone else, here, now, that's all . . . Private Holloway, and all
the Kilroys. The combined and loosened shit from the back wards,
and all the trenches everywhere, rolling and running and *avalan-
ching* down! (HE *raises his voice.)* "There's a shit-storm coming"—he says, *"There's a shit-storm coming!"*

(Siren and band music up. KERCELIK *lifts the gun from under* HOLLOWAY'S *blanket.* BUTTS *staggers to the window, taps on it, tries to run out, falls to his knees praying.)*

P.A. ANNOUNCEMENT: Honor Guard to the auditorium. Honor
Guard to the auditorium. *(Sirens and helicopters)*
KERCELIK: They're coming in.
BUTTS: Please, please, please.
KERCELIK: All right then, you take it. Take the gun.

(BUTTS sobs, helicopters roar, KERCELIK *is filled by his destiny, calling over the noise and helicopter lights, as if under-fire.)*

Stand up, soldier. Be a man. We've got wounded here. On the double! Get out there and kill! Kill! Kill-kill the phonies! Let's go, Butts, airborne!

(BUTTS crawls to HOLLOWAY'S feet. KERCELIK'S voice drops into intimacy.)

O.K. Sergeant, I'll take over. You tell about it. Make them see it from his point of view, from under the mud and shit of *his* trench. From Kilroy's and all the boys that "bought the farm"—that bought the dream—that bit the dust, so that the Zombie-in-Chief could live forever.
    (KERCELIK clicks the gun's safety off.)
You stay right here, till it's over. Take care of him. Watch over him like he was your old man—your dad, after Belleau Wood.

(KERCELIK goes to the old man and kisses him goodbye. The three men are locked together. Sound of "Hail to the Chief" from the grounds. Running in the corridor.)

Sing something for him. He's in pain . . .

(KERCELIK puts the gun into his briefcase and straightens his uniform.)

You tell 'em—"Kilroy was here."
    (HE salutes and exits.)
BUTTS: *(In the soft voice of a boy and a broken old man)* Pop?— Hey, Pop?—It's O.K. It's O.K., Pop. . . I won't leave you, Pop. . .

(BUTTS tries to sing a few words of "It's A Long Way to Tipperary," then they hear a single shot ring out. Two seconds, then a hail of bullets . . . Now, HOLLOWAY is singing. HE stands. BUTTS, like a boy at his feet, sings along. THEY are happy.)

HOLLOWAY: "In the base at Savenay,
                Where the sick and wounded lay,
AND   Running up their temperatures,
                More and more each day . . .
BUTTS: Oh, they put them all in plaster casts,
                And that's a very good sign,
                That we will stay at Savenay,
                Till the good old summertime."

END OF PLAY

Donald Freed, author of *Veterans Day*
Donald Freed's play *Circe & Bravo* was produced in DCTC's Space
theatre during the 1985-86 season and went on to a successful run
in London starring Faye Dunaway. The Robert Altman production
of Donald's *Secret Honor* has played throughout the world on both
stage and screen, and his prize-winning play *Inquest,* about the
Rosenberg-Sobell case, played on Broadway in 1970. This winter
his original play *The Quartered Man* will be produced at London's
Shaw Theatre. *Veterans Day* was selected by the DCTC as one of
six staged readings in last spring's PrimaFacie III, and next spring
will have a European premiere in London's West End starring
Harold Pinter as Kercelik. Donald's grants and prizes include a
Rockefeller Foundation Playwrights-in-Residence Award in association with the DCTC.

AFTERWORD

New Play Development at the
Denver Center Theatre Company

Theatre is energy. The primary source of energy in most theatrical exchanges is the playwright. Our need for new writers is obvious. Our responsibility to foster, nurture and develop writers is equally obvious. What is less obvious, but no less important, is the way the playwrights in our company nourish, challenge and define the work of our other artists. Our company is still in its infancy. When it matures, its greatest accomplishment will be the development of a unique company style which informs and influences our approach to each production. As this style begins to emerge, it will be heard first in the regional voices of our playwrights. If we are to have a vital American theatre, we must encourage and develop vital American playwrights.

Donovan Marley
Artistic Director

The Denver Center Theatre Company has established a four-part program to address its responsibility to encourage and develop vital American playwrights:

1. THE PLAYWRIGHTS UNIT

A year-round support system for Denver playwrights, designed to develop regional voices as a part of the daily activities of the Theatre Company.

1987-88 Unit Members
Larry Bograd
Jeff Carey
Terry Dodd
Jamie Horton
Frank X. Hogan
Maria Katzenbach
Molly Newman
Leonard Winograd

2. PRIMAFACIE

An annual play-reading series in which playwrights are selected from across the country to develop their plays in a two-week workshop, culminating in public staged readings.

3. THE PREMIERE SERIES

Full productions of new works from PrimaFacie, presented as part of the Theatre's subscription season.

4. PRIMAFACIE, AN ANTHOLOGY OF NEW AMERICAN PLAYS

The publication of our world premiere scripts made available to bookstores and theatres across the nation.

In addition, the following programs have been established to support our commitment to new play development within the Colorado community:

1. THE PLAYWRIGHTS WORKSHOP

A ten-week intensive workshop for local writers offering a creative atmosphere for developing works-in-progress and tailored to the needs of emerging writers.

2. HIGH SCHOOL PLAYWRIGHTS WORKSHOP

A collaborative effort between the Theatre and local high schools to help nurture and educate young writers.

3. NEWWORK/NETWORK

An informal organization which meets once a year, bringing together playwrights, producers, and directors of new work for the theatre, in an attempt to foster new connections and new working relationships in the Rocky Mountain Region.

4. PLAYWRIGHT OBSERVERS

An opportunity for emerging playwrights to observe our process of script development during PrimaFacie.

New Plays Developed at the
Denver Center Theatre Company

1980-81
*LATENT IMAGE by David Jones and Mark Cuddy
*CON SAFOS by Angel Vigil
THE RISE AND RISE OF DANIEL ROCKET by Peter Parnell

1981-82
*THE BALLAD OF COLORADO by Mark Cuddy and Cast
*BUCKHORN EXCHANGES by Craig Volk
*DENVER MESSIAH by Frank X. Hogan
*QUILTERS by Molly Newman and Barbara Damashek

1982-83
*RUNESTONE HILL by Laura Shamas
*A BEAUTIFUL WORLD by David Jones
*RUNAWAY TRUCK RAMP by Paul Redford and Cast

1983-84
CROSSFIRE by Ted Gross
DARWIN'S SLEEPLESS NIGHT by Merle Kessler
*DOORPLAY by Sallie Baker
ON THE VERGE by Eric Overmyer
HYDE IN HOLLYWOOD by Peter Parnell

1984-85
*RINGERS by Frank X. Hogan
MAX AND MAXIE by James McLure
*THE IMMIGRANT by Mark Harelik and Randal Myler
THE FEMALE ENTERTAINER by Elizabeth Levin

1985-86
A WOMAN WITHOUT A NAME by Romulus Linney
WHEN THE SUN SLIDES by Stephen Davis Parks
*PLEASURING GROUND by Frank X. Hogan
HOPE OF THE FUTURE by Shannon Keith Kelley
*CHRISTMAS MIRACLES by Laird Williamson and Dennis Powers
CIRCE & BRAVO by Donald Freed

1986-87
*GOODNIGHT, TEXAS by Terry Dodd
THE WORLD OF MIRTH by Murphy Guyer
RACHEL'S FATE by Larry Ketron
*SHOOTING STARS by Molly Newman

1985 PrimaFacie I
    PUBLIC LIVES by Julia Cameron
    *****DEAL WITH A DEAD MAN** by Tom DeMers
    NORMAL DOESN'T MEAN PERFECT by Don Gordon
+*****PLEASURING GROUND** by Frank X. Hogan
+ **HOPE OF THE FUTURE** by Shannon Keith Kelley
+ **A WOMAN WITHOUT A NAME** by Romulus Linney
+ **WHEN THE SUN SLIDES** by Stephen Davis Parks
    EMILY & KATE by Ruth Phillips
    NOVEMBER by J. Ranelli
  *****TELLING TIME** by Laura Shamas

1986 PrimaFacie II
  *****THE BALLAD OF THE EL GIMPO CAFE** by Jeff Carey
    CAL AND SALLY by Robert Clyman
    FAT MEN ON THIN ICE by Roger Cornish
+*****GOODNIGHT, TEXAS** by Terry Dodd
+ **THE WORLD OF MIRTH** by Murphy Guyer
    WATCH YOUR BACK by Gary Leon Hill
+ **RACHEL'S FATE** by Larry Ketron
    HEATHEN VALLEY by Romulus Linney
    AMERICAN DREAMER by Carol K. Mack
+*****SHOOTING STARS** by Molly Newman
    REUNION by Sybille Pearson

1987 PrimaFacie III
    WASPS by Roger Cornish
+ **VETS** by Donald Freed (now titled **VETERANS DAY**)
+*****KOOZY'S PIECE** by Frank X. Hogan
    GUS AND AL by Albert Innaurato
+ **TROPHY HUNTERS** by Kendrew Lascelles
    TRIPLETS by Constance Ray

*Colorado Playwright
+Selected for full DCTC production